Since his first book, *Silence in the Snowy Fields* (1962), Robert Bly has been a major—if controversial—figure in American poetry. In 1968 he won the National Book Award for his volume *The Light Around the Body*. His other books include *Sleepers Joining Hands* (1973) and *The Man in the Black Coat Turns* (1981), as well as numerous publications from small presses. In this comprehensive study, Howard Nelson examines the evolving body of Bly's work, from the rich simplicity of the first book, the passionate surrealism and political content of the second, his exploration of the prose-poem and the very brief poem, to his recent work focusing on the male soul and the powers of grief and love. Nelson offers commentaries on many individual poems while giving an overall view of Bly's accomplishment and vision.

Bly is also an important critic and theorist. The major ideas and issues that animate his essays are discussed as well as his contributions as translator, editor, and public reader of poetry. The book also includes a unique chronology, prepared with Bly's assistance and cooperation, which details important literary influences as well as travel and other experiences.

This rewarding book opens up to the reader the achievement of one of the most dynamic, original, and influential poets of the past twenty-five years.

ROBERT BLY

AN INTRODUCTION
TO THE POETRY

HOWARD NELSON

COLUMBIA UNIVERSITY PRESS

NEW YORK

1984

Library of Congress Cataloging in Publication Data
Nelson, Howard, 1947–
    Robert Bly, an introduction to the poetry.
    (Columbia introductions to twentieth-century American
poetry)
    Bibliography: p.
    Includes index.
    1. Bly, Robert—Criticism and interpretation.   I.   Title.
II. Series.
PS3552.L9Z77 1984   811'.54   83-14481
ISBN 0-231-05310-X (alk. paper)

                    Columbia University Press
            New York   Guildford, Surrey

To Stephanie

COLUMBIA INTRODUCTIONS TO
TWENTIETH-CENTURY
AMERICAN POETRY

Contents

JOHN UNTERECKER

Foreword

Perhaps the proper way for Robert Bly's poetry to be marketed is as long-playing record albums, with the texts of the poems printed in tiny type on inner liners or on the cardboard sleeves holding the records. Each of the longer books could be accommodated nicely on two-record packages. The shorter books could comfortably fit on twelve-inch singles. And the prose—well, the prose could be read as we now do read it, in paperback collections of related essays and interviews.

That—short of hearing him live—would be the right way to experience the poetry of Robert Bly. For his work is extraordinarily vocal. It cries out for the spoken voice, and Bly's voice is ideally fitted to its cadences. Though most of the books stand up very well—especially if each is read in one sitting, end to end, as printed—though they stand up well as printed words on the page—even then they work best if we give our auditory imaginations full play and read them silently, if we must read silently, at the pace of speech, listening in imagination for the full value of each of the "spoken" sounds.

I place a great deal of stress on the element of speech and speech rhythms in the poetry of Robert Bly because it seems to me it has a good deal to do with the reaction of those critics who do and those who do not respond to Bly's work. For there is no question that "readers" have a hard time with Bly's poetry whereas "listeners," by and large, grasp almost immediately not just idea but structure and style as well.

Since Howard Nelson listens so accurately, he is able, in this immensely helpful study of Bly's work, to show us central designs of both structure and style. For my own part, I'd like to use a little of my space to talk about the structure of the sound itself, the "music" of Bly's poetry, and one or two of the ways it is related to living speech. And I'd like to draw my examples from two poems quoted, for other reasons, by Nelson. In effect, what I'm about to do is to write anticipatory footnotes for up-coming pages 29 and 47.

I'd like first to consider the way Bly handles some of the words in one of his loveliest early poems, "After Drinking All Night with a Friend, We Go Out in a Boat at Dawn to See Who Can Write the Best Poem." Most of the poem is quoted by Nelson, but I want to look at all of it. Nelson uses it to show how dominant images integrate one poem into another, to show how a whole group of poems are interconnected into the larger structure of *Silence in the Snowy Fields*. I want, on the other hand, to look closely at the ways a dozen of the sounds create internal, inconspicuous, and probably largely uncalculated melodies. Here is the poem:

> *After Drinking All Night with a Friend, We Go out in a Boat*
> *at Dawn to See Who Can Write the Best Poem*
>
> These pines, these fall oaks, these rocks,
> This water dark and touched by wind—
> I am like you, you dark boat,
> Drifting over water fed by cool springs.
>
> Beneath the waters, since I was a boy,
> I have dreamt of strange and dark treasures,

Not of gold, or strange stones, but the true
Gift, beneath the pale lakes of Minnesota.

This morning also, drifting in the dawn wind,
I sense my hands, and my shoes, and this ink—
Drifting, as all of this body drifts,
Above the clouds of the flesh and the stone.

A few friendships, a few dawns, a few glimpses of grass,
A few oars weathered by the snow and the heat,
So we drift toward shore, over cold waters,
No longer caring if we drift or go straight.

And these are the sounding words—try reading them aloud!—I want to isolate (I include words from the title as part of the sound structure of the poem):

all, fall, also, all
friend, friendships
these, these, these, beneath, beneath, heat, we, we
go, oaks, boat, over, gold, stones, stone, snow, over, go
dawn, dawn
this, wind, drifting, gift, this, drifting, this, drifting, drifts,
   glimpses, drift, drift
water, water, waters, waters
strange, strange
dark, dark, dark
you, you, cool, true, few, few, few, few
morning, oars, shore

Pulled out of context in this fashion, these words seem dizzyingly repetitive, alive with echoing sound.

Technically, what I've lined up, in addition to a few patterns of full rhyme, are straight repetitions and assonant variations.

In itself, assonance—a repeating vowel sound modified by assorted following consonants—is unremarkable. It is the characteristic echoing sound in spoken or written prose. But when skillfully combined with repeating words and accented by incidental rhyme (rhyme made invisible both by burial within the line and by widely separated rhyming words, as in the three true rhymes of this poem: all/fall, you/true/few, and drift/gift), when this manipulation of sound is accomplished with sufficient delicacy, a kind of magic takes place and we both hear and do not hear a complex wave of sound. It is like walking along a stream in late spring when a dozen different bird songs are bound together by the variable sigh of wind through grass and shrubs and by the steady trickle of water over stone. We hear something both unpretentious and beautiful, something that is totally integrated into the sound of a walk by a stream.

What a poem like this one—casual in tone and perhaps casual in composition—makes use of, nevertheless, is the full range of repeating sound, from the purest "rhyme" of all, direct repetition (dark, dark, dark), which is psychologically almost inaudible, through conventional rhyme (all, fall), which our ear picks up immediately, through the subtle variations of assonance (these, beneath, heat, we), which we can hear but which we have been trained to ignore, to the most stretched partial rhyme of all, the sound structure sometimes called consonance in which the repeated sound is a consonant or consonant cluster and in which the vowel is variable. (Consonance is almost as inaudible as direct repetition itself. In this poem, it can be most vividly illustrated by the *n* and *n-plus-second-consonant* series. Again, I urge you to read these words aloud: drinking, friend, dawn, pines, wind, springs, since, strange, stones, morning, drifting, dawn, wind, sense, hands, drifting, stone, friendships, dawns, caring.)

There is no question that these linking sounds create a mosaic and, for me at least, marvelous melody. But there is also, I suspect, no question that they are assembled, most of them at any rate, without a great deal of premeditation. I can't speak for Bly, but my guess is that the big elements in the design are at least in part "thought out"—the syntactical repetitions, for example ("these pines, these fall oaks, these rocks" in the opening stanza and "a few friendships, a few dawns, a few glimpses of grass, A few oars" in the closing one). But the other repetitions and their variations and all of the complex sound systems I have so laboriously been dissecting—all of these are the kinds of effects that quite spontaneously fall into place during the muttering trials and errors that are part of the assembly of any poem.

I want to pause on this point, since too often critics (myself included when the critic's hat is perched on my head) speak of the finished poem as if all of its effects were worked out with a slide rule. So far as I can see, they never are. The poem evolves, and the job of the poet is to encourage it to evolve in a possible direction. When words sound right, they are dropped into the line; when they sound (for unexamined reasons) wrong, they are replaced by words that sound better. At its most deliberate, the process is no more than a half-conscious one. I suppose somewhere there is a poet who has once said to himself: "Well, now, let's see; I think what I want for the seventh syllable of the third line is a word that has an assonant relationship to the first syllable of the seventh line and a consonant relationship to the third and eighth syllables of the eleventh line," but if he exists anywhere on God's green earth, I've yet to hear of him.

Instead, the poet trusts to an ear that he's trained by careful listening, trying, if he's a good poet, to catch both the sounds and the syntactical patterns of living speech.

In this poem, it seems to me, Bly achieves with wonderful accuracy the slow, repetitive starts and stops, the hesitations and clarifications of a man thinking aloud.

But that's not all that it takes to make a major poem. A poem has to be more than an assembly of words that sound good. Ultimately the poem must say something and say it in such a way as to make us sit up and take notice. It has to risk statements that surprise us into the discovery of unexpected truth.

What makes this poem exciting is that its discovering speech tells us simultaneously about dawn and about an aspect both of the self and of the world that is darker and deeper than either self or dawn taken separately. Thanks to the movement of a sequence of transforming images, it opens out toward a mythic dream that hesitates above Minnesota waters and finally discovers beneath them the secret "true/ Gift" we otherwise might never encounter. What we have in a poem like this, I suppose, is a mind taking chances while its statements are being costumed in the pleasant formal disguises of meditative speech.

This relationship between chance and choice, between the luck of a poem and its formal structure, seems to me a central consideration in any discussion of Bly's work. Bly himself, as Nelson points out, has come more and more to think of this relationship as providing much of the life of art. In an essay titled "Form That Is Neither In Nor Out," Bly speaks of the satisfying poem as being dependent on its "wildness," as in a wild animal or a wild flower, where form makes freedom possible. The successful snail (his example) or panther or daisy (my examples), does not choose its symmetry (what Blake admired in the tiger) but cannot function well without it. A jagged snail just won't do; it will catch on things. A panther with one leg six inches longer than the others will stalk game like a creeping boiler factory. What wildness demands is a functioning inconspicuous order that can adapt itself easily to the needs of the moment: that can spring, claws out, when called on to spring; that can become the model of a pebble if trapped in the glare heat of noon. Wildness capitalizes on chance. The tiger doesn't choose its stripes though it does choose lairs that match some of them and a flexible territory adequate to its needs—big enough for a dependable food supply, not so large as to compel an inefficient patrol.

Bly is, of course, not the only poet to work in flexible, supple forms. Many of the late poems of D. H. Lawrence have qualities similar to those of Bly's poems—even to a similar echoing vocabulary—and we can find less precise parallels in dozens of younger poets who have looked toward Bly's achievement with disciples' admiration.

If Bly's musing, meditative poems with all of their repetitions achieve the feel of living speech, it is the speech of the conversational storyteller who is able to persuade us that we are engaged in a private one-to-one dialogue, spontaneous and unrehearsed.

A different rhetoric, a different kind of rhythm—urgent, driving—shows up in Bly's polemical poems, particularly those written in opposition to the Vietnam War. The music, on the other hand, does not really change very much. Consider "The Executive's Death," the opening poem of *The Light Around the Body:*

The Executive's Death

Merchants have multiplied more than the stars of heaven.
Half the population are like the long grasshoppers
That sleep in the bushes in the cool of the day:
The sound of their wings is heard at noon, muffled, near the earth.
The crane handler dies, the taxi driver dies, slumped over
In his taxi. Meanwhile, high in the air, executives
Walk on cool floors, and suddenly fall:
Dying, they dream they are lost in a snowstorm in mountains,
On which they crashed, carried at night by great machines.
As he lies on the wintry slope, cut off and dying,
A pine stump talks to him of Goethe and Jesus.
Commuters arrive in Hartford at dusk like moles
Or hares flying from a fire behind them,
And the dusk in Hartford is full of their sighs;
Their trains come through the air like a dark music,
Like the sound of horns, the sound of thousands of small wings.

What we have here are the same sorts of buried rhymes and slant rhymes that were seen in "After Drinking All Night. . . ." Though I won't point out all of them, a few are crucial to the sound structure of the poem. Listen to the variations on the diphthong in *dies:* dies, dies, high, fire, dying, night, lies, dying, pine, flying, sighs. Notice the straight repetitions: cool, cool; dusk, dusk; wings, wings; taxi, taxi; sound, sound, sound—and the ways some of their assonant variations are developed: cool, noon, cool, commuters, through, music; dusk, muffled, suddenly, slumped, cut, stump, commuters, dusk; sound, mountain, sound, sound, thousands.

But the big rhetoric of the poem is far different from the meditative poems. There are no hesitations in this poetry. This is the poetry of a man with answers who is speaking not to the separate, listening man but to multitudes. The poem is intended for the platform and its syntax is that of public rather than private speech. The tone is assertive at the beginning, ominous toward the end but always public, never understated, never tentative.

I once shared a platform with Bly toward the end of the Vietnam War. We were part of a panel of poets who had been assembled at the University of Maryland to read poems and to talk about "Poetry and the National Conscience." The halls we spoke and read in were crowded, partly because Bly was reading but also because then-Senator Eugene McCarthy was scheduled to do his first public poetry reading. During a question period, someone from the audience asked Bly if he felt that his poetry had become so topical that it would be forgotten as soon as the war was over. Bly's answer drew an ovation. He wasn't writing for unborn generations, he said; he was writing for the living who needed to see the corruption around them, the destruction their indifference permitted. The future would have to take care of itself; he was writing for us, now, here, and against the slaughter of Asian villagers that American bombs, American defoliants, and strafing American planes and pilots were responsible for. The statement was itself an extemporaneous poem and the cheers that followed it deafening. Later that night, at a reading before an even larger crowd, Bly's poetry with its big rhetoric and its fresh, improvisational tone brought more than five thousand people to their feet while syntax, sound, and statement combined to take on a force that seemed powerful and clean as light.

If the meditative and the polemical poems use similar melodic devices to achieve very different ends, something else seems to be happening within Bly's visionary and prophetic poems. Perhaps the nature of the audience for whom these poems are written has something to do with the changed character of sound and tone. For just as the hesitant meditative poems seem to be addressed to a single listener and the aggressive polemical poems seem addressed to a very large live audience (an audience concerned with issues as immediate as a present war), the visionary and prophetic poems—many of which are collected in *This Body Is Made of Gopher and Camphorwood* and most of which are in the form of prose poems—seem addressed not so much to a living audience as to an as-yet-unborn one. Nelson (following Bly) links these poems to Old Testament roots and to writers such as Blake and Kabir. But no matter how the style is evolved or what writers are echoed, the prose poems are constructed on a language that shifts suddenly from very flat statement to the most ornate embellishment. It is as if Bly wants to graft onto the common man's prose a rhetoric for archangels.

Critics find it difficult to comment on such poetry, I think, because, like all of us, they are of this time and this place. That is, they try to read it as if they were reading either the meditative poems or the polemical ones. They listen for the familiar melodies and the familiar kinds of statements of those poems and, of course, don't find them and are uneasy. I also share some of that discomfort. Yet if I try to project myself into a future in which the flesh and blood Robert Bly has been washed out of everybody's memory, the visionary poems take on a different quality. Forgetting the cadences of Bly's human voice, I listen to a speaker who has become a prophet anonymous as Solomon, a persona rather than the person from Minnesota, and I find the abstractions that once troubled me become manageable parts of a phantasmagoria of pure being. The language—like that of Blake toward the end of his career—becomes strange: archaic, almost so archaic as to be primitive, and yet oddly grand.

But I have moved beyond my project, which was to comment on patterns of sound, into the territory of statement and structure and style, the provinces of this fine book.

And it is a fine one—not just because it illuminates difficult or even obscure material, though it does, but because it manages to go beyond the texts of the poems to show us something of the texture of another man's life and thought. The kind of discoveries that Nelson makes are rare in criticism and relatively rare in life. Yet because within the frame of critical detachment, he is paradoxically willing to run the risks of sympathetic identification, Nelson is able to show us the human dimension of art: the root probe of anger and anxiety and love—and of doubt—that troubles the writer and that nudges him into creation. With modesty and with a quiet insight, Nelson helps us understand Robert Bly's concern for truth and his achievement of a body of work that is frequently beautiful, sometimes provocative, and almost always muscular in technique and as tender and tough and unpredictable as the breathing earth itself.

Preface

I first encountered Robert Bly in the pages of *Silence in the Snowy Fields*. As I read the poems in that book for the first time, I felt in them something fresh and peculiarly powerful. Since then I have read Bly's work steadily, and as I've studied it and watched it unfold my initial sense that this is a poet of special vision and force has remained, and deepened. In this study I have tried to describe Bly's vision and identify the distinctive powers and gifts of his work (not overlooking what I take to be its weak or problematical points). To do this I've tried to strike a balance, commenting on a substantial number of individual poems, and at the same time giving a sense of the ongoing themes and development of Bly's poetry as a whole, book by book. It is a body of work, I should add, that is still very much a work-in-progress.

Bly is a critic as well as a poet, and I have brought into this commentary on his poetry some of the major points of his criticism. Bly's criticism is an important part of his contribution; it is also useful in reading his poetry. As William Matthews has said in an essay on Bly, "Poets who are also critics write not only about other poems but always, in an elaborate code, about their own—both those they have written and those they aspire to write."[1]

We live in a period in which the interview has become a major—or at least ubiquitous—genre. Bly has given many interviews, a number of which have been collected in *Talking All Morning*, in the University of Michigan Press's Poets on Poetry series. This is a very lively book, and I have quoted from the interviews often. I note this because it should be kept in mind that comments in an interview are conversational, influenced by the interviewer and the circumstances; they are not the same as statements made in an essay, where the writer shapes and revises his thoughts and words at his own pace. I hope that I have not taken any of the comments from interviews out of context or placed more weight on them than is appropriate, but I have wanted to convey the flavor and energy of Bly's mind, and to this end the interviews are a rich source. Also, like his criticism, the interviews contain much that is useful in understanding his poetry.

I want to express my gratitude to a number of people. Friends tell me that there is such a thing as a word processor, which is an incredible aid in writing a book. I don't have one, and so I want to thank first my typists, Joan Cofrancesco and Henry Nelson, my father, whose patience through many revisions has been indispensable. Cayuga County Community College has been excellent in its support of this project, and I should mention individually Helena Howe, William Schwab, Thomas Steenburgh, Margaret Savage, Creston Munger, and Daniel Labeille. I am also indebted to the State University of New York for a grant that enabled me to take time off from teaching to work on this book. The staff of the Cayuga County Community College Library has helped me track down various source material, and I want to thank Douglas Michael and Kathleen Long in particular.

I am also indebted to Susan Wolstenholme, John Clarke, Robert Muhlnickel, and Jenny Hammett, who read or listened to various parts of the manuscript and offered helpful comments; and to John Unterecker, for his advice, criticism, and support throughout the project. I would also like to thank Jon Rossman, who has encouraged me in many ways, and who sent me, when the book was nearing completion, the following quotation from *I Don't Care If I Never Come Back*, by Art Hill: "What I am doing here is saying goodbye, because the book is about to end, and it's hard to say goodbye to anything that's been so much a part of your life for so many months. I worry about all the things I wanted to say, but didn't, and all the really terrific things I never even thought of, but will after it's too late. For those omissions, as the Spanish say, *no hay remedio*—there is no remedy. But I wish there were."

Robert Bly has assisted me in the preparation of the Chronology (I haven't asked him, however, to interpret any of his poems—that, I figure, is my job, not his); and he has been generous in granting me permission to quote a number of his poems in full. I am very grateful for this cooperation. This debt of gratitude is added to the larger one I feel toward him for his work, which has challenged and enriched me greatly, and continues to do so.

Finally, I say thanks to my wife Stephanie, to whom I would like to dedicate this book.

Howard Nelson
Scipio, New York

Acknowledgments

Grateful acknowledgment is made to the following:

Beacon Press, for permission to quote from *The Kabir Book: Forty-Four of the Ecstatic Poems of Kabir.*

Bruce Bennett, for permission to reprint his poem "Tracking the Rabbit Whose Tracks I Discovered This Morning in My Backyard."

Robert Bly, for permission to quote from *Silence in the Snowy Fields; The Loon; The Sixties; I Never Wanted Fame: 10 Poems and Proverbs by Antonio Machado; Lorca & Jimenez: Selected Poems; Jumping Out of Bed; Ducks;* and a letter to the author.

City Lights Books, for permission to quote from *The Teeth Mother Naked at Last.*

Doubleday & Company, for permission to quote from *The Man in the Black Coat Turns* (published by the Dial Press) and from *The Collected Poems of Theodore Roethke.*

Harper & Row, for permission to quote from *The Light Around the Body; Sleepers Joining Hands; The Morning Glory; This Body Is Made of Camphor and Gopherwood; This Tree Will Be Here for a Thousand Years;* and from Rainer Maria Rilke's *Duino Elegies,* translated by Stephen Garmey and Jay Wilson.

David Ignatow, for permission to quote from a letter to the author.

Alfred A. Knopf, for permission to quote from *The Collected Poems of Wallace Stevens.*

John F. Nims and *Poetry,* for permission to reprint "The Moose," copyright 1981 by The Modern Poetry Association.

Mrs. E. O. G. Turville-Petre, for lines from the *Elder Edda* translated by E. O. G. Turville-Petre in *Myth and Religion of the Far North.*

John Weatherhill, Inc., for permission to quote from *Pilgrim of the Clouds: Poems and Essays by Yüan Hung-Tao and His Brothers,* translated by Jonathan Chaves.

Chronology

The focus of this chronology is Bly's life as a writer; it identifies teachers, readings, literary friendships, publications, and other experiences that have been particularly important and characteristic in the course of his life in writing. Some of these items rely on Robert Bly's personal recollection, and while I have tried to verify dates against written records, this has not been possible in every case; a few items are estimations which may be off by a year or two.

1926   Robert Elwood Bly born on December 23, the second child of Jacob Thomas Bly and Alice Aws Bly, in Madison, Minnesota, a small farming community in the western part of the state.

1932–40 Attends one-room schoolhouse, Lac Qui Parle County, District 94.

1940–44 Attends Madison High School.

1944   Graduates from high school. Enlists in Navy, October; taken into a special radar program. While in this program, meets Marcus Eisenstein and Warren Ramshaw, the first men he had met who had a strong interest in literature. Buys his first book of poetry, Carl Sandburg's *Poems of the Midwest*, and later, *Leaves of Grass*.

1946–47   Upon discharge from the Navy, enrolls at St. Olaf's College, Northfield, Minnesota. Studies writing with Arthur Paulson.

1947–50   Transfers to Harvard, Fall 1947. Majors in English; studies with Archibald MacLeish, F. O. Matthiessen, John Kelleher. Under Kelleher's guidance, reads Thoreau and Yeats. Also studies German, Greek, and Latin. Reads Robert Lowell's *Lord Weary's Castle* and Richard Wilbur's *The Beautiful Changes*, "the dominant books" (Bly's words) of contemporary American poetry at that time; virtually memorizes *Lord Weary's Castle*.

Works on staff of *The Harvard Advocate*; becomes Literary Editor in his junior year. Meets Donald Hall. Other literary friends and acquaintances: Richard Wilbur, John Ashbery, Kenneth Koch, Frank O'Hara, Adrienne Rich, George Plimpton, Will Morgan, John Hawkes.

Meets future wife, Carolyn McLean.

Graduates, *magna cum laude*, 1950. Delivers the class poem.

Leaves Harvard having resolved to write poetry as his life's work. Moves to cabin in northern Minnesota.

1951–53   In January of 1951, goes to New York City, where he stays for two years, living alone, supporting himself with part-time jobs as clerk, typist, house painter, etc.

Important reading during this period: Rilke, Jacob Boehme's *The Three-Fold Life*; the *Tao Te Ching*; Horace; Virgil's *Georgics* and *Eclogues*; Rudolph Steiner. Reads and translates Pindar, and writes an essay (unpublished) on Pindar's metrics. (In 1982 Bly said: "My longing for some meter possible in English, yet not iambic, comes from the experience of Pindar's astounding poems.")

Writes "Where We Must Look for Help," "On the Ferry Across Chesapeake Bay," and "With Pale Women in Maryland," which would later appear in *Silence in the Snowy Fields*.

1953   Moves to Cambridge; continues living alone. Directs first American production of Yeats' *Player Queen* for the Poets' Theater.

1954   Travels to Iowa City, August. Enrolls in M.A. program at University of Iowa. Takes Paul Engle's workshop; teaches Freshman Composition and "Greeks and the Bible." Literary acquaintances: Marguerite Young, Kim Yong Ik, W. D. Snodgrass.

1955   Marries Carolyn McLean. Leaves Iowa in June; moves to a farm in Minnesota.

1956   Returns to Iowa in January. Submits as master's thesis *Steps Toward Poverty and Death*, a collection of poems. Receives master's degree.

1956–57 In Norway on Fulbright Grant to translate Norwegian poetry. In the Oslo library reads for the first time the poetry of Pablo Neruda, Georg Trakl, Juan Ramon Jimenez, Gunnar Ekelöf, Harry Martinson.

1957–62 Returns to Minnesota, Summer 1957. Lives on farm near where he was born. Occasional stays in New York City. Money he earns comes through translating (e.g., Selma Lagerlöf's *The Story of Gösta Berling*; *Reptiles and Amphibians of the World*, a textbook) and occasional teaching.

Important reading during this period: Antonio Machado; Lorca; R. H. Blyth's *Haiku* and *Zen in English Literature and Oriental Classics;* Chinese poetry; Ortega y Gasset's *Meditations on Quixote* and *Revolt of the Masses;* D. H. Lawrence's *Fantasia of the Unconscious;* Kierkegaard; Meister Eckhart.

1958   Begins writing the "country poems" which would later appear in *Silence in the Snowy Fields;* the first: "Three Kinds of Pleasures."

With William Duffy as coeditor, publishes first issue of *The Fifties.*

Meets James Wright.

1959   Works on a book of poems called *Poems for the Ascension of J. P. Morgan,* which was never published (selections from it appeared in *New World Writing*).

The Fifties #2 publishes the first poems by James Wright in "his new manner"—i.e., the poems that would become *The Branch Will Not Break.*

Meets Louis Simpson, David Ignatow. Visits William Carlos Williams. Often visits Donald Hall in Ann Arbor.

Meets Galway Kinnell, James Dickey.

During a stay in New York, receives as a gift from Jackson Mathews, *Two Essays on Analytical Psychology* by Jung.

1960   Meets John Logan. Visits William Carlos Williams with James Wright.

1961   First book publication by the Sixties Press: *Twenty Poems of Georg Trakl,* translations by Bly and James Wright.

Meets Kenneth Rexroth.

Translates *The Story of Gösta Berling*.

1962 Birth of first daughter, Mary.

The Lion's Tail and Eyes: Poems Written Out of Laziness and Silence, poems by Bly, James Wright, and William Duffy, published by Sixties Press.

Meets Ruth Ray.

Silence in the Snowy Fields published.

1963 "A Wrong-Turning in American Poetry" published in *Choice*.

Translates Francis Ponge's "object poem," "The Oyster."

Birth of second daughter, Bridget.

1964 Writes sequence entitled *Homage to Max Ernst* (eventually published in *Kayak* #55, 1981).

Awarded Amy Lowell Traveling Fellowship; lives in England for five months; then moves to Paris. Writes "My Three-Year-Old Daughter Brings Me a Gift," first "object" prose poem. Meets Pablo Neruda in Paris; visits Vincente Aleixandre in Madrid. Visits Machado's grave in south France. Meets Tomas Tranströmer.

1965 Back in the United States. Gives a number of poetry readings, which have become and will remain his major source of income.

Writes first Vietnam War poem, "At a March Against the Vietnam War," November. Begins work on long autobiographical poem which would become "Sleepers Joining Hands." Begins keeping dream journal.

Awarded Guggenheim Fellowship.

Receives as a gift from James Wright *One Hundred Poems of Kabir*, translated by Rabindranath Tagore and Evelyn Underhill; does not read it seriously until several years later.

1966   Organizes first anti-Vietnam War poetry readings at Reed College and the University of Washington. Founds, with David Ray, the organization American Writers Against the Vietnam War. The anthology *A Poetry Reading Against the Vietnam War* is published. Becomes increasingly active in antiwar readings with James Wright, Galway Kinnell, Denise Levertov, Lawrence Ferlinghetti, and others. Speaks poems more and more from memory.

The Sixties Press brings out *Forty Poems Touching on Recent American History* and *The Sea and the Honeycomb: A Book of Tiny Poems*, both edited and introduced by Bly.

1967   *The Light Around the Body* published; translation of Knut Hamsun's *Hunger* published.

Present at Pentagon demonstration and draft card turn-in with Dr. Spock and others.

Reading Blake and Jacob Boehme.

Publishes in *The Sixties* #9 his review attacking James Dickey's *Buckdancer's Choice*.

Meets Gary Snyder.

Birth of first son, Noah.

Receives Rockefeller Foundation Grant.

1968   *The Light Around the Body* wins the National Book Award for poetry. In his acceptance speech, Bly attacks American publishers for not actively opposing the war,

1972   Received first mask from Keith Gunderson; begins using masks in readings.

Received first mask from Keith Gunderson; begins using masks in readings.

First Kabir versions published as *The Fish in the Sea Is Not Thirsty* by Lillabulero Press. *The Seventies* #1 (later reissued as *Leaping Poetry*) published.

Continues work on "Sleepers Joining Hands."

Awarded Gugghenheim Fellowship.

1973   *Sleepers Joining Hands* and *Lorca & Jimenez: Selected Poems* published.

Important reading: *Parzival;* Denis DeRougemont.

1974   Teaches course for local citizens entitled "The Discoveries of Freud and Jung and How They Apply to Life in Madison, Minnesota."

Meets dulcimer player Gary Parks, who makes him a dulcimer.

Reads first poems of Rumi.

1975   Begins using dulcimer in readings.

Begins study of fairy tales; reads Marie-Louise Von Franz's *The Feminine in Fairy Tales*. Other important reading: *The Cloud of Unknowing; The Secret of the Golden Flower*, with introduction by Jung.

Organizes, with Peter Martin, the First Annual Conference on the Great Mother. At the conference, teaches classes on *The Odyssey* and lectures for the first time on fairy tales.

The Morning Glory published. *Friends, You Drank Some Darkness*, translations of Harry Martinson, Gunnar Ekelöf, and Tomas Tranströmer, published. *Selected Poems of David Ignatow*, edited and with commentary by Bly, published.

urges defiance of draft laws, donates prize
the draft resistance movement.

Twenty Poems of Pablo Neruda, translations by
James Wright, published by the Sixties Press

Travels in England, Sweden, and Norway
meditation with Trunpa Rinpoche in Scotland

Visits Tomas Tranströmer in Sweden.

1969   First edition of *The Morning Glory* (twelve pros
published by Kayak Press.

Reads Jung intensively for the first time; rea
Neumann's *The Great Mother: An Analysis of t*
type.

Tennessee Poetry Journal devotes special issue
work. Bly meets Stephen Mooney, the editor,
comes a student of astrology through him.

1970   City Lights Books publishes "The Teeth-Mot
ked at Last." The Seventies Press publishes
Poems of Tomas Tranströmer.

In September, goes with family to live for mos
year in California. Writes the Point Reyes poem
included in *The Morning Glory.*

1971   Begins reworking the Tagore-Underhill translat
Kabir.

Meets Andrei Voznesensky in Vancouver.

Returns home from California in May. Birth of
son, Micah.

Neruda & Vallejo: Selected Poems, published by l
Press.

Bly's only brother, James, dies in car crash.

1972   Received first mask from Keith Gunderson; begins using masks in readings.

First Kabir versions published as *The Fish in the Sea Is Not Thirsty* by Lillabulero Press. *The Seventies #*1 (later reissued as *Leaping Poetry*) published.

Continues work on "Sleepers Joining Hands."

Awarded Gugghenheim Fellowship.

1973   *Sleepers Joining Hands* and *Lorca & Jimenez: Selected Poems* published.

Important reading: *Parzival;* Denis DeRougemont.

1974   Teaches course for local citizens entitled "The Discoveries of Freud and Jung and How They Apply to Life in Madison, Minnesota."

Meets dulcimer player Gary Parks, who makes him a dulcimer.

Reads first poems of Rumi.

1975   Begins using dulcimer in readings.

Begins study of fairy tales; reads Marie-Louise Von Franz's *The Feminine in Fairy Tales*. Other important reading: *The Cloud of Unknowing; The Secret of the Golden Flower*, with introduction by Jung.

Organizes, with Peter Martin, the First Annual Conference on the Great Mother. At the conference, teaches classes on *The Odyssey* and lectures for the first time on fairy tales.

The Morning Glory published. *Friends, You Drank Some Darkness*, translations of Harry Martinson, Gunnar Ekelöf, and Tomas Tranströmer, published. *Selected Poems of David Ignatow*, edited and with commentary by Bly, published.

urges defiance of draft laws, donates prize money to the draft resistance movement.

Twenty Poems of Pablo Neruda, translations by Bly and James Wright, published by the Sixties Press.

Travels in England, Sweden, and Norway. Studies meditation with Trunpa Rinpoche in Scotland.

Visits Tomas Tranströmer in Sweden.

1969   First edition of *The Morning Glory* (twelve prose poems) published by Kayak Press.

Reads Jung intensively for the first time; reads Erich Neumann's *The Great Mother: An Analysis of the Archetype.*

Tennessee Poetry Journal devotes special issue to Bly's work. Bly meets Stephen Mooney, the editor, and becomes a student of astrology through him.

1970   City Lights Books publishes "The Teeth-Mother Naked at Last." The Seventies Press publishes *Twenty Poems of Tomas Tranströmer.*

In September, goes with family to live for most of the year in California. Writes the Point Reyes poems, later included in *The Morning Glory.*

1971   Begins reworking the Tagore-Underhill translations of Kabir.

Meets Andrei Voznesensky in Vancouver.

Returns home from California in May. Birth of second son, Micah.

Neruda & Vallejo: Selected Poems, published by Beacon Press.

Bly's only brother, James, dies in car crash.

1976   "Being a Lutheran Boy-God in Minnesota," published in *Growing Up in Minnesota*.

Meets Etheridge Knight.

Second Annual Conference on the Great Mother.

Important reading: Marie-Louise Von Franz's *The Shadow and Evil in Fairy Tales*; Ouspensky; Vidyapati; Chandidas.

1977   *This Body Is Made of Camphor and Gopherwood*, *The Kabir Book*, and *The Loon* published.

Participates in symposium, Chinese Poetry and the American Imagination, New York, April. The Third Annual Conference on the Great Mother takes place, now called Conference on the Great Mother and the New Father.

Important reading: Philip Slater; Ester Harding; William Irwin Thompson; Gaston Bachelard; Mircea Eliade.

1978   Writes play: *The Thorn Bush Cock Giant*. Tours with the Great Mother Traveling Troupe.

Two documentaries on Bly are made: a film, "A Man Writes to a Part of Himself," by Minnesota filmmakers; and a PBS program by Bill Moyers.

Attends International Poetry Festival in Rotterdam.

Important reading: John Perry; Ernst Becker.

1979   Important reading: Ernst Becker's *The Denial of Death*; Rudolph Steiner; Joseph Campbell; James Hillman. Meets Campbell and Hillman.

Finishes work on the anthology *News of the Universe*.

June: Robert and Carolyn Bly divorce.

This Tree Will Be Here For a Thousand Years published.

1980   *News of the Universe* and *Talking All Morning* published.

Participates in Writers' Week Festival in Adelaide, Australia. On return trip visits Bali, where he meets I Wayan Wija, poet and master of the "shadow play."

Death of James Wright.

June: Marries Ruth Ray. Moves to Moose Lake, Minnesota. Carolyn Bly lives nearby; they share custody of the children.

Attends Conference on Rudolph Steiner in California.

Important reading: Owen Barfield's *Poetic Diction;* James J. Y. Liu's *The Art of Chinese Poetry;* the Provençal poets; Ponge. Memorizes passages from *Beowulf* and medieval English poetry.

1981   *Selected Poems of Rainer Maria Rilke* published. Following his long-time editor Frances McCullough, moves from Harper & Row to the Dial Press, which publishes *The Man in the Black Coat Turns.*

"The Image as a Form of Intelligence" and "What Whitman Did Not Gives Us" published.

Gives memorial reading for James Wright, with Galway Kinnell, New York, March. Participates in anti-nuclear-arms poetry reading at Town Hall, New York, May. Participates in Lindisfarne Conference on Pythagoras.

Important reading: Frances Yates; Rafael Lopez-Pedraza's *Hermes and His Children;* Anna Akhmatova; Gurdjieff.

Of Solitude and Silence (earlier issued as *Poetry East* 4/5), first book-length collection of criticism on Bly, published. *Plainsong* devotes special issue to Bly.

1982   Annual Mother Conference becomes A Conference on Form.

Teaches course in mythology in Greece for the University of California.

Translation of *The Economy Spinning Faster and Faster*, poems by Göran Sonnevi, published.

Participates in Russian and American Writers Conferences, Kiev, July.

Six Comments on Poetry by Robert Bly

In a poem, as in a human body, what is invisible makes all the difference.[1]

What astonished me in Chinese poetry and still does is the way so many Chinese poems begin: "Well, the porch was wet today when I walked out." . . . These Chinese are amazing in the way they'll root the poem instantly in the body—"Mist today, huh? I notice my little blue flower doesn't look quite so bright this morning."[2]

. . . what is needed to write good poems about the outward world is inwardness.[3]

. . . when writers talk hysterically about the human because of failure of imagination and exhaustion; when they can think of nothing else that is exciting; when they are *reduced* to the human, then what is human is barren. I am not urging a nature poetry either, but rather a poetry that goes deep into the human being, much deeper than the ego, and at the same time is aware of many other things. The confessional poets tend to believe that the human being is something extremely important *in itself*. That is why they are always telling us every fact about their operations. Poets of that sort will accept calmly the extinction of the passenger pigeon or the blue whale. These are the poets to whom Nerval was talking when he suddenly turned and said: "When you gather to plan, the universe is not there."[4]

The whole capitalist system, we know, is against those peak moments; if you're working on the production line you have to leave it. And all capitalism tries to dull you with television so you don't recognize your own peak moments when they come. . . .

Finally, your unconscious says, "The hell with this guy, this person's a creep, I'm going back in the seed, I'll be reborn, better luck next time, I hope in New Guinea!" And what you should be trying to do in life is to prevent your unconscious from making that decision. To me this is what poetry is involved with.[5]

Poetry I think is a healing process.[6]

ROBERT BLY

CHAPTER I

Silence in the Snowy Fields

> If I reached my hands down, near the earth,
> I could take handfuls of darkness!
> A darkness was always there, which we
>   never noticed.
>   —"Snowfall in the Afternoon"

A first reading of Robert Bly's first book, *Silence in the Snowy Fields*, is likely to be a mysterious or mystifying experience. Certainly many readers have found in the short, quiet, mostly rural poems he gathered there, with their pronounced simplicities and repetitions of scene and syntax, something new and refreshing. To others the book has seemed baffling or annoying. In an essay written in 1969, William Heyen gave a good description of his own, negative reaction (later, as the essay goes on to say, much revised); it touches on many of the problematical aspects of the book:

> For several years I disliked what Robert Bly had done in *Silence in the Snowy Fields* (1962). Indeed, I was surprised that the book had even made it into print. His risks, I felt, were all the bad ones. And his dustjacket remarks to the effect that "any poetry in the poems . . . is in the white spaces between the stan-

zas" offended me. I didn't expect these poems. . . . I thought
that his collection was a mistake, a group of journal jottings.

Where was his "heightened speech?" How, if to suggest
something is to create it and to state something is to destroy it,
could he write lines such as "I have awakened at Missoula, Mon-
tana, utterly happy" ("In a Train") and "There is a privacy I love
in this snowy night" ("Driving to Town Late to Mail a Letter")?
Didn't he know such bare statements were against the rules?

How could he employ the "pathetic fallacy" with such care-
lessness? I looked on such images as

And I know the sun is sinking down great stairs
Like an executioner with a great blade walking into a cellar . . .
                                          ("The Clear Air of October")

as combinations of cliché and absurdity.

Didn't he know enough not to use the word "strange"? Why
did he repeat the words "dark" and "darkness"dozens of times?
How could he be naive enough to use so many exclamation marks
when everyone knows that this shows his language isn't bearing
the weight of his emotion? How, in the Age of Eliot, could he
write poems that defied serious inquiry and involved explication?
What did these poems *mean?* I couldn't surround them, couldn't
imagine discussing them. What could one say about them?

Silence in the Snowy Fields was like a cluster of gnats.[1]

Heyen uses the phrase "against the rules" advisedly: for all
its quiet and pastoral qualities, *Snowy Fields* was a rebellious book.
Written at the end of a period in our poetry when irony, highly
worked surfaces, and intellectual density were prized over other
effects and possibilities, a poem like this brief one, titled simply
"Love Poem"—

> When we are in love, we love the grass,
> And the barns, and the lightpoles,
> And the small mainstreets abandoned all night.

seemed an affront to literary sophistication. Different readers
can argue a long time over the loveliness or banality of such a

poem; as Louis Simpson said after quoting it in his review of *Snowy Fields*, "this kind of writing will strike you either as totally poetic, or not poetry at all."[2]

In the poems of *Snowy Fields* Bly was flying in the face of what he saw as narrow and atrophied poetic standards, just as he was rethinking, in his complementary roles as critic and editor, the nature and resources of poetry. In 1958 he founded, with William Duffy, *The Fifties*, "a magazine of poetry and general opinion." *The Fifties* (later *The Sixties* and, for one issue, *The Seventies*) quickly established itself as an important and original force in American poetry, principally because of the translations it published and because of the critical essays by Bly that appeared in it (often under the pseudonym "Crunk")—essays which have more than once been compared in their freshness and impact to the criticism of Ezra Pound in the second decade of the century. In an essay in the first issue of *The Fifties* Bly wrote, "There is an imagination which assembles the three kingdoms within one poem: the dark figures of politics, the world of streetcars, and the ocean world. . . . We need poets now who can carry on a sustained raid into modern life, and in work after work, carry on the green and vigorous waters of this profound life."[3] On the inside of the front cover this declaration appeared: "The editors of this magazine think that most of the poetry published in America today is too old-fashioned." *The Fifties* was an instrument of iconoclasm and exploration.

While it is the simplicity and quiet of *Snowy Fields* that first strike the reader, the book was a key contribution to the period of great restlessness, energy, and originality in American poetry that began in the 1950s and continued throughout the 1960s. In 1960 Frost, Eliot, Pound, Williams, Moore, and Jeffers were all still alive; Stevens was just five years dead. Whatever was not clear, it was clear that something magnificent was ending. The influence of New Criticism had become an orthodoxy which many, widely various poets found constricting. Allen Ginsberg's *Howl* appeared in 1956, *Kaddish* in 1961. Donald M. Allen's anthology *The New American Poetry 1945–1960* gathered a range of poets of varying ages, presented in five geographical/poetic groups, and a battery of "Statements on Poetics," none of which derived their standards from John Crowe Ransom, Cleanth Brooks, or Yvor Winters. Robert Lowell, in the 1959 *Life Studies*, moved away from traditional meters and highly wrought diction into freer forms and colloquial language, just one of the first and most influential poets in what was becoming a large-scale migration. Theodore Roethke also explored more open forms, and, more importantly, continued his explorations of shores and rivers far from the palace of reason (which he referred to in one poem as "That dreary shed, that hutch for grubby school-boys!"[4]) *The Fifties/Sixties* was busy with its work of trying to clear ground for younger poets and to internationalize and re-imagine American poetry. The careers of a strong and diverse generation of poets, born in the 1920s—James Dickey, Denise Levertov, John Logan, Louis Simpson, Robert Creeley, Kenneth Koch, Galway Kinnell, W.S. Merwin, James Wright, Anne Sexton, Philip Levine, Adrienne Rich, to give a partial list— were gathering force and recognition, as were those of certain somewhat older poets, notably William Stafford and David Ignatow. (Other poets, who had gained reputation earlier and who are often among the victims of the unavoidable slights of summaries of this sort, people such as Richard Wilbur and Howard Nemerov, contributed not to the creative restlessness of the period, but only to its creative achievement.)

One common denominator among the poets who came to prominence in the early sixties (possibly the only one) was dissatisfaction to greater or lesser degrees with traditional metrical forms and rhyme. So an anthology that brought a number of them together, *Naked Poetry* (1969), carried the subtitle *Recent*

American Poetry in Open Forms. While his work represented as emphatically as anyone's a turning away from rhyme and meter, Bly commented in an essay which appeared in that anthology that he preferred the term "free verse" to "open form," "because it implies not a technique but a longing." He went on to say:

> I refuse to say anything at all about prosody. What an ugly word it is! In the true poem, both the form and the content rise from the same place; they have the same swiftness and darkness. Both are expressions of a certain rebellious energy rising in the psyche: they are what Boehme calls "the shooting up of life from nature to spirit." What is important is this rebellious energy, not technique.[5]

Early in his career Bly had studied prosody, and he wrote most of his earliest poems in meter; later, he would investigate set measures again. But throughout most of his poetry an impatience with matters of prosody has been apparent, and a statement such as the one above is important for understanding his work. And in *Snowy Fields*, beyond all matters of style, beyond the radical plainness which is so pronounced that it transforms into something not so plain after all, what is startling and essential is, first, the attention it pays to the physical world, and second, its rendering of profound moments and motions in a man's inward life.

Identifying literary influences on *Snowy Fields*, Bly has cited Kenneth Rexroth, J. M. Synge, translations by Frank O'Connor from medieval Irish poetry, and "some Twentieth Century Spanish poets," especially Antonio Machado, "the father of that book."[6] One can also sense Wordsworth in the background, and William Carlos Williams should be mentioned as a father-figure for all American poetry written in colloquial language—for Bly's commitment to the colloquial is a consistent principle throughout the various kinds and styles of poetry he has written. But probably the strongest literary presence in *Snowy Fields* is Chinese poetry—that is, Chinese poetry as we have come to know it through the body of translations that make up one of the most beautiful and influential strands in modern poetry in English.[7] In their surfaces and textures, and I think in their longings as well, many of the poems of *Snowy Fields* feel more like these Chinese translations than any other work. Rexroth is a strong link to the Chinese, though in the structure of the line, where Bly favors end-stopping, the *Snowy Fields* poems resemble the translations of Arthur Waley and others more than those of Rexroth, with their elegant, glancing enjambments. Simplicity of diction, a flat music, trust in straightforward declarative sentences, an inclination to speak through images, titles that are artfully artless, celebration of simplicity and idleness and a steadying relationship between the poet and the natural world, a tone which is a mixture of quiet and intensity, the ability to make an elliptical presentation create profound undercurrents—all of these are elements shared by *Snowy Fields* and the Chinese translations. Both are poetry which is plain, delicate, and sturdy. Bly has said that he considers ancient Chinese poetry the greatest ever written,[8] and it is not hard to see why a poet interested in "the connection between poetry and simplicity"[9] would be drawn to it. But beyond simplicity, the Chinese translations often capture a rare sense of a union of the physical and the spiritual, a deep connection between landscape and emotion. And it may be in this quality that *Snowy Fields* bears the most significant resemblance to Chinese poetry.

The book carries an epigraph from Jacob Boehme: "We are all asleep in the outward man." One could read this statement two ways. For Boehme it would mean that we are caught up in the outer—i.e., material, temporal, social—world, and therefore are not awake to our true spiritual or inward nature. But with regard to *Snowy Fields*, we might read it somewhat differently.

There is little overt social content in *Snowy Fields;* in fact, other than the poet himself there are few people in evidence at all. This is deliberate: in order to awaken the inward man, Bly moves off into solitude. But in terms of the outer world in its most immediate sense—the world of the senses and the body and the physical place which a person inhabits—the man we meet in *Snowy Fields* is far from being asleep; in this sense he is an exemplary exception to Boehme's statement. Bly said in 1966: "I suppose . . . *Silence in the Snowy Fields* has something to do with my conviction that unless American poetry can grow naturally out of American ground, we may as well give up now and quit." [10] With respect to "American ground," the outer world is brought strongly into *Snowy Fields*. Much of Bly's work belongs among the best regional writing this country has produced. A native of Minnesota, he writes with great sensitivity to both the detail and mood of his place, and one cannot think of his poetry without forming pictures in one's mind of the rural Midwestern landscape. But his poems are not regionalism of the superficial or strictly external variety. His scenes of farms, woods, and lakes are deepened; they have spiritual resonance. The inward world is entered in *Snowy Fields* through the outward world: the soul is known through the body and the places it moves among.

This "inward/outward" terminology, derived from Boehme and the Protestant mystical tradition to which he belongs, can become somewhat awkward, but it would be pointless to try to avoid it, because it is central to Bly's thought. Like two of the other teachers to whom he is most deeply indebted, Blake and Jung, Bly is interested in wholeness; like them, he speaks in dichotomies because he does not want to be split in half. And again like Blake, he is a believer in possibility: "What is now proved was once only imagined." [11] Reaching what is only imagined, which would include wholeness itself, is a slow process, a long journey, lasting perhaps longer than any of our lives. But it is a journey of which the movements and momentary illuminations of *Snowy Fields* are a part.

Snowy Fields was not just a collection of the poems Bly had ready for publication in 1962. Some of the poems that would appear in his second book, *The Light Around the Body*, had already been written. When he gathered the poems of *Snowy Fields*, he created a book of unusual unity, both in tone and in purpose. One can easily conceive of it as a single poem, and when it is read in this way its impact is greater than the sum of its parts. It is not a work of minimalism, but rather of concentration: the concentration of using few words, and that of knowing what one wants to concentrate on. The book contains forty-four poems, divided into three groups. The organization is not rigid or inevitable, but it does reflect a sequence that is basic to the book's work and effect: an experience of solitude (Eleven Poems of Solitude), which brings expanded or deepened awareness (Awakening), which leads to a state of being which contains both stillness and direction (Silence on the Roads). Though its laconic style and spare, shadowy scenes may at first make *Snowy Fields* resemble a cloud of gnats, actually it has the solidness and the value of ritual. The silence that lines the poems is not slight. It hovers over the land, and around a man who knows he is wounded, and returns to certain springs to drink.

In looking at individual poems in *Snowy Fields*, we should begin with one that has a special importance: "Return to Solitude." Bly placed it second in the book, but it is appropriate to discuss it first, for most of the poems in *Snowy Fields* begin in the experience it describes.

Bly has been emphatic about the value of solitude, particularly for writers; his remark, "my advice to anyone if he wants to write is to go and live by himself for two years and not talk to anyone," [12] is indicative. Of course all writers know solitude at least to some extent—the solitude of the blank page—but for some it is more than just the time of work; it is a root into an essential landscape, a shack by a pond or a hut in a desert. When Bly advises young writers to go and live alone, he is essentially suggesting that they do as he did. Following his graduation from Harvard in 1950, he spent the next three years living by himself, mostly in New York City, supporting himself through various part-time jobs. He maintains a certain privacy about those years, but it is clear that he has come to regard them as a crucial experience in his spiritual life—an instinctive withdrawal into the wilderness, a night journey, an awakening. They contained depression and alienation—"I understood Sartre's *Nausea* very well in those days" [13]—and ecstasy. Bly would write later, in the autobiographical poem "Sleepers Joining Hands": "I felt the road first in New York, in that great room/reading Rilke in the womanless loneliness./ How marvelous the great wings sweeping along the floor." That "great room" refers to the main reading room in the New York Public Library, which Bly has called "the most wonderful place in the world—no matter how poor or neurotic you are, they'll give you a book anyway." [14] And he has also said of this period of solitude in New York, "it was those years in which I learned everything that I tried to bring into poems." [15]

(Those who have attended Bly's readings, which regularly run to two and three spirited hours, or have read his interviews, which are both numerous and extremely lively, will note a certain incongruity between his insistence on solitude and silence on one hand and such outpourings of extraversion on the other. It is the first of many paradoxes we will encounter in considering Bly and his work. An introvert and an extravert live together in Bly's body. He welcomes them both, although in certain later poems—"Falling into Holes in Our Sentences" in *This Body Is Made of Camphor and Gopherwood*; "Written at Mule Hollow, Utah" in *The Man in the Black Coat Turns*—the extravert comes in for criticism.)

It is easy in reading *Snowy Fields* to form an impression of it too much dominated by the book's peaceful elements. In a number of important instances the poems depart from the peaceful, and within the brevity and spareness of "Return to Solitude" there is a windblown, nearly violent quality. Solitude here is a dynamic experience, with the power to change a person's life. There are indeed clear, cold springs in *Snowy Fields*, but in "Return to Solitude" we find ourselves not looking into a still pool, but making a "return to the sea."

In poetry and in criticism, Bly always tries to speak in images, and there are certain broad and rich ones that his imagination picks up naturally; they are part of his basic vocabulary. The sea is one of these, as is water in general; other key examples are darkness, trees, and roads. Needless to say, the meanings of such ancient, primary images are not fixed and do not have clear borders; that is one of their advantages. The associations of the sea with primordial life, formlessness, the womb, the abyss, the infinite, tidal movements, creatures both beautiful and terrifying, are obvious enough, and certainly do not exhaust the possibilities. To some extent, the image of the sea was supplanted in our vocabulary (though not in our souls) when we developed the phrase "the unconscious"—a term almost as usefully ambiguous as "the sea," though less useful with respect to visualization and connotative richness.

The poem's second stanza is a small catalogue which elaborates briefly on the sea we are returning to. It is "the sea of solitary corridors,/And halls of wild nights,/explosions of grief." The stanza then adds another dimension, as the sea is trans-

formed further into "the sea of death." The death here is that
which is felt when the self ventures outside its usual boundaries.
It is a reaching out and mingling which for some poets is crucial
to being fully alive. The experience is different at different times
and for different individuals. For Whitman, merging with nature and other people seemed both possible and desirable. For
Roethke, it was a dive down among other life forms—exhilarating, nourishing, and, since he was often unsure about his ability
to return, terrifying. In Bly's case, the dive is a baptism, not a
drowning. The poems in *Snowy Fields* take us out into broken
cornstalks, a lake at sunset, grass, falling snow, a horse's gaze,
and in doing so they take us also into psychic waters beyond the
shores of the conscious mind. It is a baptism not into certainty
but into a new or renewed strangeness, which the third stanza
of "Return to Solitude" describes with a fine understatement:

> What shall we find when we return?
> Friends changed, houses moved,
> Trees perhaps, with new leaves.

That captures both the astonishment—disorienting, a little
frightening—of finding oneself in a familiar but altered place,
and the freshness of new life. The new leaves on those trees,
whose roots stretch down into the darkness of earth, express
Bly's hope. He believes that transformation arises from hidden
sources, and that solitude allows this rising and rebirth to take
place.

   We might take three poems from the first section to suggest
three sources of the subtle and distinctive power of *Snowy Fields*.
There is of course some oversimplification in this scheme, since
these elements occur together in various ways throughout the
book. The poems I will discuss are "Three Kinds of Pleasures,"
"Hunting Pheasants in a Cornfield," and "Driving Toward the

Lac Qui Parle River," and the elements I want to draw attention to are imagery, instinct, and intuition. To begin, here is "Three Kinds of Pleasures" in full:

I

Sometimes, riding in a car, in Wisconsin
Or Illinois, you notice those dark telephone poles
One by one lift themselves out of the fence line
And slowly leap on the gray sky—
And past them, the snowy fields.

II

The darkness drifts down like snow on the picked cornfields
In Wisconsin: and on these black trees
Scattered, one by one,
Through the winter fields—
We see stiff weeds and brownish stubble,
And white snow left now only in the wheeltracks of the combine.

III

It is a pleasure, also, to be driving
Toward Chicago, near dark,
And see the lights in the barns.
The bare trees more dignified than ever,
Like a fierce man on his deathbed,
And the ditches along the road half full of a private snow.

Often a poet's special sensitivity to particular subjects, moods, or objects is as important to the strength and distinctiveness of his work as his way with language. This is true of Bly, and one notices in reading his poems that his imagination responds remarkably to light and darkness. Throughout *Snowy Fields* we encounter many lights and shadows; sunlight and moonlight are mentioned often, and darkness continually. Many of the poems are set in a specified part of the day, and night and dusk dominate. Bly has commented, "It seems that man's unconscious opens around twilight. . . . This idea I didn't learn from Jung, but I learned it myself noticing that many of the poems in *Snowy Fields. . . .* were written at dusk."[16] And in the poems, one can indeed sense in the gathering darkness a new, darker intelligence gathering as well. The play of light and dark in *Snowy Fields* reflects the conscious mind and the unconscious opening to one another. It is important to note that for Bly the darkness is not sinister, but rich; he welcomes it. Like consciousness, the small lights in barns move us because of the vast surrounding dark, and the darkness is beautiful because of the specks and shards of light that shine within it.

Read quickly, the stanzas of "Three Kinds of Pleasures" seem to be mere snapshots, three frozen glimpses. But as one lingers over them, it becomes apparent that these scenes are alive, and they are full of motion. The telephone poles "lift themselves," and "slowly leap on the gray sky"; darkness "drifts down"; the trees have been "scattered"; the poet is driving, moving past delicate lights—the small lights in barns, the faint glow of snow in ditches. In this subtle sense of motion, as in the play of light and dark, Bly describes a countryside but also a psychic state. When he says that the telephone poles "slowly leap on the gray sky," he is not merely making a picturesque metaphor; that leaping comes from a leaping in the soul of the man looking across the countryside. And yet the landscape is itself marvelously real. . . .

One of the things Bly first attempted to do in his career as a theorist was to redefine the term "image." He proposed that Imagism in its Hulme-Pound-Lowell formulations was misnamed. Seeing in Imagism an excessive drive toward objectivity, he calls the kind of image which that movement concentrated on "pictures"; a poem made up of pictures is "an extension of the eye, rather than the brain."[17] Williams, according to Bly, "asks poetry to confine itself to wheelbarrows, bottlecaps, weeds. . . . Keeping close to the surface becomes an obsession."[18] The difference between a picture and an image as Bly wants to define it is that an image carries not just sense impressions but psychic content as well. There is some oversimplification of Imagism in Bly's criticisms—for example, Pound did call for "Objectivity and again objectivity, *and expression*" [19] (italics mine); he defined image as "that which presents an intellectual and emotional complex in an instant of time." [20] So he was interested in image as more than an extension of the eye. Still, one can see why Bly would find Pound's conception of image unsatisfactory. Bly has never been an advocate of objectivity in poetry; to him, it is largely strength and originality of subjective response that breathe life into a poet's work. But beyond that, by Bly's standard, Pound's definition is lacking in another way. The phrase "intellectual and emotional complex" misses the spiritual and unconscious levels that Bly feels are essential. He once remarked, "Pound almost never mentioned Rilke. . . . Why not? Because he's too inward for Pound." [21] And in one of his early, key formulations, Bly defined a poem as "something that penetrates for an instant into the unconscious." [22]

Bly gave this definition in "A Wrong-Turning in American Poetry" (1963), one of his most provocative and influential essays. The piece is a broad criticism of three generations of American poets: "the generation of 1917," Pound, Eliot, Williams, Moore, "the objectivist generation"; "the Metaphysical Generation . . . Eberhart and Tate as well as the *New Masses* poets"; and "the generation of 1947," Shapiro, Lowell, Berryman, Schwartz, Jarrell, "the Hysterical Generation." [23] Through these generations Bly traces what he sees as a destructive movement toward objectivity and absorption in the data of the outer world, and away from the unconscious and the intense spiritual life he finds in the poetry of Rilke, Machado, Juan Ramon Jimenez, Lorca, and Cesar Vallejo.

In "A Wrong-Turning in American Poetry" Bly criticizes

not only "pictorialism" but also Eliot's "objective correlative," a term which he calls "astoundingly passionless." [24] Eliot had said:

> The only way of expressing emotion in the form of art is by finding an "objective correlative"; in other words, a set of objects, a situation, a chain of events which will be the formula of that particular emotion; such as when the external facts which must terminate in sensory experience are given, the emotion is immediately evoked. [25]

For Bly, Eliot was making the poetic process seem too much like "a controlled experiment [which] can be repeated any number of times" [26]—an analogy he would never choose to describe poetry. Also, in Eliot's statement effect preceeds image: the poet knows what he wants to express and only needs to find the vehicle for expressing it. It all sounds very self-conscious, as if Eliot were trying to eliminate the unknown from the poem. This is the last thing Bly wants. If a poet were actually to write according to such a method, "the impulse to the poem [would be] broken. True freshness and surprises [would be] impossible." [27]

Bly's emphasis on and way with the image has been the focus of much of the critical discussion of his work, and it was the image that became the hallmark of the movement he seemed to be leading in the 1960s, frequently referred to as "deep image poetry," a term which Bly himself avoids. "Deep image" and "deep image poetry" have proven somewhat slippery subjects over the years. Many definitions have been given, sometimes in highly abstract and laborious critical language at a far extreme from the spirit of its subject, for the "deep image" is essentially a union of the physical and the mysterious. Bly's own comments on the image have been pungent and, until a 1981 essay called "Recognizing the Image as a Form of Intelligence," fragmentary. Here are three comments by Bly that seem especially noteworthy.

Let's imagine a poem as if it were an animal. When animals run, they have considerable flowing rhythms. Also they have bodies. An image is simply a body where psychic energy is free to move around. . . . An image is not anything unusual. It is simply language used in such a way that psychic energy can continue its flow.[28]

The important thing about an image . . . is that it is made by both the conscious and the unconscious mind.[29]

I insist the image is a physical thing.[30]

Bly wants the image to be both physically and psychically alive, and he wants its reverberation to be felt beyond the rational and even the conscious mind. In "Recognizing the Image as a Form of Intelligence" he says:

. . . the image joins the light and dark worlds. It is a house with a room for each. An image may join the world of the dead with the world of the living; it makes a house with a room for each. . . . It may connect what we know with what we don't. . . . It may join what is invisible with what is visible. . . .

It's possible there is another sort of image, which the ancients knew about. It is less like a container and more like an arm. It reaches out of human consciousness to touch something else. We find it in Blake's "Tiger," and other poems of his . . .

We do feel a gap between ourselves and nature. We can remain in the gap, and let the two worlds fall apart farther and remain separate. Or a human being can reach out with his left hand to the world of human intelligence and with the right hand to the natural world, and touch both at the same time . . . I recently came across an image that ancient Norwegians created for Thor: lightning over a ripe barley field. There it is again: the ancient Gothic imagination was unwilling to accept the severe categorizations of outer and inner, divine and human, intelligence and matter, that Aristotle and Descartes acquiesce in.[31]

In poems written twenty years earlier, Bly was himself creating (or finding) images which united the senses, the conscious mind, and the unconscious, and which reached out with right and left arms to link the world of a solid natural scene and an invisible human longing. The imagery of poems like "Three Kinds of Pleasures" brings us closer to the earth, and at the same time it wakens and expresses the inner man.

Another poem which finds strange power in a simple scene is "Hunting Pheasants in a Cornfield." It has the same sort of spare, sharply observed, resonant description as "Three Kinds of Pleasures," but in it something else comes into play as well. One of the lucky outcomes of Bly's interest in "the connection between poetry and simplicity" was that at times, after he had stripped away verbal ornament, irony, social details, and discursive thinking, he arrived at something very old. "Hunting Pheasants in a Cornfield" brings us down to a level of experience where a man moves as if by instinct, where familiar objects become oddly compelling, and where he begins to feel himself surrounded by huge stretches of time. He finds himself enacting an unconscious ritual, in which the simplest acts take on the power of myth. When this happens, it is apparently the body which first becomes aware of it.

The poem describes a walk in a field, in the middle of which stands a willow tree. When the poet reaches the tree, he is aware of a fascination with it, felt in the body: "The body is strangely torn, and cannot leave it." Here is Jung's description of what happens when we find ourselves within the force-field of a myth:

> The moment when this mythological situation reappears is always characterized by a peculiar emotional intensity; it is as though chords in us were struck that had never resounded before.[32]

The poem evokes with great delicacy the link of "peculiar intensity" between the man and the tree. The first three stanzas describe the attraction. The poet's movements suggest those of an animal: "I walk around and around it. . . . / At last I sit down beneath it." There is a sharpening of the senses that is also ani-mallike: "Its leaves are scattered around its trunk . . . / Brown now, and speckled with delicate black./ Only the cornstalks now can make a noise." A significance that lies behind the physical perceptions edges toward consciousness as he watches "the sun moving on the chill skin of the branches," a light that is like the poet's attention, moving so far only on entrancing surfaces. In the last stanza the previously hidden significance of the tree breaks through:

> The mind has shed leaves alone for years.
> It stands apart with small creatures near its root.
> I am happy in this ancient place,
> A spot easily caught sight of above the corn,
> If I were a young animal ready to turn home at dusk.

One is tempted to rewrite this stanza, inserting the word "tree" for "mind," but the directness of the original has its ap-peal. Three strands come together in this stanza: the tree as an image of the mind, solitary, passing through cycles of loss and renewal, rooted in earth and darkness; the sense of timelessness in an "ancient place," which the poet inhabits and which inhab-its the poet; and the sense again of entering a kind of awareness connected with animals. This combination brings to the surface the instinctual quality that runs throughout the poem. In the tree he encountered in that field, Bly found an old and rich pres-ence, an image that could be called primordial. That adjective recalls Jung again, who said that "the primordial image might suitably be described as the instinct's perception of itself, or as the self-portrait of an instinct."[33] The scene Bly sketches in "Hunting Pheasants in a Cornfield" becomes such a portrait. The last two lines summarize the experience: "A spot easily caught sight of above the corn,/ If I were a young animal"—which man is—"ready to turn home at dusk"—which is one way to describe turning back toward what is instinctual in our nature, and feeling at moments what it is like to be deeply alive in the universe, at home in it in the way we imagine the animals to be.

Soon after the first issue of *The Fifties* was published, Bly received a letter from James Wright. Wright was teaching at the University of Minnesota, across the state from Bly's home in Madison, and he was at the time discouraged about his poetry. While it was being published and well received, it did not seem to him to touch the deeper springs of emotion and imagination. Wright found in *The Fifties* an encouraging note, or at least a kindred dissatisfaction with the prevailing conception of poetry. When the two poets met soon afterward, they became friends, and throughout the 1960s they collaborated on a number of translation projects. They collaborated in another way as well, as they influenced and suppported one another in the development of an alternative to what Wright called "the poetry of calcium."[34]

Both Bly and Wright are poets of strong intuitive intelligence. The desire to give intuition full play in poems must have been one thing that drew them to one another; it is one reason why *Snowy Fields* and Wright's *The Branch Will Not Break* strike common chords. In 1962, together with William Duffy, they put out a small collection of their poems, called *The Lion's Tail and Eyes*. In the introductory note Bly said: "One purpose of poetry is to forget about what you know, and think about what you don't know. . . . The poem expresses what we are just beginning to think, thoughts we have not yet thought."[35] They were interested in writing poems of intuitive thought and perception, rather than direct or rational statement. That interest is in evidence throughout *Snowy Fields*, and is exemplified particularly well in the poem "Driving Toward the Lac Qui Parle River." In fact, if "Hunting Pheasants in a Cornfield" offers a sort of self-portrait of instinct, this poem does the same for intuition.

The first two stanzas contain elements that are already becoming familiar: dusk; subtle light ("The stubble field catches the last growth of sun"); sharp yet mysterious details of the landscape ("The soybeans are breathing on all sides./ Old men are sitting before their houses on carseats"). As in "Three Kinds of Pleasures," the poet is driving in a car, a "solitude covered with iron." These stanzas establish the joyous yet brooding mood that Bly loves and evokes so often in his poems. But it is in the third stanza that the poem becomes magical.

> Nearly to Milan, suddenly a small bridge,
> And water kneeling in the moonlight.
> In small towns the houses are built right on the ground;
> The lamplight falls on all fours in the grass.
> When I reach the river, the full moon covers it;
> A few people are talking low in a boat.

It is a stanza of highly intuitive description, and in the images of the "sudden" small bridge and the people talking in the boat—just out of hearing, down close to the water—it gives what can be taken as a description of intuition itself.

As in many of the poems in *Snowy Fields*, in "Driving Toward the Lac Qui Parle River" things are sinking, drifting down, gravitating to the earth and low places. The houses "are built on the ground"; the moonlight is down upon the water; the people in the boat are there too, and even their talking seems drawn down. In two striking metaphors, beautiful and jarring to reason, water kneels, lamplight "falls on all fours in the grass." They too are involved in the bowing and sinking of things, which is felt before it is consciously noticed or understood. The poem, in its last stanza especially, expresses movements that are fundamental to *Snowy Fields:* movements toward the earth and into what lies beyond the rational, well-lit parts of the mind. (There is also, in the first stanza, the complementary movement of a rising joy: "I am happy,/ The moon rising above the turkey sheds.") We are taken just far enough into consciousness of these currents, and no farther; they remain as "thoughts we are just beginning to think."

The Lac Qui Parle River is an actual river in western Minnesota, but its name has a fortuitous appropriateness in this poem, and in this book: in *Snowy Fields*, the inward waters often find a voice. In "Three Kinds of Pleasures," "Hunting Pheasants in a Cornfield," and "Driving Toward the Lac Qui Parle River," with their images that carry inner correspondences and their attentiveness to instinct and intuition, we can see ways in which they do so.

There is another reason for the quiet intensity of this "simple" book. It conveys a sense of solitude that is joyous, yet it contains also pain and loneliness, though these are most often left submerged, implicit. It is easy to overlook them. For example, Donald Hall (Bly's close friend since their days together at Harvard) has written of *Snowy Fields*: "The *Silence* poems are soft and frequently happy, even in their melancholy somehow secure. They are the less complicated, more primitive aspect of Bly's vision. . . . They are psychically the earliest, approaching the uroboros." [36] Hall's description is one that the reader of *Snowy Fields* can well understand, yet it misses a dimension of the book. The consciousness embodied in *Snowy Fields* is in fact quite complicated, and there is more longing than security in these poems. The uroboros is "the circular snake biting its tail, . . . the symbol of the psychic state of the beginning, of the original situation, in which man's consciousness and ego were still small and undeveloped." [37] *Snowy Fields* is not a book of "the original situation." The man we encounter in it has left these fields and welcoming dusks and is returning to them in the poems. It is when the ego is developed and has firm walls, inside of which the person has tasted a profound isolation, that experiencing what is outside the walls comes as a draft of new life.

This loneliness is not necessarily for other people (in *Snowy Fields* this kind of loneliness is barely addressed); it can be for a part of one's self as well. In the second section of *Snowy Fields*, the ache of inner loneliness is dealt with more explicitly, and in one key poem we find a direct description of the lonely room the poet has fled from. This poem is "A Man Writes to a Part of Himself," which Philip Dacey, in an excellent analysis, has called "a lens through which to view the business Bly is about in his work at large."[38]

As I mentioned earlier, Bly is a poet who longs for wholeness; in fact, if we look at his poetry in its broadest outlines, we see that it is a continuing and complex effort to overcome fragmentation and alienation. In "A Man Writes to a Part of Himself" Bly expresses inner fragmentation in terms of a separation between a husband and wife. The man who writes the poem-letter is in a city, where he lives a life that outwardly seems happy and consequential—he describes himself as "laughing,/ with many appointments"—but privately is barren and cold: at night he goes "To a bare room, a room of poverty,/ To sleep among a bare pitcher and basin/ In a room with no heat." The woman, meanwhile, is far way, "starving, without care." She is, in fact, far away not only in distance but apparently in time as well. She is pictured living in a cave, "rained on . . . / Water dripping from [her] head, bent/ Over ground corn." This gap in time, as well as the phrase "like a wife," makes it clear that it is the woman, not the poem's title, that is to be taken metaphorically. The husband is cheerful in public, busy, apparently ambitious, but in private, in his inner life, he is impoverished and lonely. The wife, though neglected and in danger of starvation, is nonetheless the keeper of the cave and the corn and the rain, and all the nourishment and life associated with them.

Bly's use of a separation between a man and a woman as a metaphor for inner fragmentation reflects a fundamental aspect of his thought. He sees the psyches of both men and women as naturally androgynous, and he views Western culture as unbalanced, encouraging a sharp split between the masculine and feminine. In "A Man Writes to a Part of Himself," and in his poetry as a whole, Bly yearns for a reconciliation. The poem ends with these lines: "Which of us two then is the worse off?/ And how did this separation come about?"

And what has the man abandoned in leaving the feminine part of himself? Reading *Snowy Fields* itself provides a good answer, for in it a man is returning to much that we might wish to call feminine: earth, water, intuition, feeling, receptivity. It is probably coincidental that "A Man Writes to a Part of Himself" occurs precisely at the center of the book, midway through the middle section, but in any case it is central in more than position. Bly could have used the title of this poem as the title of the book as well. The man who wanders among the snowy fields has left the barren, lonely room (or at least he leaves it during the moments the poems characteristically describe), but he has not forgotten it.

There are other poems in the Awakening section that make the awareness of fragmentation and grief explicit. The section opens with two poems that swerve away from the mood and manner of the first section and give glimpses of the more wildly surreal style that would dominate Bly's next book. In the first, "Unrest," Bly speaks of "a strange unrest [that] hovers over the nation," and he gives a brief expressionistic summary of a man's first twenty years of life in contemporary America:

> A lassitude
> Enters into the diamonds of the body,
> In high school the explosion begins, the child is partly killed,
> When the fight is over, and the land and the sea ruined,
> Two shapes inside us rise, and move away.

This is a capsule version of the description of the process of fragmentation that Bly would give later, in the first section of

"Sleepers Joining Hands." The second poem, "Awakening,"
presents a swirling, sensuous vision—a vision of life itself—that
is both beautiful and apocalyptic.

> The storm is coming. The small farmhouse in Minnesota
> Is hardly strong enough for the storm.
> Darkness, darkness in grass, darkness in trees,
> Even the water in wells trembles.
> Bodies give off darkness, and chrysanthemums
> Are dark, and horses, who are bearing great loads of hay
> To the deep barns where the dark air is moving from corners.

In "Where We Must Look for Help" Bly works from the
version of the Flood found in the Epic of Gilgamesh, in which
it is a raven rather than a dove that is the messenger of deliver-
ance. Bly changes the raven to a crow:

> On the third day the crow shall fly;
> The crow, the crow, the spider-colored crow,
> The crow shall find new mud to walk upon.

Bly has related this poem (one of his earliest) to Jung's idea of
the Shadow, and to his own realization during his years in New
York City that "if any help was going to come to help me out
of my misery, it would come from the dark side of my personality."[39] Surely the blackness of the crow is related to all the
other darknesses of *Snowy Fields*. And as significant as the crow
itself is the mud we see it walking upon. As with the minglings
of light and darkness that appear in many of the poems, the mud
represents a fusion, earth and water together—we might say body
and soul. *Snowy Fields* is book of lights and darknesses, water
and earth.

Among the other poems in the section are a powerful rendering of depression (titled simply "Depression"), in which earth
and darkness offer obliteration rather than nourishment; a fine
poem on the necessity of facing the fact of death straightfor-

wardly ("At the Funeral of Great-Aunt Mary"); and a masterful quiet poem of human grief and vulnerability, "Afternoon Sleep."

At the beginning of "Afternoon Sleep" the poet is awakening from sleep and dreams. "I awoke happy," he says, "for I had dreamt of my wife." But his dreams had also contained "the loneliness hiding in grass and weeds/ That lies near a man over thirty, and suddenly enters." On waking, the poet drives out to the deserted farm of Joe Sjolie, a bachelor and Norwegian immigrant (or son of immigrants). At some point in the past, Sjolie "grew tired, he sold his farm,/ Even his bachelor rocker, and did not come back." This poem is unusual in *Snowy Fields*, as it is the only one in the book that deals with another person's life in a detailed way. Detailed? Well, the details are few and spare, but each carries extraordinary weight. A world of unstated significance exists in the simple explanation that Joe Sjolie "grew tired." The man has utterly broken off his old life; he "did not come back." When he went, he left his dog behind, locked in a shed; when it was discovered, "The dog refused to take food from strangers." These homely details about a dog occupy only two lines, yet they have a sharp and ragged edge of grief.

As the poet approaches the house, "Alone on a hill, sheltered by trees," the uncut grass lies matted on the ground. Two more profound, uncommented-upon details appear. First, the door is standing open—a mute statement of final abandonment. Then, when the poet goes inside, he finds "old abandoned books,/ And instructions to Norwegian immigrants." With this last image, enormity—years, plans, hopes, voyages, irrevocable departures—enters this brief, brooding poem. It is a poem of great subtlety and a dignified sadness.

Why did the poet go to this farm? Apparently it was at the prompting of his dream. The dream, with its thoughts of his wife and of loneliness, suggests a state related to that which was described in "A Man Writes to a Part of Himself": it is a dream of love and isolation. And such a dream could well lead a person unconsciously to a place like Joe Sjolie's farm. In a way the poem feels like "Hunting Pheasants in a Cornfield," in that an almost instinctual force pulls the poet to a place where a mood sharpens and a realization hesitates on the border of conscious recognition. Again, there is a ritual-like quality in the experience, in the way the poet moves, and in the way inward significance wells up through simple objects. "I awoke happy," Bly tells us at the beginning of the poem, but when he walked into Sjolie's farmhouse his mood was shadowed by other emotions. Anyone who has walked through an abandoned house has perhaps felt something of what the poem quietly, surely captures, which is the grief that comes with the knowledge that our lives, with all their hopes, struggles, comforts, and loneliness, ultimately pass away into time.

There are other poems in the Awakening section which are indeed poems of simple pleasure and joy—the joy of awakening to the present moment in all its fullness; for example, the tiny poems of three to five lines which take simplicity to extremes that are striking even by the standards of *Snowy Fields*. But I think it is important to emphasize the poems in which loneliness and the sense of fragmentation break the surface, for in the total effect of *Snowy Fields* these feelings are crucial. Their weight can be felt also in poems where they are not explicitly mentioned. Let me quote here from an essay by Michael Quam, who like Bly grew up in rural Minnesota. Looking back, Quam says:

[A] haunting and pervasive sense of guilt and of the limits to happiness, the hard road of salvation by faith and faith alone, the severe restraints on any spontaneity—for the body is corrupt and thus cannot be trusted—produced in some people a brooding and dangerous streak of violence that often turned inward. Those who could not bear up killed themselves emotionally and physically. Strangely careless automobile accidents occurred, some so grisly that the details lived on as a kind of gruesome folklore. When I was a boy, Lac qui Parle County was dry, yet some people had no difficulty drinking themselves into oblivion. The great well of feeling and desire that exists in all people could not be tapped. Instead of drawing upon these life-giving waters, so many went down, down, to drown. Because they could give it no voice, their love for one another and for the natural world turned from wonder and joy to blankness and despair. . . .

As a young man I fled, frightened by the dark side of my heritage, feeling stifled and alone. . . . *Silence in the Snowy Fields* . . . broke through the barrier I had so carefully constructed against my past. To see the experiences of my childhood now used as images in poems of such depth and intensity was stunning. For Robert went back and faced it all, all the sorrow, all the richness; and for me he redeemed that small part of the world that was for so many years my whole world.[40]

One need not share Quam's and Bly's background and region to feel in *Snowy Fields* a power that deepens, reveals, and perhaps even heals. In the essay cited earlier, William Heyen said: "For years I felt that Bly's poetry pointed at a mysterious and dissatisfying nothingness that was a non-subject. But he has one subject that speaks out from the spaces between lines, stanzas, and poems and unites them. The Self."[41]

After reading *Snowy Fields* one probably recalls first the images of snow, trees, and darkness that appear in it so often. But there is another image that is as important as these: the road. It is another of those old rich images I referred to earlier, basic to Bly's vocabulary and vision. The book's third section, Silence on the Roads, opens with a poem that sets before us the image of the road with a luminous purity: "After Working." After two stanzas of remarkable evocation of moonlight—not just how it looks but how it *feels*—the poem concludes with this stanza:

> We know the road; as the moonlight
> Lifts everything, so in a night like this
> The road goes on ahead, it is all clear.

Most poets would try to disguise such an ancient symbol a little
more within a dramatic situation, but Bly disguises it not at all,
and once again simplicity somehow succeeds: the moonlit road
captures a sense of life itself stretching on before us with a rare
and radiant clarity. These lines can perhaps help to explain the
peculiar power felt in earlier roads in the book, such as those in
"Three Kinds of Pleasures" and "Driving Toward the Lac Qui
Parle River."

   The repetition of certain key images unifies *Snowy Fields*,
and also enriches it. We can see such repetitions working especially well in the book's final section. But first a transition must
be made, and a small poem by Antonio Machado, which Bly
has translated, may be helpful in making it:

> All things die and all things live forever;
> but our task is to die,
> to die making roads,
> roads over the sea.[42]

The image of the road appears again in the poem "Silence":
"Something homeless is looking on the long roads—/ A dog lost
since midnight, a small duck/ Among the odorous reeds,/ Or a
tiny box-elder bug searching for the window pane." But elsewhere, as if Bly is heeding the words of Machado, "the father"
of *Snowy Fields*, the road leads out across water. The sea, encountered first in "Return to Solitude" and repeatedly after that,
appears once again. Roads and voyages over water become the
prevalent images in the last section. "The road goes on ahead; it
is all clear," and yet we move across waters whose depths we
can never know.

   The weaving of repeated images is often fascinating. "Night"
ends with this stanza:

> Alive, we are like a sleek black water beetle,
> Skating across still water in any direction

We choose, and soon to be swallowed
Suddenly from beneath.

This poem is followed by one whose title carries the book's oddly formal informality to considerable length: "After Drinking All Night with a Friend, We Go Out in a Boat at Dawn to See Who Can Write the Best Poem." As the ancient Chinese poets often did, Bly here celebrates the comradeship of poets and an escape from worldly concerns. These pleasures are like a fragrance in a cool breeze in the poem's lines:

> This morning also, drifting in the dawn wind,
> I sense my hands, and my shoes, and this ink—
> Drifting, as all of this body drifts,
> Above the clouds of the flesh and the stone.
>
> A few friendships, a few dawns, a few glimpses of grass,
> A few oars weathered by snow and the heat,
> So we drift toward shore, over cold waters,
> No longer caring if we drift or go straight.

It is a fine and grateful passage, but its echo of the water beetle is unmistakable, and so the praise of the moments and satisfactions of earthly life takes on a certain added shadow.

Then in the next poem, "Old Boards," the most mundane objects bring us once again to a road over water. Looking at weathered boards lying on the muddy ground, Bly says:

> This is the wood one sees on the decks of ocean ships,
> Wood that carries us far from land . . .
>
> . . . .
>
> This wood is like a man who has a simple life,
> Living through the spring and winter on the ship of his own desire.

These enriching repetitions of images are one reason why this book should be read as if it were a single poem. In *Snowy Fields* moments of drifting and joy occur within a journey which never loses its mortal and moral dimensions. The morality is that of choosing to live with depth and intensity, and of openness to the undiscovered life.

The poem which gives the most striking variation to the imagery of journeying over water is "Snowfall in the Afternoon." Bly placed this poem last in the book, and it can hardly have been arbitrary choice. As I quoted in full the poem that opens *Snowy Fields*, let me do the same with the one that closes it.

SNOWFALL IN THE AFTERNOON

I

The grass is half-covered with snow.
It was the sort of snowfall that starts in late afternoon,
And now the little houses of the grass are growing dark.

II

If I reached my hands down, near the earth,
I could take handfuls of darkness!
A darkness was always there, which we never noticed.

III

As the snow grows heavier, the cornstalks fade farther away,
And the barn moves nearer to the house.
The barn moves all alone in the growing storm.

IV

The barn is full of corn, and moving toward us now,
Like a hulk blown toward us in a storm at sea;
All the sailors on deck have been blind for many years.

The snow, the grass, the cornstalks; the darkness, lying in low places; dusk, and something within a human being, descending, reaching down "near the earth"; the figure of the ship at sea, which by now should be predictable yet appears here with its greatest impact: much of what has given the book its special atmosphere and power come together in this poem. An outer darkness is speaking to an inner darkness, in the fundamental rhythm and ritual of the book. In the imagery of the second stanza the darkness in the grass becomes a spring from which the poet can lift up water in his hands to drink. The joy of finding the water, which "was always there," acknowledges the thirst which is not mentioned. But Bly did not choose to end with an image of cool springs or still waters, but rather with one that carries not only mystery but pain as well.

The description of the barn in the deepening storm is one of the most remarkable passages in Bly's poetry, and it demonstrates his gift for capturing, in only a few lines and images, a moment of perception and the *almost* ineffable awareness it fosters. As the cornstalks fade and the barn looms against the whitened ground and dusk, the barn appears to be moving closer. With that, it suddenly becomes a ghostly ship heaving off some coast in stormy seas. At first the ship seems like something out of an ancient mariner's haunted memory. But the power of the image does not come only from its strangeness, but also from a recognition that the ship and its sailors are somehow ourselves. The water journeys of the previous poems have prepared us for the ship, but not for these blind men. It is impossible to reduce such intuitive images to paraphrasable meanings without simplifying them drastically, but we might nonetheless say that the blind sailors are all that our lives contain but which we have not yet met or seen. *Snowy Fields* leaves us looking toward the sea.

Bly has said of the writing of *Snowy Fields:* "when the poems of *Silence in the Snowy Fields* came, I set them down with very little rewriting, maybe one or two lines only. Most of them were written outdoors and they arrived complete as they came on whatever little piece of paper I had with me."[43]

The phrasing seems right. Though their clean language and simple stanzas clearly reflect craft, one can easily believe that these poems "arrived," and the poet was simply attentive enough to write them down. The circumstances of composition are interesting but not so important. What is important is the effect of the poems, and in them art, instinct, spontaneity, and ritual seem to come together as one thing. As to their being written outdoors, that doesn't come as a surprise. Reading these poems, one doesn't think of them *not* being written among the fields, trees, lakes, and silences they describe. *Snowy Fields* takes us to its place, where we find a world that is utterly real yet subtly transformed. Transformed through a man awake to inner and outer correspondences, intuition, the dusky borders of consciousness, joyous solitude but also an inner loneliness, and "the ship of his own desire."

CHAPTER 2

The Light Around the Body

> The heart leaps
> Almost up to the sky! But laments
> And filaments pull us back into the
> darkness.
> —"Wanting to Experience
> All Things"

To those who were looking for another book in the vein of *Snowy Fields*, Bly's second collection, *The Light Around the Body*, was a jolt. In both content and style it seemed to forsake the world of the first collection. On closer consideration it becomes apparent that both books spring from common convictions and purposes: both are based in an awareness of spiritual fragmentation and a sense of the soul's journey. But on first impression they seem to be antitheses, moving at different speeds through different realities. Actually, Bly had not suddenly and utterly changed his poetry: some of the poems in *The Light* were written earlier than most of those in *Snowy Fields*, and in certain spots at least, as in the poem "Unrest," the style and concerns of *The Light* had already been in evidence in the first book. Bly has always tried to create books that have a certain unity, whether of style, intention, or theme. He achieved a distinctive unity so well in *Snowy Fields* that when he gathered the woolier and more public poems that make up *The Light*, it seemed to many readers that his work had undergone a complete transformation.

Even in the context of the world of contemporary poetry, with its extreme diversity, passionate contentiousness, and partisanship, Bly is a writer with a special gift for arousing widely differing and often polarized responses. This was certainly the case with *The Light*, a product of the polarized 1960s and the most widely reviewed and controversial of all Bly's books. Two basic facts of the book's history are symptomatic: Wesleyan University Press, which had published *Snowy Fields*, rejected it; when published by Harper & Row, *The Light* went on to win the National Book Award for poetry for 1968. To begin, let me set up a collage of selected comments as a backdrop for discussion:

> . . . the correctness of a writer's social theories is no guarantee of literary achievement. Today Robert Bly's protest poetry might stand as evidence that political and social involvement is still no guarantee.
>
> My objection is not to the content but to the poems as poetry. His lines are too often trite, flat, unimaginative—merely rhetorical.[1]
>
> —Richard Calhoun

> The sadness in *The Light Around the Body* is a sadness for America. The book quietly, but firmly, translates the inward mystery and melancholy . . . into an expansive public language.[2]
>
> —Paul Zweig

> The Bly (sic) sees the world in blacks and whites, weird oversimplifications resembling the machinations of Eli Siegal but much less competent. He thinks in cartoon stereotypes rather like the comic strip of Mr. Mum: no vision of "the psychic life of America," only the Strange World of Robert Bly.[3]
>
> —Smith (in *The Smith*)

Bly is one of the few poets in America from whom greatness can be expected. He has original talent, and what is more rare, integrity.[4]

—Louis Simpson

. . . Bly fails through flatness. In our time the distinction between art and documentation, writing and journalism, poetry and note-keeping, has been persistently narrowed. . . . In Bly's little flat poems the distinction has been eroded altogether. . . . Again and again in his book I respond to what is true, wishing it were poetry as well.[5]

—Hayden Carruth

Bly claims that he and the poets he most admires have written the first valid political poems in our history. Now, I'm not sure what he means by this, but if his claim is that he has found a medium which bears the weight of political protest poetically, I'm fully in agreement. I can't think of a poem in *The Light Around the Body*, no matter how stark, which is open to the charge that it is essentially journalistic or propagandistic.[6]

—William Heyen

. . . The poems are inert and humorless, the "I" disappearing almost completely. Which does not elevate Bly's analysis to the status of objective fact, but rather shortcircuits it by depriving it of the moral energy which would give it social force. . . . As it stands, *The Light Around the Body* is an honorable failure.[7]

—Herbert Leibowitz

The poems in *The Light Around the Body* are, generally speaking, a big advance over those in his first book. Not only has he achieved an effective style, but he has achieved effective substance. His poems are active, and they are active on broad levels of experience.[8]

—Kenneth Rexroth

. . . *The Light Around the Body* is, at its worst, a document in the triumph of a kind of pseudo-poetry which Robert Bly has been importantly instrumental in fostering since the '50s: a Cult of Goodness. This is a poetry in which the poet sounds rather like

a hairy All-American Pen Woman. I believe someone should say
something against it, and what needs saying is that it leads to just
another kind of sentimentality, another kind of shrill melodra-
matic posturing, and worse, another kind of arrogance.[9]

—William E. Taylor

Bly's poems do not attest to Bly's virtue. . . . The point about
Bly's political poems is clear or ought to be: the violence is Bly's
own. Certainly he understands his own murderousness, and no
man can protest war if he does not understand himself a mur-
derer.[10]

—Donald Hall

One can begin with *The Light* by granting it at the very least an
important place in the poetic debate of its time.

Published in 1967, *The Light* is a book of fierce political and
social protest; the Vietnam War, which gives the middle section
of the volume its name, looms in it heavily. None of the critics
quoted above say that such content is wrong for poetry, but
clearly in undertaking it as boldly as he did in this book Bly
walked knowingly into the perennial argument as to the place of
protest and politics in poetry. He took part in the argument in
his essays as well. In "Leaping Up Into Political Poetry" he
wrote:

Many poets say flatly—and proudly—that they are "not political." If a tree said that, I would find it more convincing than
when a man says it. I think it is more conceivable that a tree
could report that it grew just as well in the Johnson administration as in the Kennedy administration or the Lincoln administration. But a modern man's spiritual life and his growth are increasingly sensitive to the tone and content of a regime.[11]

And the issue of a poet's consciousness and handling of historical and social realities was crucial in what is perhaps Bly's most
famous essay, "The Collapse of James Dickey," [12] a blistering
review of Dickey's prizewinning *Buckdancer's Choice*, attacking especially the poems "The Firebombing" and "Slave Quarters."

Bly's anti-war activity was not limited to his writing. With David Ray, he founded American Writers Against the Vietnam War, a group which staged readings on campuses around the country and published an anthology called *A Poetry Reading Against the Vietnam War.* The anthology, though long out of print, remains a devastating and eloquent collection. Bly's best-known anti-war action occurred at the National Book Award ceremonies in 1968. Bly turned his acceptance speech into an attack on the war, a castigation of institutions—universities, churches, publishing houses—for not acting against it, and finally an act of civil disobedience: as he handed his prize money over to a representative of the draft resistance movement, he counseled him to defy the draft and to counsel others to do so in turn. The hall filled with cheers and boos.

In his acceptance speech Bly said:

> . . . if the country is dishonored, where will it draw its honor from to give to its writers? . . . I know I am speaking for many, many American poets when I ask this question: since we are murdering a culture in Vietnam at least as fine as our own, have we the right to congratulate ourselves on our cultural magnificence? Isn't that out of place?[13]

We can see here, and in the preceding quotation, Bly's polemical abilities, but beyond that something else as well: his insistence on seeing poetry in a context larger than the merely literary. He persistently views poetry in terms of the life of the spirit and of consciousness, which he views in turn in a perspective that reaches beyond the individual human being.

This study is concerned with Bly's own poetry and not directly with his translations, but anyone wishing to get a full sense of Bly's career and contribution will want to take a long look into his translations as well. It's quite possible that his translations have had an even greater influence on contemporary American poetry than his original work, though the distinction is difficult to draw very sharply, as his sensibility and poetic values have been strongly reflected in the translations, and likewise in his own poetry he has been deeply influenced by many of the poets he has translated. Charles Molesworth has commented, "One might well say, as Eliot said of Pound and Chinese poetry, that Bly has invented South American poetry for our time,"[14] though Bly himself has nodded to H. R. Hays, whom he says "is to the translator of South American poetry as Madame Curie is to the x-ray."[15] In any case, it is for his translations of South Americans—chiefly Pablo Neruda and Cesar Vallejo—and of Spanish poets such as Lorca, Juan Ramon Jimenez, Antonio Machado, and Vincente Aleixandre that Bly is best-known as translator. He has also done important work in translating Scandinavian literature (poetry by Tomas Tranströmer, Harry Martinson, Gunnar Ekelöf, and Rolf Jacobsen; novels by Knut Hamsun and Selma Lagerlöf) and German (chiefly Rilke).

In 1956 Bly received a Fulbright Grant to go to Norway to translate Norwegian poetry (in spite of the fact that he did not know the language when he was chosen). It was not Norwegian work, however, that had the greatest impact on him during this trip. In the Oslo library he encountered for the first time the poetry of Neruda, Jimenez, Vallejo, and Georg Trakl. The effect of these discoveries was at least twofold. First, Bly became convinced, since these writers were little-known in the United States, that American poetry had grown complacent and narrow, isolated from important international literary movements, badly in need of transfusions from outside the English tradition. To provide such transfusions was the primary motivation for the founding of *The Fifties*. Second, these poets gave Bly new ideas as to the very possibilities of poetry: "I felt avenues opening into kinds of imagination that I sort of dimly sensed somewhere off on the horizon, but I had never actually seen in English. . . . Wonderful imagery, exuberance, and enthusiasm."[16] Neruda startled him especially: "When I first read those poems I saw freedom in them . . . freer than any of my poems had ever been. . . . It was a great discovery and excitement for me to translate those deep surrealist poems of Neruda, because I was in the presence of freedom for the first time in my life."[17]

The impact of the poets Bly had discovered in Oslo was evident in *Snowy Fields* in relatively subtle ways: we saw the landscape first, and then noticed the scattering of poems and images within poems that cast a strange glow of surreality over it. But in *The Light* the influence of Spanish surrealism flows powerfully into Bly's work; what bits of Minnesota landscape as remain seem torn loose, swirling among images of war and nightmare. And Neruda provided inspiration in more than his surrealism: he was also an example of a poet who takes on ambitious political and historical themes passionately and as a matter of natural development and responsibility. Bly called the introduction he wrote for a collection of Neruda translations "Refusing to be Theocritus,"[18] taking a reference from a poem in which Neruda describes his own arrival at political poetry. *The Light* represented a similar refusal on Bly's part.

Where *Snowy Fields* had a single one-line epigraph from Jacob Boehme, the various sections of *The Light* carry a total of six epigraphs, four of them from Boehme. The first is this:

> For according to the outward man, we are in this world, and according to the inward man, we are in the inward world. . . . Since then we are generated out of both worlds, we speak in two languages, and we must be understood also by two languages.

Bly is strongly aware of this dichotomy, which, oversimplifying somewhat, is the split that separates the social man from the spiritual man. But in *The Light* his effort is not to speak in two separate languages, but to forge a language that contains the realities of both worlds: he wants this language to take account of both public, historical brutalities and breakdowns, and the inward reservoirs where dream, spiritual longing, and moral outrage mingle. So what we have in this book is a man alive in the middle of the twentieth century facing the grimmest realities of his country's present and past, responding to a spiritual challenge taken from a Christian mystic of the sixteenth century, and reaching for a means to speak into "the Spanish tradition . . . which grasps modern life as a lion grabs a dog, and wraps it in heavy countless images, and holds it firm in a terrifically dense texture."[19] It is a startling mix, and the poems that embody it were something new in the history of American poetry.

There are two aspects of *The Light* that need to be taken into account if the book is to have its full effect. The first is its intention, the nature of its vision. Bly has said that the impetus behind his poems on the Vietnam War was the desire to discover "where it came from inside us."[20] He believes that it is possible to speak of a national psyche, which the people of a country are inside, and which is within each person. Writing in 1967, he said:

> It's clear that many of the events that create our foreign relations come from more or less hidden impulses in the American psyche. It's also clear I think that some sort of husk has grown around that psyche, so that in the fifties we could not look into it or did not. The Negroes and the Vietnam war have worn the husk thin in a couple of places now. But if that is so, then the poet's main job is to penetrate that husk around the American psyche, and since that psyche is inside *him* too, the writing of political poetry is like the writing of personal poetry, a sudden drive by the poet inward.[21]

Bly's own poetic intentions are consistently more than a little reflected in his essays, and this statement is a prime example of that. During the Vietnam years Bly felt impelled to try to break through the husk he speaks of and to imagine what the national psyche might look like. Most American literature of social criticism has been in a more or less realistic mode. The way we see America in *The Light* is not in the realistic tradition at all. In one poem, "Johnson's Cabinet Watched by Ants," Bly begins by borrowing a scene of midnight devil-worship from another non-realist who was interested in portraying the hidden, shared psyche of his culture: Hawthorne. Hawthorne was considerably more subtle in his blend of the inward and the outward, but what Bly tries to do in *The Light* is essentially what Hawthorne did in "Young Goodman Brown," the story from which the scene is taken: to envision the night side of his society's soul.

In a 1970 interview Bly was asked, "Would you say we've gone a little too far in our worry about 'asethetic distance' these days?" Bly's response was interesting: "What is 'aesthetic distance'?"[22] And *The Light* does seem to exist in a world where that concept is a foreign one. Personal vision and anger are both given free rein. Some of the book's "indiscretions" are flaws, some are virtues, and some are both or neither. For example, the anti-rational images and shifts Bly employs here are responsible for many of the most penetrating moments in the book, and also for many of the most impenetrable. Another aspect which both is and is not a weakness is the heavy use of stereotypes. Bly's attention in his poetry has always been weak in what we might call "the middle ground." By this last phrase I mean the ground that lies between solitude and the natural world on the one hand, and "the psyche of the nation" on the other: the ground of the commonplace, complicated realities of ordinary human lives and relationships; the ground we are on when we read Chekhov. With a few exceptions, Bly's poems do not demonstrate much skill or inclination for writing about people other than himself, although in his later poetry he has made an effort to overcome this limitation. Throughout most of his work the emotional content is very much "I-centered," and he has been more at home dealing with emotions through images than through distinct, fully described human circumstances. Symptomatically, one of the most moving poems in *The Light*, "Come With Me," expresses grief through objects—images of metal shavings on work benches, shredded tires along thruways, "Black and collapsed bodies, that tried and burst,/ And were left behind." There is a marvelous depth and poignancy to these images, but in *The Light* there is very little depth or roundness to the people, and they can be referred to simply as "accountants," "ministers," or "the poor." There are several dramatic monologues in *The Light*, but even these do not really describe people: in "The Busy Man Speaks" and "Counting Small-Boned Bodies" we are given portraits of psychic diseases, and "Three Presidents" and "Andrew Jackson's Speech" are caricature, not characterization. The references to contemporary figures take the same tendency further, and these lines in particular have been objected to more than once:

> Men like Rusk are not men:
> They are bombs waiting to be loaded in a darkened hangar.
> ("Asian Peace Offers Rejected
> without Publication")

As William Matthews pointed out, these lines, while "half-true, are also half-false: a major problem is that men like Rusk *are* men." [23] Less sympathetic critics accused them of a Calley- or Hitler-like spirit of dehumanization.

Bly's tendency to think in types and categories is strong and deep, reflected not only in the stereotypes of *The Light* but at other times in other ways as well: for example, in his affinity for Jung's theory of psychological types, [24] or in his groupings of poets in essays such as "The Three Brains." [25] His bias against office and business "types," so prominent in *The Light*, goes back to his childhood. In an autobiographical essay published in 1976

Bly described the attitude that prevailed in his farming family toward the "men from town, who did not work with their hands," as one of suspicion. He went on to give this account of the bank clerks who were sent out to the fields at threshing time to watch out for their employers' interests in the operation:

> How we pitied these creatures! Getting out of the car with a white shirt and necktie, stepping over the stubble like a cat so as not to get too much chaff in his black oxfords, how weak and feeble! What a poor model of a human being! It was clear the teller was incapable of any boisterous joy, and was nothing but a small zoo animal of some sort that locked the doors on itself, pale from the reflected light off the zoo walls, light as salt in a shaker, clearly obsessed with money—you could see greed all over him. How ignoble! How sordid and ignoble! What ignobility![26]

That kind of pity is the sharpest sort of derision. Yet it is hard not to respond to the vividness and enthusiasm of the passage— as long as one is not the person who happens to be in the oxfords. It is a tricky mixture of unfairness, lack of compassion, and truth. In *The Light* the early habits of mind revealed there are very much alive.

But while there are valid objections to be raised against such one-dimensional renderings of human beings and whole classes of human beings as we find in *The Light*, what Bly is doing here does not amount to mere finger-pointing. In 1959 he had published in *New World Writing* a group of poems called *Poems for the Ascension of J. P. Morgan*,[27] certain pieces of which later went into *Snowy Fields* and *The Light*. In a headnote he commented, "The place and influence of J. P. Morgan today is about the same as that of Christ in the Middle Ages." When executives and businessmen appear in *The Light*, they are not just a particular culpable class of people, but paradigms of values and forces as dominant within the national psyche as those men are in its affairs and institutions. My point is that while the poems attack and satirize certain groups and individuals, they do so within a large conception of shared social and psychic responsibility. In another of the book's harsh statements, in "Turning Away from Lies," Bly says, "No one in business can be a Christian." But that statement, narrow and arrogant on one level, is on another melancholy and inescapable. We are not a nation of John Woolmans, and the cross-purposes of Christian values and capitalist values are simply an astounding irony our culture has long held inside it. At certain times and in certain events such as the Vietnam War, that irony becomes especially apparent and acute. So in reckoning with *The Light* it is necessary to understand its purpose and perspective. Many critics have spoken of the book in terms of satire, and that view is no doubt correct—though it is satire with very little laughter. Given its overall tone, mood, and effect, however, it seems more accurate to think of *The Light* as prophecy—like satire, a genre that by its nature sacrifices the individual to a larger truth. As Bly lays out before us his vision of the soul of America, he does so with the objectivity and moderation of a Blake or Jeremiah. And does he have any special prophetic grasp of hidden truths? In some of the strongest poems of social criticism here—my list would include "Watching Television," "Come With Me," "The Great Society," "Hearing Men Shout on Macdougal Street," "Sleet Storm on the Merritt Parkway," "Counting Small-Boned Bodies," and "Hatred of Men with Black Hair"—Bly memorably evokes, turns into images, bitter currents buried in our history and therefore in ourselves. The poems are troubling not merely because of their racked and smoky strangeness.

The second fundamental aspect of *The Light* that needs to be taken into account is its structure. If *Snowy Fields* was a unified collection and, as I've suggested, something of a sequence as well, *The Light* represents a similar but more difficult and determined effort to make a book that coheres. Its progression is clearly purposeful, and in fact is crucial to its overall meaning and impact. We might look back for a moment here at Bly's earliest collection of poems: the work he submitted as his master's thesis at the University of Iowa in 1956. In some ways— most noticeably its use of iambic meter, frequently rhymed— this collection was unlike any of those Bly was to publish. But in two respects at least it sets a pattern he would later follow. Already at this stage we see Bly setting up groups of poems within the manuscript in an effort to produce something other than a miscellaneous collection, and taking for his organizing principle the spiritual journey. The thesis was titled *Steps Toward Poverty and Death,* and it was divided into three sections, the titles of which Bly took directly from the three parts of Rilke's *Book for the Hours of Prayer:* The Book of the Monkish Life, The Book of Pilgrimage, The Book of Poverty and Death. When Bly came to put together *The Light,* he worked to organize it in such a way that the book as a whole would constitute a statement, larger than any of its individual poems. And rather than putting the poetry of religious meditation and ecstasy aside while dealing with heavy social and historical content, he sets the public and the private, the historical and the spiritual, the more-than-profane and the sacred, side by side. The protest poems for which *The Light* has been best-known occur for the most part in the first three sections of the book: The Two Worlds, The Various Arts of Poverty and Cruelty, The Vietnam War. But there are two more sections, and their titles indicate the direction Bly moves in: In Praise of Grief, A Body Not Yet Born. The book that begins by depicting the dark interiors of public and historical realities curves into a more private spiritual vision. The realities of the outer world and historical time are not forgotten, but the poet, having immersed himself in them, turns to see what may be left for the inward man. What he finds are energies in opposition to the forces of death and corruption described in the earlier sections: it is the energies of the inward man that finally offer the strength to struggle and survive and the possibility of new life. To say that Bly in these last sections "retreats into the refuge of the inward man,"[28] as Herbert Leibowitz did in his review, mistakes the matter. It is not a retreat but a necessary dialectic. In the book's structure we see again its prophetic character: social criticism is based in spiritual values and a vision of transformation. For Bly it could not be otherwise, for his social vision is always integral with his sense of the life of the spirit.

The first group of poems, The Two Worlds, plays variations on the Boehme-inspired vision of the inward and outward realities. America as Bly describes it here is a culture that does not recognize the need to be "generated out of both worlds," and consequently the two are splitting apart; at times it seems that they have already irrevocably done so. In this section we find "Johnson's Cabinet Watched by Ants," with its Hawthornesque depiction of the double lives of "the citizens we know during the day": "Tonight they burn the rice-supplies; tomorrow/ They lecture on Thoreau; tonight they move around the trees,/ Tomorrow they pick the twigs from their clothes;/ Tonight they throw the fire-bombs, tomorrow/ They read the Declaration of Independence; tomorrow they are in church." Commonplace aspects of American life are seen with a similar sort of night-vision. In "The Executive's Death" Bly gives a surreal rendering of "lives of quiet desperation." The comparisons Bly uses when he says, "Merchants have multiplied more than the stars of heaven./ Half the population are like the long grasshoppers/ That sleep in the cool of the day," seem at first glance flatly arrogant, but thinking of shopping malls with fifty glowing stores or suburban neighborhoods with no people on the streets, only the hum of an air conditioner here and there, we may decide that they are less judgments than vivid expressionistic reports.

The desperation comes in when one of the executives, who "walk[s] on cool floors" "high in the air" plunges suddenly into a dying dream: "As he lies on the wintry slope, cut off and dying,/ A pine stump talks to him of Goethe and Jesus." Brought down from the cool floors of prestige and manipulative power exercised at a distance, almost abstractly, he is lectured to by a stump, lowly, rooted, an image of grief, about the inward life that he had ignored. Then the poem circles back to the imagery of the opening lines, giving a description of commuter trains that conveys both panic and pathos, and links contemporary life with the world of biblical plagues:

> Commuters arrive in Hartford at dusk like moles
> Or hares flying from a fire behind them
> And the dusk in Hartford in full of their sighs;
> Their trains come through the air like a dark music,
> Like the sound of horns, the sound of thousands of small wings.

Most people who think about it recognize in television a more or less poisonous, or at least sedative and addictive, influence. In "Watching Television" Bly describes the dark side of hours in front of the flickering screen, and what he shows us is an inward disfigurement:

> The detective draws fifty-five million people into his revolver,
> Who sleep restlessly as in an air raid in London;
> Their backs become curved in the sloping dark.
>
> The filaments of the soul slowly separate:
> The spirit breaks, a puff of dust floats up,
> Like a house in Nebraska that suddenly explodes.

The handling of the images here is skillful. As the watchers are "drawn" into the gun, it is as if they are pulled out of themselves: the state they are in now is not so much consciousness as restless waking-sleep. And as the poem puts them inside a bullet, their backs take on the curve of its shape. A weird metamorphosis takes place. The people become very old, bent over in "the sloping dark," and at the same time they have been pulled back into a womb of repressed violence. The final image of the house exploding is also deft in its ominousness. First we view it from a distance, small and silent, "a puff of dust"; it recreates the inconsequential, abstracted quality of television violence. Bly saves the word "explodes" until the very end, and the effect is that of trance giving way suddenly to destruction. When he says, "The filaments of the soul slowly separate:/ The spirit breaks," he states outright what the poems in the first section of *The Light*, and the two sections that follow it as well, express in other ways again and again.

In some poems Bly describes the split between the two worlds, the soul's separation, dramatically: "The Busy Man Speaks" is a dramatic monologue, and "Romans Angry about the Inner World" tells a story. The first of these is one of Bly's best-known poems, and its notoriety has been due to at least three factors. First, it is a key poem in terms of the masculine/feminine dichotomy that has been of central importance in Bly's thinking. It is also notable for its innate rhetorical power, but added to this has been the dramatic performance Bly gives the piece in his public readings. I would like to digress here briefly, and say a few words about Bly as a reader, or performer, or sayer, of poems. One needs to do so somewhere in a study of this poet, for his work in this area is by no means an insignificant aspect of his talent and contribution.

Not everyone views the proliferation of the poetry reading that has occurred in the past twenty years or so as a positive development. For instance, there are those—represented in a segment of almost any college English department—who are uncomfortable at the idea of poetry getting up off the page, and skeptical that there could be more than three or four living poets worth listening to. Of course there are some valid reservations to be raised about the poetry reading phenomenon, but certainly it is fundamentally proper and healthy that poetry—the basic stuff of which is sound, and the aim of which is communication and, at times, incantation—is being read aloud to audiences across the country. Bly has been one of the poets most active and creative in the revival of the poetry reading.

It is appropriate to mention Bly's readings in the midst of discussing *The Light*, for it was during the period surrounding this book that he began to think seriously about what a poetry reading might be beyond a poet standing at a lectern and reading, poorly or well, from a book: "we hear so many poets read in a flat and dull voice," Bly has remarked; " 'I want the poem to stand on its own feet,' they say, as if their voices were not feet." [29] Bly had done more than just put expression in his voice. With the advent of the anti-war readings staged by American Writers Against the Vietnam War, Bly began to read in public more often, and also to work consciously with the possibilities of the oral presentation of poetry. Opinion, humor, physical presence, and personality are among the resources Bly brings to bear in his readings, but beyond these his work involved an effort to recover ancient means and powers—namely, memory, dance, music, and masks.

The term "reading" itself is not quite accurate with respect to Bly. During the anti-war readings he became aware of the greater immediacy and contact with one's audience that can be achieved if a poem is spoken from memory. Bly began to speak poems more and more "by heart" and less from the page. This also freed the body to move about, and the hands for gestures; gradually this freedom evolved into the dance—spontaneous, strange, incongruous, often lovely—of Bly's readings: a tall, thickset, not overly graceful man carving curves in the air with his hands, swaying, moving, to the rhythms of his feelings and words. And in 1975 Bly learned to play the dulcimer and began to use it to accompany certain poems. With its simplicity and drone, the dulcimer lends itself beautifully to poetry; the words are not overpowered by the music, as has often been the case in collaborations between poets and jazz combos. Yeats said in his essay "Speaking to the Psaltery":

> Since I was a boy I have always longed to hear poems spoken to a harp, as I imagined Homer to have spoken his, for it is not natural to enjoy an art only when one is by oneself. . . . Images used to rise up before me, as I am sure they have arisen before nearly everybody else who cares for poetry, of wild-eyed men speaking harmoniously to murmuring wires while audiences in many-coloured robes listened, hushed and excited.[30]

Bly and his dulcimer are capable of bringing those images to life; those who have heard him speak some of the poems from *Snowy Fields* to the dulcimer have shared one of the finest lyrical experiences in contemporary American poetry.[31]

As in the poetry itself, sometimes in Bly's readings flamboyance and didacticism become obstacles to "the true gift." But more often he reveals himself to be a poet with extraordinary gifts for making poetry live in the air and in the flesh. Patricia Goedicke has described a Bly reading, and some of those gifts, very well:

> The voice is high, flat, a narrow Middle Western twang. Nasal, metallic. Faintly unpleasant? And the torso, unencumbered by the familiar poncho, is surprisingly stiff, the satin-looking blue pinstriped vest outlining the awkwardly elegant instep of the spine. Where is the hushed, primordial hum I have been hearing in my head all these years, reading Robert Bly's poems for myself?
>
> He is about to give a reading, in New York, and from what I hear I am afraid I won't like it. After all these years swimming underground, in the miraculous silences of those poems. But he begins, and I settle down. I am prepared for large dance movements, the swooping Sufi gyrations friends have described to me. But at first there is only a slightly irritable tapping, on the lec-

tern, of long bony fingers. Then the hands lift, begin to weave a little, in small tight circles, pretentious maybe, self-conscious? But then, suddenly, not. As the poetry takes hold—this time it is James Wright's poetry; the occasion is a Memorial for Wright— the hands take hold with it, then the whole stiff torso relaxes, expands, begins to breathe; the business-suited man with the corona of white hair turns into a sleek horse, then into a gangling giraffe rearing and swaying, up there like a motionless wind on the stage.

No doubt I exaggerate (and the motions at this reading were restrained! Probably because he was reading Wright's poems, not his own). But the performance was remarkable. What happened to the voice? I forgot it . I understood, I "knew," I rode with the poems only. And at the end the dulcimer came out. For the last poem, Wright's "Milkweed." Little pieces of the spirit blew over the auditorium, small tufts of seed on the winged metal notes of the dulcimer.[32]

The reading Goedicke describes took place in 1981. The mood of Bly's readings during the Vietnam War was rather different, of course, as one can well imagine from reading *The Light* or the later "Teeth-Mother Naked at Last," a long dramatic diatribe which was in fact largely composed aloud during readings.

The fourth ancient element, the mask, brings us back again to *The Light*. One afternoon in 1972 in Minneapolis, the poet Keith Gunderson, with whom he was to give a reading that evening, gave Bly a rubber Halloween mask. During the reading Bly put the mask on and spoke a poem through it. He did so as a joke, but he noticed that the mask had an unnerving effect on the audience, and in later readings he began to experiment with masks as visual accompaniments for poems. It was poems with dramatic personae to which the use of masks most clearly lent itself, and it is two of the persona pieces in *The Light*—"The Busy Man Speaks" and "Counting Small-Boned Bodies"—with which Bly has done his most notable mask work. For "The Busy Man Speaks" he wears the original mask—a Nosferatu-like man, bald, hook-nosed, leering. The performance is highly theatrical; the effect is bizarre, unsettling, and powerful. But in addition to sheer dramatic effect, the presentation makes clear that in spite of the title's not overly subtle pun, the poem is no mere attack on businessmen but a description of inner forces, a coarsening and debasement of the spirit. As performed by Bly or on the page, the poem is strong and frightening.

Bly says that he had not yet read Jung or Erich Neumann or other "psychic archeologists" on the subjects of the masculine and feminine in the psyche when this poem was written,[33] so once again, as with "A Man Writes to a Part of Himself," we see him dealing intuitively with the dichotomy which he would work with more elaborately and systematically later. The Busy Man renounces a dozen "mothers," all of them connected with emotion, intimacy, suffering, inwardness, or the natural world. He then declares his allegiance to a series of "fathers": the father of righteousness, the father of cheerfulness, the father of perfect gestures. In making these choices and these vows he becomes the purely outward man. For this he receives a conventional re-ward—money—and one less often spoken of: rocks, the hard-ness and purity of spirit that is also the barrenness of the desert, "the landscape of zeros"—a phrase that neatly ties together the world of great amounts of money and spiritual emptiness.

The poem is a caricature of one-sided soul. The Busy Man is seemingly upright, his qualities are ones that his society ap-proves, yet the narrowness of his supposed virtues disfigures him. He is worldliness and cynicism in apotheosis. What is perhaps most frightening in his speech is his self-assurance. He accepts his condition as if it were health, a reason for pride. He lacks not only the values and energies of the feminine, but also any desire to come into contact with them. This arrogance in itself is as important an aspect of his disease as his alienation from any of the various mothers.

It may be worth mentioning that while the poem's intention is to depict a masculine soul as it appears when its connections with the feminine are severed, at the same time it caricatures one-sidedness it caricatures the masculine as well. Apparently nothing of much value is in the keeping of the fathers—only some cheerfulness and impressive gestures, and a righteousness that is invisibly but clearly prefixed by the word "self." Later in his work we will see Bly making a concerted effort to examine and honor the masculine soul, and when he does so it will be not only to tend wounds that have resulted from cultural forces but also perhaps to redress slights he himself might have committed. Earlier, he periodically reminded his readers and listeners—and himself—of the danger of denigrating and turning away from "masculine consciousness." After reading "The Busy Man Speaks" during a 1970 interview, Bly was asked, "Is it accurate to say that you feel the masculine principle is destructive?" He responded:

> When it gets too far from the feminine, yes. Most western men are. But masculine consciousness in itself is not evil. Far from it. In its highest levels, it is pure light. There must be a balance between two poles of consciousness. Before and during the Middle Ages Celts and Gauls were moving into masculine consciousness, keeping a tremendous amount of feminine consciousness. The Cathedral of Chartres is deeply feminine. At the same time, a great masculine drive built it.[34]

And in the 1973 essay "I Came Out of the Mother Naked," he commented: "Right now we long to say that father consciousness is bad, and mother consciousness is good. But we know it is father consciousness saying that; it insists on putting labels on things. They are both good."[35]

In the introduction to *A Poetry Reading Against the Vietnam War* Bly wrote: "The Vietnam War . . . resembles the long-term effort of the Romans to set up a military colony in Palestine. To the Romans, Palestine was Asia, or its porch, as Vietnam is to us—and of course they had to contain the Persians."[36] Where that statement stays in the historical dimension, "Romans Angry about the Inner World" uses the example of ancient Rome to dramatize the split between the inner and outer worlds. The poem describes the torture and execution of a religious martyr. Once again the inward/outward dichotomy is joined with that of the feminine and the masculine. The persecutors, presumably, are male, but the martyr is a woman; and she is apparently a devotee of a Mary or other Mother cult: the torturers exclaim as they tie her legs, "Here is a woman/ Who has seen our mother/ In the other world!"

In this poem Bly makes the word "executive" interchangeable with "executioner." The point is not only to attack Johnson and MacNamara, but to have the oppression of religion which the poem describes stand for a psychological repression as well. The executioners kill the spiritual woman, and the executives, representatives of the one-sided consciousness that understands only the values and realities of the outer world, in effect try to wipe out the inward and feminine energies. "Romans Angry about the Inner World" restates the conflict dramatized in "The Busy Man Speaks," but with a difference. Where the Busy Man is contemptuous of those energies, the executives/executioners are aware of a world counter to their own only enough to be threatened by it:

> The other world is like a thorn
> In the ear of a tiny beast!
> The fingers of the executives are too thick
> To pull it out!
> It is like a jagged stone
> Flying toward them out of the darkness.

They want to be "reassured" by the woman, and when she refuses they kill her. Both the arrogance of the Busy Man and the insecurity-leading-to-violence of these "Romans" are aspects of the psychic disintegration Bly repeatedly depicts in the poems with which he opens *The Light.*

In the second section, The Various Arts of Poverty and Cruelty, Bly again plays variations on a theme. The section carries another epigraph from Boehme:

> When we think of it with this knowledge, we see that we have been locked up, led blindfold, and it is the wise of this world who have shut and locked us up in their art and their rationality, so that we have had to see with their eyes.

There are two other epigraphs as well: a line from an old liturgy, and this from Freud: "What a distressing contrast there is between the radiant intelligence of the child, and the feeble mentality of the average adult." The quotations from Boehme and Freud announce the theme, not separate from that of the first section but an extension of it: the betrayal of consciousness and of the human spirit. The opening poem, "Come with Me," with its rich images of defeat and despair, serves as an invocation, calling us into a world filled with such images. A center has not held, and Bly sets before us the spectacle of a culture falling apart from its inner decay, blighted, withering, turning back on itself. Physical things rebel and long to escape into the wilderness: "The dams reverse themselves and want to go stand alone in the desert." The society's supposed spiritual leaders are also desperate for escape: "Ministers . . . dive headfirst into the earth" ("Those Being Eaten by America"). "Written in Dejection near Rome" presents passivity and alienation as the two alternatives possible in such a society. Those with enough consciousness to be aware of the decadence "will abandon their homes/ to live on rafts tied together on the ocean." With the most conscious people gone, the rest of the population is one step closer to inertness: "those on shore will go inside tree trunks,/

surrounded by bankers whose fingers have grown long and slender,/ piercing through rotting bark for their food." While Bly's portrayal of ordinary citizens is harsh here and elsewhere, it should be noted that he does not portray alienation as a reason for self-congratulation, as Cummings or Jeffers or Ginsberg tend to do. In Bly's depiction those who have lost their relationship with the broader community and those who are left behind both suffer from the exile.

As in the first section, Bly is expressing a vision that combines social and psychic dimensions, and he intersperses among his images of pervasive spiritual breakdown specific public figures and episodes. "The light in children's faces fading at six or seven" ("Those Being Eaten by America") represents one kind of loss; a president lying about an invasion ("Listening to President Kennedy Lie about the Cuban Invasion") represents another. Three presidents get special attention in the section. In "Andrew Jackson's Speech," Jackson is imagined speaking against the backdrop of the Detroit riots. In his National Book Award acceptance Bly referred to Jackson as "the General Westmoreland of 1830," noting that Jackson's second annual message, in which he talked about the Indian problem, resembled an administration speech on Vietnam: "It was another speech recommending murder of a race as prudent policy, requiring stamina."[37] In the poem Jackson is the fanatical defender of "honor," that of his wife and that of the country, both of which he mentions in the same breath. He accuses the poor of betraying the revolution, and his entire speech, rising "in the noisy streets of Detroit," is a mixture of chivalric ideals, violence, and delusion.

Jackson also speaks briefly in "Three Presidents," where we also hear from Theodore Roosevelt and John Kennedy. The poem presents what we can imagine as a surreal news conference in which the presidents are asked, "What would you like to be?" Each responds in turn in an unaccustomed language which has the revealing strangeness of dream. Their speeches tell us something about the presidents themselves, but beyond that they are, like "The Busy Man Speaks," expressionistic renderings of certain kinds of consciousness. Jackson's four-line speech is as fleeting as the image he chooses to express his wish: he wants to be a white horse that runs across the countryside, an image that conjures up a romanticized masculinity. Bly uses Roosevelt to represent another variety of exaggerated masculinity. The "big stick" psychology here becomes quite talkative, and Roosevelt brags about how he slept in his underwear in the White House, "ate the Cubans with a straw," and haunted Lenin's dreams. When he comes to make his wish, he chooses to be a stone:

> As for me, I want to be a stone. Yes!
> I want to be a stone laid down thousands of years ago,
> A stone with almost invisible cracks!
> I want to be a stone that holds up the edge of the lake house,
> A stone that suddenly gets up and runs around at night,
> And lets the marriage bed fall; a stone that leaps into the water,
> Carrying the robber down with him.

The scene describes a strength and solidness the underside of which is a high instability. A sense of justice and firm action is joined with a kind of mania; the robber is drowned, but suddenly the foundation stone is missing. The poem is an attack on machismo as a support for a house—a symbol of the self in and out of dreams— and for the marriage bed inside it.

Neither of these caricatures makes its subject totally unattractive. Jackson's romanticism and Roosevelt's rough, unapologetic vigor both have their appeal. But the sketch of Kennedy is easily the most complex and interesting of the three. Bly has said in introducing this poem that he found in the personality of Kennedy something "very beautiful, and evasive also."[38] The monologue he gives him in this poem suggests this combination very well. Kennedy wants to be "a stream of water falling—/

Water falling from high in the mountains, water/ That dissolves everything,/ And is never drunk, falling from ledge to ledge, from glass to glass." The images capture a combination of idealism and extraordinary egotism; the smoothness, style, and charisma which could create an illusion of Camelot; the megalomania of a man who wanted to wash away the logjam of government by committee and replace it with dynamism emanating from an individual—himself.[39] Both Theodore Roosevelt and John Kennedy represent powerful arrogance, but it may be that the kind Bly sees in Kennedy is the more dangerous, because it is less straightforward, and more beguiling. (The poem was written, incidentally, while Kennedy was still alive, when such a critical reading of Kennedy was far less common than it has become in later years.) When Bly has Kennedy say at the end of his speech, "And when I ascend the third time, I will fall forever,/ Missing the earth entirely," he is describing a longing which is counter both to the grounding he had affirmed in *Snowy Fields* and the heavy grief and passion he honors in *The Light*.

Writing in 1981, David Ignatow said of *The Light*: "It was then and is now a legitimate attempt to nail down the national and personal feelings of a native American in words that are meant to startle us awake by their angled vision. At times, certain poems remind me of Picasso's Guernica for their frightfulness and maddened vision of destruction."[40] The comparison to Guernica seems an apt one, and a number of poems in the book resemble painting in their effect: their assembled images become nearly visual compositions. In The Various Arts of Poverty and Cruelty, for example, there are two particularly striking "American landscapes"—"The Great Society" and "Sleet Storm on the Merritt Parkway."

In "The Great Society" the landscape is permeated by a disturbing blend of restlessness and torpor. People seem caught in a kind of simmering daydream: "Dentists continue to water their lawns even in the rain;" "The janitor sits troubled by the boiler,/ And the hotel keeper shuffles the cards of insanity./ The President dreams of invading Cuba." Bly makes handfuls of shard-like images capture a bleak and foreboding atmosphere. In the final stanza he takes us to "the far shore," and ends with an image that simultaneously suggests both despair and decapitation; it could be out of either Edward Hopper or Hieronymus Bosch:

> On the far shore, at Coney Island, dark children
> Play on the chilling beach: a sprig of black seaweed,
> Shells, a skyful of birds,
> While the mayor sits with his head in his hands.

Earlier in the poem we encounter another striking image—bizarre, funny, melancholy:

> Hands developed with terrible labor by apes
> Hang from the sleeves of evangelists:

The image telescopes an evolutionary span of time in an instant, outdoing other poems such as "After the Industrial Revolution, All Things Happen at Once" and "Hearing Men Shout at Night on Macdougal Street," which do something similar with historical time. On one hand, a child begins to lose "radiant intelligence" at six or seven. On another, after hundreds of thousands of years, after the struggle to stand upright, to chip stones, to create a little area of consciousness in the immense night, mankind arrives at Billy Graham and Jerry Falwell. And it isn't only evangelists who may not have been worthy of all that effort; the poem calls the entire "Great Society" into question. *The Light*, and Bly's other work also, contains many references to the long past. These references imply the largest context of Bly's conviction that "there is a road." Betrayals of intelligence and inner life are not only breakdowns in the life of individuals and of a society, but of the evolutionary labor itself. The compressed, rich images of *The Light* are its key power. Through them Bly is able to express not only emotions and moods, but ideas as well.

In "Sleet Storm on the Merritt Parkway" the landscape is rendered in a realistic style—the only case in *The Light* in which this is so. Yet the poem is no less successful, for the absence of surreal effects, in describing a profound disillusionment. Moving through the world of suburbs and thruways, the poet says:

> Seeing the sheets of sleet untouched on the wide streets,
> I think of the many comfortable homes stretching for miles,
> Two or three stories, solid, with polished floors,
> With white curtains in the upstairs bedrooms,
> And small perfume flagons of black glass on the window sills,
> And warm bathrooms with guest towels, and electric lights—
> What a magnificent place for a child to grow up!
> And yet the children end in the river of price-fixing,
> Or in the snowy field of the insane asylum.

It is a straightforward and touching lament for the middle class dream. Then the poem turns to the anguish of living in a country that partly lives up to its ideals but whose history is full of their betrayals:

> The sleet falls—so many cars moving toward New York—
> Last night we argued about the Marines invading Guatemala in 1947,
> The United Fruit Company had one water spigot for 200 families,
> And the ideals of America, our freedom to criticize,
> The slave systems of Rome and Greece, and no one agreed.

Bly concluded an earlier poem in this section, "Listening to President Kennedy Lie about the Cuban Invasion," with the simple statement, "There is a bitter fatigue, adult and sad." That describes the mood of "The Great Society" and "Sleet Storm on the Merritt Parkway" and a number of other poems in the first two sections. In the eight poems that make up the third section, The Vietnam War, the bitterness and fatigue remain, but violence and a sharper desperation dominate.

Bly's Vietnam poems are different from many of the poems written about the war in that in addition to raising protest they also attempt to understand the war's relationship to the national psyche. As I have mentioned, Bly said that he wrote these poems about the war because he "was interested in where it came from inside us." The first two sections of *The Light* suggest one source: the split between the inner and outer worlds. But the poems that deal directly with the war look further. Again and again, they evoke some hidden thing: " . . . something inside us/ Like a ghost train in the Rockies/ About to be buried in snow!/ Its long hoot/ Making the owl in the Douglas fir turn his head" ("Asian Peace Offers Rejected Without Publication"). It is hidden inside us, and hidden, less well, in our history.

> . . . there is something moving in the dark somewhere
> Just beyond
> The edge of our eyes: a boat
> Covered with machine guns
> Moving along under trees
> It is black,
> The hand reaches out
> And cannot touch it—
> It is that darkness among pine boughs
> That the Puritans brushed
> As they went out to kill turkeys
>   ("At a March against the Vietnam War")

The essential source Bly sees in *The Light* for the Vietnam War is the European-American heritage of racist oppression and violence. This in turn, as the reference to the Puritans suggests, he relates to a profound fear and antagonism toward all that which is perceived as "dark," "primitive," or "other." Both the extermination of the Indians and America's disastrous crusade in Vietnam share this deep root. "Hatred of Men with Black Hair," a dense phantasmagoria of a poem, expresses this idea most strongly. It culminates in this powerful image:

Underneath all the cement of the Pentagon
There is a drop of Indian blood preserved in snow:
Preserved from a trail of blood that once led away
From the stockade, over the snow, the trail now lost.

In these poems Bly is forcing his reader to look at that lost trail. In his essays, and in "The Teeth-Mother Naked at Last," which will be discussed in chapter 3, Bly offers other sources, other theories. In *The Light*, it is this "hatred of men with black hair," fed by and feeding a lurking hatred of part of our own nature— "We were the ones we intended to bomb!" Bly says in "Driving through Minnesota during the Hanoi Bombings"—that he presents as the hidden thing out of which a Vietnam War can grow.

The poems are uneasy with distance, and struggle against it. Before evoking that "something moving in the dark somewhere" in "At a March against the Vietnam War," Bly gives images of the march itself. It is a sunny fall day; the marchers, "bundled in coats/ and sweaters," are protected against even the discomfort of chilly air. The incongruous aspect of the march, its distance from the realities of the war in more than miles, is not lost on the poet, and he notes: "Looking down, I see feet moving/ Calmly, gaily,/ Almost as if separated from their bodies." Similarly, "Driving through Minnesota during the Hanoi Bombings" begins with images of lakes and grass, and then breaks jarringly into scenes of mutilation in Vietnam, and this prophecy:

These instants become crystals,
Particles
The grass cannot dissolve. Our own gaiety
Will end up
In Asia, and in your cup you will look down
And see
Black Starfighters.

The poems try to cross the distance between who we think we are and the hidden thing inside us. Failing to do so, *The Light* seems to say, we continue down a road that ends in the final dehumanization described in "Counting Small-Boned Bodies," deservedly one of the best-known poems in the book. Here distance has triumphed aboslutely:

COUNTING SMALL-BONED BODIES

Let's count the bodies over again.

If we could only make the bodies smaller,
The size of skulls,
We could make a whole plain white with skulls in the moonlight!

If we could only make the bodies smaller,
Maybe we could get
A whole year's kill in front of us on a desk!

If we could only make the bodies smaller,
We could fit
A body into a finger-ring, for a keepsake forever.

The reference is to one of the peculiarities of the Vietnam period: body counts, reported routinely on the evening news. Again creating a mask, Bly imagines the body-counter himself, who turns out to be a rather cheerful being who sits at a desk and has a taste for scenic vistas, efficiency, technical ingenuity, and expensive trinkets. He is, in short, a citizen of a modern business-dominated, technological, affluent society. The poem manipulates scale and distance with great effectiveness. In his mania for making the bodies smaller—their shrinking suggests their reality receding further and further away—the speaker does not seem to notice or care that all the while they are moving closer to him. The bodies—never regarded as human from the outset—move in three dream-like steps in toward him, from the moon-lit plain to the desk to the ring. The implication is clear, and contained perfectly within the images and their movement: when one succeeds this well in distancing the suffering and death of other human beings, in making them smaller and smaller, one ends up engaged to death itself. The final phrase plays on a well-known advertising slogan, but in this context it takes on a terrible psychological meaning.

After the anguish and fury of the social and anti-war poems, Bly places the group of poems which he titles In Praise of Grief. We begin to curve toward the more private (though still shared) aspect of the vision of *The Light*. The last section, called A Body Not Yet Born, continues that arc, with poems that are intensely inward—mystical, apocalyptic, erotic, evolutionary. As I suggested earlier, it would be mistaken to construe this movement as flight from the outward realities faced in the previous poems. Bly has created a book which insists that public events have spiritual meaning. By ending with the private poems, Bly affirms the soul, the life and death of which *The Light* has brooded on from its first poem onward.

The tragic sense is based in the conviction that if grief is our lot, we may at least become more human through it. *The Light* shares this conviction. In "A Home in Dark Grass," Bly says:

> We did not come to remain whole.
> We came to lose our leaves like the trees,
> The trees that are broken
> And start again, drawing up from the great roots,

For Bly, this is a key article of belief. The poem that meditates most directly on the potentially redeeming nature of grief is "The Fire of Despair Has Been Our Saviour." The title has the effect of a simple affirmation of faith, but a complex relationship exists between the words "despair" and "saviour." It is this paradoxical relationship that the poem expresses.

The season is autumn. The bare trees, "Heaven's roots," which have been and are here again images of cycles of regeneration, are not enough now. "How easily we see spring in your black branches," the poet says. But that the trees will be reborn carries no inward correspondence, and he wanders, depressed, adrift, detached. The problem lies, of course, within him—in a failure of feeling. He cannot find the connection with the natural world and with experience itself that gives life intensity. It is connectedness and intensity that translate in Bly into a sense that "the road" exists.

> This autumn, I
> Cannot find the road
> That way: the things that we must grasp,
> The signs, are gone, hidden by spring and fall, leaving
> A still sky here, a dusk there,
> A dry cornleaf in a field; where has the road gone?

Adrift in the present, the poet's mind casts back into the past. He thinks of the Middle Ages, which he imagines as a time possessed of a sharpness and intensity that he lacks: " . . . iron ringing iron/ At dawn, chill wringing/ The grass, clatter of saddles,/ The long flight on borrowed stone/ Into the still air sobered by the hidden joy of crows." He thinks back further, to the Ice Age, when man's protection from death, cold, and pain was small: "Another child dead,/ Turning bone stacks for bones, sleeves of snow blowing/ Down from above, no tracks in the snow . . . " But these sufferings, while they forced man to grow "Horny scales/ From sheer despair," were also "instants/ Finally leading out of the snowbound valley." The intensity of grief and awe-fulness has led us forward. If we lose the capacity for such deep feelings, as the poet believes he may have here, we lose everything, as individuals and as a species.

The poem seems to end in complete despair. Neither the intensity he imagines in past ages nor the consolation of nature's promise of renewal are quite real to him: " . . . where has the road gone? All/ Trace lost, like a ship sinking,/ Where what is left and what goes down both bring despair./ Not finding the road, we are slowly pulled down." We seem to have arrived at the point of defeat, yet in the phrase "slowly pulled down" there is at least basis for hope. Images of sinking and drifting down appear frequently in Bly's poetry, and they are almost always signs of a positive motion in the psyche. The sinking ship represents the possibility of psychic oblivion, yet it may also be that this despair, this sinking, can become the grief that deepens being, the death out of which life is resurrected. If we think of a writer like Melville, it is clear that both his authority and his humanity derive from the unmistakable sense that this is a man who has been pulled down often, powerfully. In the poem's last line we are left at the moment of despair which contains within it the potential for redemption. Being pulled into the depths may spell the death of feeling, but it may also become the depth of feeling that carries life forward. Those earlier ages struggled hard. Modern man has his own agonies to struggle against, and his despair, his alienation from the fundamental rhythms of life and from his own experience, are not least among these. In this regard, it is in being pulled down that he may be saved.

"The Fire of Despair Has Been Our Saviour" is one of Bly's earliest poems. It was included, in a substantially different version and under the title "The Man Who Sees the Hill of Despair from Afar," in his Master's thesis collection at the University of Iowa. He worked on the poem for years, and after *The Light* was published he again became dissatisfied with it, particularly with the last line, which he considered inconclusive.[41] The gap between the last line and the affirmation that "the fire of despair has been our saviour" does represent a considerable ambiguity. But I think the poem succeeds, and partly because of its ambiguity. If we are awake to the positive as well as the negative implications of the phrase "pulled down," we feel a turning at the end of the poem—a downward curve—toward the possibility of redemption. It is not a promise, but only a subtly felt shift. In this the poem catches, just firmly enough, an elusive, crucial, paradoxical turning point in the life of the spirit.

What distinguishes *The Light* from much of the surrealism that proliferated in American poetry in the 1960s and after—largely through Bly's influence both as poet and translator—is its passion and moral energy. Its effects are not merely bizarre, amusing, or outrageous. They arise from strong emotion, felt in the body; they are not just products of the mind at play. So it is in the places where surrealism seems to descend to oddness, where it crosses the line between a penetrating strangeness and self-parody, that *The Light* is weakest. By this standard, the poem "Opening an Oyster" is the low point in the collection. When Bly begins the poem, "We think of Charlemagne/ As we open oysters," he is assuming a good deal in his use of the plural pronoun. The rest of the poem follows a progression of images which as often as not turn funny against themselves. "Westward the ice peaks/ Like vast maternity hospitals turned white by oyster shells!" Such a mixture of urgency and arbitrary weirdness is at odds with the real passion and moral earnestness of *The Light*.

As the emphasis shifts in the last two sections from outer to inner events, rage and "a bitter fatigue, adult and sad" give way to a different form of intensity, flowing from a series of visions of transformation. The long past was invoked earlier: hands developed through the labor of apes hung from the sleeves of evangelists ("The Great Society"); "half-evolved antennas of the sea-snail/ [sank] to the ground" when emotional intimacy was refused ("Suddenly Turning Away"). As we move to the final section, A Body Not Yet Born, the past that lies beyond history enters the poems strongly. In Praise of Grief ends with "Looking at Some Flowers," where the poet suddenly becomes aware, in one of those moments of pure intuition which are the mark of much of Bly's best work, that the ground the house stands upon is "only free of the sea for five or six thousand years." In that moment, the psyche opened through the flowers' association with death, millennia are reduced to relative insignificance, and our distance from the sea, the primordial mother that bears and swallows us, is revealed as a slender margin. In A Body Not Yet Born we find further evocations of the long past. "Moving Inward at Last" describes the psychic turning its title announces through images of cave times. "Evolution from the Fish" sees in love-making a manifestation or recreation or continuation of the evolutionary process itself:

> This nephew of snails, six feet long, lies naked on a bed
> With a smiling woman, his head throws off light
> Under marble, he is moving toward his own life
> Like fur, walking. And when the frost comes, he is
> Fur, mammoth fur, growing longer
> And silkier, passing the woman's dormitory,
> Kissing a stomach, leaning against a pillar,
> He moves toward the animal, the animal with furry head!

It is a lovely and ecstatic imagining, and the sense that evolution is not only a matter of the past gives these poems a fine and fiery longing. "Evolution from the Fish" ends with these lines: "Do/ Not hold my hands down! Let me raise them!/ A fire is passing up through the soles of my feet!" Even poems which make no specific reference to prehistory have a certain archaic simplicity and mystery about them. Returning to the comparison to visual art (masks, landscapes) used earlier, we might say that in the last section Bly creates an atmosphere like that which surrounds cave art:

> An owl on the dark waters
> And so many torches smoking
> By mossy stones
> And horses that are seen riderless on moonlit nights
> > ("Riderless Horses")

The images of the poems often appear like talismans, intimations of ancient origins and an unknown destination.

It is a poem about conversation, simple human intimacy, that brings the first glimpse of new life. It is from this poem, "Looking into a Face," that both the final section and the book take their titles.

LOOKING INTO A FACE

Conversation brings us so close! Opening
The surfs of the body,
Bringing fish up near the sun,
And stiffening the backbones of the sea!

I have wandered in a face, for hours,
Passing through dark fires.
I have risen to a body
Not yet born,
Existing like a light around the body,
Through which the body moves like a sliding moon.

The first stanza is alive with sexual energy and the sense of the primal past; consider, for example, how concisely and delicately the image of the stiffening backbones of the sea suggests two movements toward erectness. The second stanza turns toward transfiguration, and its complex closing image captures beautifully the intimation of the unknown which is not completely so. Jung said, "we must always reckon with the presence of things not yet discovered."[42] That is what "Looking into a Face" and that last section of *The Light* as a whole try to do. Bly does not do this at all in the form of discursive speculation, but rather through the assertion of images rising from intuition and the body in moments of intensity. The image he draws of the "body not yet born" is convoluted and luminous; it is hard to know whether it has been elaborately worked, or if it is the product of an instant's burst of inspiration. The idea of having risen to a body that is not yet born is a difficult one for the rational intel-

ligence to deal with, and reason will have difficulty also with a
passage such as the one in "Wanting to Experience All Things"
where Bly says:

> We cannot see—
> But a paw
> Comes out of the dark
> To light the road. Suddenly I am flying,
> I follow my own fiery traces through the night!

How can one speak, in the past tense, of rising to what is not
yet born? How does a paw light up the road? How do we follow
traces that trail behind our own flight? These figures are surreal,
they are nonrational, they are koan-like; above all, they are clasps
that join that which lies behind us with that which lies ahead.
The poet reaches backward and forward. He links the mammal
paw and the road; the traces behind us suddenly are also the
path before us; the stiffening backbones of the sea bring us to
the body still to be born. There are moments when transfiguration is not just a faraway abstraction. These poems are made
from such moments.

The apocalyptic glimpses of A Body Not Yet Born take
various forms and tones. In "Hurrying Away from the Earth" it
is the "shadow of slums and of the conquering dead" and the
sound of "the iron chairs scraping in asylums" that give the sense
of final things. In "The Hermit" the revelation is in the image
of a man who has seemingly escaped from the wheel of suffering
and identity. "A Journey with Women," while it contains some
images that tread the line between the sublime and the ridicu-
lous very tenuously, is a wondrously strange description of a
night's spiritual and sexual journey; in it, as in "Evolution from
the Fish" and to a degree in "Looking into a Face," eros is the
energy that carries us out of our former selves, "carries us . . .
through the darkness between the constellations."

Bly ends *The Light* with another poem which promises revelation: "When the Dumb Speak." The poem begins with a catalogue of elements of the inward life: the experience of the dark night when the "I" is known as a small and floating thing ("There is a joyful night in which we lose/ Everything, and drift/ Like a radish"); the experience of the sea beyond the ego, and the rhythms of the risings and fallings of the soul's life ("Rising and falling, and the ocean/ At last throws us into the ocean,/ And on the water we are sinking/ As if floating on darkness"); the strength of the body's desire ("The body raging/ And driving itself, disappearing in smoke"); solitude ("Walks in large cities late at night/ Or reading the Bible in Christian Science windows"); a consciousness that includes war and the events of history ("Or reading a history of Bougainville"). After all this, "Then the images appear:"

> Images of death,
> Images of the body shaken in the grave,
> And the graves filled with seawater;
> Fires in the sea,
> The ships smoldering like bodies,
> Images of wasted life,
> Life lost, imagination ruined,
> The house fallen,
> The gold sticks broken,
> Then shall the talkative be silent,
> And the dumb shall speak.

In *Snowy Fields*, Bly concluded with an image of blind sailors approaching through a storm; here, we encounter in the book's final lines the dumb who shall speak. I don't think that it is accidental that Bly ends both books with images of the human when it is not whole. These images signify his awareness that we are fragmented or damaged creatures, and also his sense that the dark, wounded, or silenced parts of our being contain truth that we must hear as we journey toward our individual and collective spiritual destinies. They signify, too, a deepening of consciousness.

For all its ominous, cloudy prophecy, "When the Dumb Speak" amounts to an affirmation of faith, and the same can be said of *The Light* as a whole. *The Light* contains many images of life betrayed, disfigured, brutalized, "wasted." One would not want to call the book optimistic—to do so would be to trivialize it—yet it does not, ultimately, give in to ennervation or despair. As with *Snowy Fields*, *The Light* is best understood when read entire. Its overall movement contains much of its meaning. Intensely contemporary, it holds inside it a consciousness of the long past and intimations of an unknown future, and therefore it has the effect not only of protest but of a difficult, profound, shared journey as well. Faced with degradation and annihilation, the spirit struggles against them. This confrontation is felt throughout the collection; this struggle makes of *The Light*, a book that contains much ugliness and raggedness, a moving and coherent poem. Like *Snowy Fields*, *The Light* is one of the key books of American poetry of its time; one would not have an adequate sense of the poetry of the 1960s without reckoning with it. In *Snowy Fields*, Bly looked at his native landscape and found it alive with spiritual meaning. In *The Light* he looks passionately at historical events, present and past, and sees in them the conflict between the forces of death and the sources of life that exists in all moments of human time.

CHAPTER 3

Sleepers Joining Hands

. . . the whole genius of modern
poetry lies in its grasp of flowing
psychic energy.
—Robert Bly, 1972

In a review of Peter Matthiessen's *The Snow Leopard*, Donald Hall
makes a comment which says something fundamentally important about our time, and which is also pertinent to a consideration of the work of Robert Bly.

> Perhaps decades from now it will be obvious that in the last years
> we have moved beyond a three-century-long secular interpreta-
> tion of man's passage on earth. "For this is the Kali Yuga," Mat-
> thiessen writes toward the end of this book, "the Dark Age, when
> all the great faiths of mankind are on the wane." I suspect that
> they have begun to wax again, but of course the majority of con-
> temporary academics and intellectuals, journalists and profession-
> als, remain secular, considering themselves liberated from super-
> stition, like bright-eyed Victorians. Therefore they are liberated
> into a shallowness which is historically extraordinary, as hu-
> manly extreme as anything we remember from an earlier Dark
> Age: any children's crusade, any inquisition. . . . It will not do.[1]

Bly would agree. Throughout his work, both poetry and prose, he resists the pervasive historical anomaly Hall speaks of. As we have seen in his first two books, whether he is writing of rural Minnesota or the Vietnam War, Bly is a poet of the inward life. His concerns and attitudes are fundamentally religious. For him the secular interpretation of experience is unacceptable, and the rationalism, positivism, and objectivity which reinforce it are impoverished and impoverishing. An estimation of life that finds it possessed of divine and natural mystery (a distinction harder to draw after reading him) is both the root and the flower of Bly's work.

In describing the poem, Bly has been apt to say that it is "something that penetrates for a moment into the unconscious"[2] or "a wave on a flow of growth inside a person"[3]—a rather different emphasis from that given, say, by Frost's phrase, "a momentary stay against confusion." He seeks a balance, but one that will be open-ended and dynamic; while he is interested in the still point, what he is more interested in is the motions of the spirit—and the intellect's and the body's motions—around it. This fundamental attitude is reflected in many ways in Bly's work—I mean his total vocation as poet, writer, thinker—from his persistent search for new models (not so much of style as of consciousness), to his refusal to limit himself to a particular type of poem, to the experimentation and challenging vitality of his public readings, to his longing for a poem to reach out to the unknown. The desire for a richer, active balance leads him, as we have seen, into fields at dusk as well as into contemplation of contemporary affairs and history, into the plainest and most finely tuned pastorals and the fierce protest and dense surrealism of his political and social poems. It also leads him into areas of investigation beyond the conventional boundaries of literature—into religion, psychology, mysticism, anthropology, folklore, astrology, and at times, as in his essay "The Three Brains," even some science. Obviously it is not having read widely that makes Bly a unique figure among his contemporaries. Rather it is the way in which his roving studies are reflected, aggressively or subtly, in his thinking and writing. Bly is a man of many theories, speculations, and unexpected conjunctions. An essay on Wallace Stevens, for example, relates Stevens to "Dr. Jekyll and Mr. Hyde," the psychological and cultural phenomena underlying it, and more. Commissioned by the Sierra Club to do an anthology of poems related to ecology, he produces a book that is also a treatise on the history of human consciousness in its relationship to nature since Descartes.[4] Some have called his theorizings reckless, and no doubt there is some degree of truth in this charge—though also some resentment toward an intelligence that is omniverous, extremely energetic, original, and unusually at ease with its own promptings, and which dares to try to relate everything that comes within its ken. As Bly wrote once, "all thinking experiences in one century seem to be related, and knowledge of one forward impulse helps the impulses in other fields to find their way through the soggy brain tissue."[5] And as Bly is a poet, most often it is poetry which he uses as a common denominator in his speculative assimilations. This makes him all the more aggravating to those who prefer to keep poetry more or less compartmentalized.

To the more sympathetic he is eclectic and invigorating. Hall has described him as "a huge hummingbird [moving] from Jung flower to Zen flower, from Buddha to the Great Mother."[6] He is nothing if not—for want of a less baggy word—romantic, and he believes with Blake that there is no progression but through opposites, and with Emerson that "consistency" is an overrated and potentially dangerous virtue. Bly fits well Emerson's metaphor for true consistency: the ship tacking before the wind which, while seeming to alter its course constantly, when viewed from a height and distance is seen to have a clear direction. Bly revealed himself to be on such a zig-zag course in his first two books, and in the poetry and essays that followed he continued to tack with remarkable imagination and moral purpose. With its apocalyptic feelings, relentless desire for inward truths, and wild and profuse imagery moving between outrage and nightmare, *The Light* was decidedly not a book written under the aegis of reason, order, or moderation. Yet the poems in that book have a compression, a hardness and bitterness, that temper its expansive and rhetorical urges. It was in his next full-size collection, *Sleepers Joining Hands*, that Bly's centrifugal impulses became truly dominant. Bly is a poet in the Whitman tradition in various important respects, but merely in terms of the expansiveness that we associate with the adjective "Whitmanesque," *Sleepers* revealed him as an inheritor of Whitman much more sharply than either of his first two books. In much of the book Bly adopts a longer, more fluid line than he had used previously, and the drive toward expansiveness leads him to longer poems as well: his longest political poem, "The Teeth-Mother Naked at Last," and the title poem, a sequence in five parts which runs to nearly four hundred lines, but seems longer. The book's large embrace is inclusive and, in desire if perhaps not in effect, synthesizing. The poems included here represent Bly at his most delicate, concise, and mysterious, in the "Six Winter Privacy Poems" which open the book, and also at his most sprawling and difficult, in the title poem which closes it. In between there is a selection of poems which, among other things, made it harder to maintain the impression of "two styles" which many readers had formed after the first two books, and a speculative essay on the dynamics of consciousness, focusing on the archetype of the Great Mother. *Sleepers* is a rich and adventurous collection—in some ways the most fascinating of Bly's books. This is of course not necessarily to say that it is his best. (My own nomination for that distinction would be the quietly intense, darkly luminous *Snowy Fields*.)

In the late 1970s Bly began to talk more in his essays and readings about the importance of sound, which he had talked little about earlier, and form, a subject he had frequently bridled at in his attacks on iambics and "mere technique," and in his insistent emphasis on the image and the psychic content and motion of the poem. His new thinking about form was not simply reactionary; he did not say that free verse and the image had been a mistake, and that the iamb or the sonnet, or "composition by field," were the true way after all. But he did say: "I have been thinking that we have not been very faithful servants of art. . . . By 'we' I mean the poets of my generation. We have been lively and fierce servants, but was it of art? Or was it of art but not the work of art?"[7] In 1975 he invented a set form of his own, the ramage, which has a prescribed number of syllables (eighty-five) and concentrates on a particular vowel sound. When he talks about form it is clear that he is still trying to guard against what is too mechanical. Like others before him who are by gifts and temperament more at one with free verse but who long for some of the tensions, symmetries, and pulses of more regular forms (and most readers of American poetry can probably, by the 1980s, understand such a longing), he speaks of form in terms of nature:

> . . . when we speak of form as a wildness, and consider a poem's form as drawn from the careful economy of nature, we then can imagine the poem as a being that moves fast, can leap in the air, escape from tigers or professors, and live for generations, even during lean times.[8]

The power of analogy does not desert him. Here is his description of "form that is neither in nor out":

> The drummer Michael Meade from Seattle told me that the ancient Celtic women would sometimes lay hard conditions on a man who wanted to sleep with them. Conflicting loyalties and obligations often made going to bed dangerous for both parties. And besides, no woman wants to go to bed with a man who can't solve riddles, or is too straight-laced, or has no playfulness in his soul. So she might say, you can come to me, but neither in the day nor the night, and neither riding nor walking, and you should be neither in the house nor out.

> We see the threshold coming in here—on the threshold one is neither in the conscious or unconscious, neither in this world nor the other world. That is where true form takes the poem. And thresholds belong to all inbetwixt and between places, to the heron that is neither land bird nor sea bird, or mercury that is neither metal nor liquid. So the wise man might arrive riding a sheep, or lying across a short pony, with his legs dragging, so he is neither riding nor walking, at dusk, which is neither day nor night, and he wouldn't call to her until the pony's front legs were inside the house and the back legs outside. Then they could do what they wished.

> Free verse is a little like walking over the threshold right into the house, and saying, I'm a Protestant, I don't believe in all of this, let's just go to bed. And writing in an overly human form, too regular, is a little like riding the horse right up to the threshold, all four hooves outside, putting the head in, and saying, I'm a Catholic, we can cancel the conditions, come out and marry me.

> But writing in an inbetween form, a form for which one has gone to nature, a form the artist has drawn from her subtle abundance of snail shells and herons, that is like arriving at the inbetwixt time, neither night nor day, neither walking nor riding, and the horse neither inside nor out.[9]

And he has taken Whitman to task (respectfully) in an essay called "What Whitman Did Not Give Us." Among the deficiencies of Whitman's legacy Bly includes "care for small sounds, care for pauses": he criticizes Whitman's concentration on "the flow of creativity . . . rather than the shape and weight of a jar." [10] Applying the animal analogy to Whitman's work, he comes up with this: "If we imagined a typical lengthy Whitman poem as an animal, it would be something about a mile and a half long which would be killed by the first lion that entered the forest. It would be too long, with not enough bone structures between head and tail." [11] Obviously there is something of a son's criticism of a father here. But the point of this digression on form is to suggest that Bly is criticizing—not very obscurely— himself as well as Whitman. Bly may have had in the back of his mind the prose poems which had dominated his writing for a number of years when he criticized Whitman for concentrating too much on flow and not enough on "the shape and weight of a jar." It seems to me, however, that it is many of the poems in *Sleepers*, rather than "Crossing Brooklyn Ferry" or "Out of the Cradle, Endlessly Rocking," that are in danger from the lion.

For example, though the title poem has been hewn out of what were originally several thousand lines, it is still a sprawling creation, and one that lacks the rhythm and parallelisms which contribute so greatly to the coherence and power of a Whitman poem of similar length. And the expansiveness of *Sleepers* manifests itself in the book's language. The poems that dominate the collection are streams of images, again in an impassioned, Neruda-inspired surrealist style, but caught up in a greater flow of rhetoric than the poems in *The Light*. For the most part *Sleepers* is a poetry of sweep and the extravagant gesture. Sometimes the poems move and gather force beautifully, but sometimes the movement is impeded by lines which are clumsy or unconvincing. Here are the openings of two poems:

> You United States, frightened by dreams of Guatemala,
> building houses with eight-mile-long wings to
> imprison the Cubans . . .
> ("Condition of the Working Classes: 1970)

We are writing of Niagara, and the Huron squaws,
the chaise longue, periwinkles in a rage like snow,
Dillinger like a dark wind.
                                ("Calling the Badger")

The first is more predictable, less transformed by imagination,
than almost anything in *The Light;* the second combines an unconvincing use of the plural pronoun with exotic details that
sound like a parody of Wallace Stevens. Or, for example, these
lines from the title poem: "The feminine creature at the edge of
town,/ men with rifles all around." In their rhythm, image, and
unfortunate rhyme, they would be right at home on an old al-
bum by the Doors. The religious impulse weighs heavily in some
lines, turning awkward and self-congratulatory:

I am passive, listening to the lapping waves,
I am divine, drinking the air . . .
                    ("Water Drawn Up Into the Head")

inwardness, inwardness, inwardness,
the inward path I still walk on . . .
                    ("The Night Journey in
                    the Cooking Pot")

Dramatic effects also seem at times artificial, histrionic:

A woman whispers to me, urges me to speak truths.
"I am afraid that you won't be honest with me."
                    ("Meeting the Man Who Warns Me")

These are snippets, and picking them out like this is somewhat unfair to the total experience of the poetry they occur
within. But I think it is fair to say that Bly's use of language,
highly individual and open to risks at all times, becomes most
uneven when he writes in his more expansive, extravagant style,
and that the poetry in this mode sometimes succumbs to mere
inflation. It is also the case, however, that he is one of the few
American poets capable of, or much interested in, flying in his

poems—of achieving a sweeping forward motion, of dipping and soaring on the wings of his images. He sometimes crashes, yet without this element something large and frequently marvelous would be missing from his work.

The expansive and flowing quality of the work in *Sleepers* was reflected in/reflective of his major critical focus during the 1970s. Where he emphasized the image earlier, he now turned his attention to association. The first (and only) issue of his magazine that bore the logo *The Seventies* was a collection of essays, translations, and other poems forming a sort of manifesto on the powers and varieties of association in poetry, and beyond poetry as well. When reissued in book form by the Beacon Press, the collection was titled *Leaping Poetry: An Idea with Poems and Translations*, and the "leap," used broadly to signify any nonrational link or shift in a poem, became a term widely used in the discussion of contemporary poetry.

In focusing on association Bly had not really turned away from the image, the primary catalyst in the associative process. As we have seen earlier, Bly wants in the image a conjunction of the physical and the unknown, the sensory impression and the inner reverberation. With association he is again speaking of touching the known and the unknown:

> In ancient times, in the "time of inspiration," the poet flew from one world to another, "riding on dragons," as the Chinese said. Isaiah rode on those dragons, so did Li Po and Pindar. They dragged behind them long tails of dragon smoke. . . .
>
> This dragon smoke means that a leap has taken place in the poem. In many ancient works of art we notice a long floating leap at the center of the work. That leap can be described as a leap from the conscious to the unconscious and back again, a leap from the known part of the mind to the unknown part and back to the known. . . .
>
> Thought of in terms of language, then, leaping is the ability to associate fast. In a great ancient or modern poem, the consid-

erable distance between the associations, the distance the spark
has to leap, gives the lines their bottomless feeling, their space,
and the speed of the association increases the excitement of the
poetry.[12]

The image as Bly sees it is a thing that contains two worlds;
association is movement from one place to another. While also
recognizing and admiring the poetry of "steady light," "written
by a poet who remains by choice roughly in one part of the
psyche" (the work of Robert Creeley and Robert Francis are
given as examples, along with Shakespeare's sonnets and "some
Wordsworth poems"),[13] and while still writing poems which associate in quieter, sparer, more earthbound ways, Bly's interest
in *Sleepers* lay particularly with a profuse, kaleidoscopic associative style. Working from the belief that "the real joy of poetry
is to experience this leaping inside a poem,"[14] he wanted to examine and develop "the ability to associate fast," "freedom of
association." (This last phrase ought not to be taken as synony-
mous with "free association" in the sense that proponents of au-
tomatic writing use the term. Bly prizes spontaneity but also
believes in revision. For him the free flow of the mind in and
of itself is neither avant-garde nor necessarily very interesting.)

Bly's ideas on association are related to another focus in his
thought: his study of the mythological and psychic realm of the
Great Mother, embodied chiefly in the essay at the center of
Sleepers, "I Came Out of the Mother Naked." The mascu-
line/feminine dichotomy that we have seen developing previously comes to its fullest articulation in Bly's work in this essay.
What had been a matter of images arrived at intuitively in poems
such as "A Man Writes to a Part of Himself" and "The Busy
Man Speaks," in this essay is worked out into a systematic theory of consciousness, though the thinking and writing it contains are a long way from abandoning intuition. "I Came Out of
the Mother Naked" is a rich speculative weave—not without

certain gaps; it brings together an enormously ambitious range of material within its eighteen pages. It contains, among other things, Bly's most direct summary of the qualities of feminine and masculine, mother and father, consciousness:

> Mother consciousness was in the world first, and embodied itself century after century in its favorite images: the night, the sea, animals with curving horns and cleft hooves, the moon, bundles of grain. Four favorite creatures of the Mother were the turtle, the owl, the dove, and the oyster—all womb-shaped, night, or ancient round sea creatures. Matriarchy thinking is intuitive and moves by associative leaps. . . .
>
> When masculine consciousness became aware of itself, it took for its main image the bright blue sky surrounding the sun—its metal then was gold: Apollo had gold sun rays around his head. . . . In thinking, Socrates sounds the note: avoid myths—which are always stories of the Mother anyway—and think logically, in a straight line. . . . Father consciousness tries to control mammal nature through rules, morality, commandments, and tries to reach the spirit through asceticism. The Chinese describe it as the cold, the clear, the south side of the mountain (on which the light always falls), the north side of the river (always in sunlight), the rational, the spirit, the hard.
>
> In mother consciousness there is affection for nature, compassion, love of water, grief and care for the dead, love of whatever is hidden, intuition, ecstasy. The Chinese describe it as the north side of the mountain (always in shadow) and the south side of the river (always in shadow); also as the valley of the world.[15]

The essay takes its primary ideas from Johann Bachofen, the nineteenth-century scholar who proposed that patriarchal societies were preceded by matriarchies, from Jung, and from Erich Neumann. Pushing beyond the masculine/feminine dichotomy, it concentrates on the feminine side. Drawing on Neumann's *The Great Mother: An Analysis of the Archetype*, Bly describes a further division. Mother consciousness is not one thing, but contains the force-fields of four different mothers: the

Good Mother, "who brings to birth and nourishes what is born"; the Death Mother, whose "job is to end everything the Good Mother has brought to birth"; the Ecstatic Mother, associated with dance and the muses and whose name is self-explanatory; and the Stone or Teeth Mother, whose reign is stupor and psychic annihilation.[16]

To some (I include myself in this group) the heavy and systematic use of the masculine/feminine terminology will be problematical. Rooted in thousands of years of myth and religion, the deepest images and stories our species possesses, it nonetheless contains hazards. For example, thinking about archetypes can easily skid into thinking in stereotypes; instead of helping us to grasp complex human phenomena, it may end up reducing them to abstract simplifications. Bly says, "A woman radiates her energy whether she wants to or not; she has it from birth. But a man's spiritual life, as we know, is full of curious accidents."[17] "As we know. . . ." One may be surprised to hear that men have a corner on curious spiritual accidents.

But most often Bly's use of these images and schematics is fascinating and provocative, largely because of his ability to link the archetypes (a word, by the way, which he avoids; he manages not to use it at all in "I Came Out of the Mother Naked," which is rather remarkable considering his subject matter) and his generalizations to vivid examples. In these examples, Hölderlin's long insanity is seen as living in the same house with the Stone Mother; the brutal, pious racism of a tract by two apologists for the extermination of the Indians is an instance of father consciousness gone crude; and the change that took place between Woodstock and Altamont is seen as the Death and Stone Mothers stepping in and presiding at the second gathering in the places of their benevolent and ecstatic sisters, who clearly had been present at the first. Even a reader who begins with a basic skepticism toward such terms as mother consciousness and the Stone Mother is likely to emerge from this essay feeling that he has been given a rich and useful set of metaphors—in some respects more adequate than the terminology used by more orthodox psychology.

The concerns of *Leaping Poetry* and "I Came Out of the Mother Naked" meet in the sentence, "Matriarchy thinking is intuitive and moves by associative leaps." By definition "matriarchy thinking" is related to the unconscious; it is friendly toward it, where masculine or Socratic thinking is not. Rapid association, freedom of association, have at least the potential then of taking us inside the realm of intuitive knowledge, of the shadowy, of "whatever is hidden." In Exodus 20:4 we find this commandment: "You shall not make yourself a graven image, or any likeness of anything that is in heaven above, or that is in the water under the earth." The Father-God wants the image-making powers of the psyche suppressed. In *Sleepers* we find Bly disobeying that commandment as vigorously as he can. One poem in fact—as if in answer to Yahweh's prohibition—is titled "Water Under the Earth," and it is a litany of images in praise of "what is beneath us" and "underground rivers." In the essay Bly calls the Puritans "fanatic father types"; in a poem called "Pilgrim Fish Heads" he sketches a Puritan settlement and Puritan consciousness, which holds the Indian as its enemy largely because of his connection with water:

> And the Indian, damp, musky, asking for a bed.
> The Mattapoiset is in league with the salamander,
> he has made treaties with the cold heads of fishes.
> In the grave he does not rot, but vanishes into water.
> The Indian goes on living in the rain-soaked stumps.
> This is our enemy, this is the outcast,
> the one from whom we must protect our nation,
> the one whose dark hair hides us from the sun.

Water, and hair. In "Hair," one of the wildest associative poems Bly has written, images of hair weave together many other images of psychic life and death (one can see the four mothers, if one is looking for them, peering out through the strands), and here water is also present. At the beginning of the poem a drunk movie star's tousled hair associates with a whirlpool, and we seem to be pulled into it, into the underwater world where the images dwell. Near the end of the poem we find ourselves under the earth as well, a long way down:

> Under the ground the earth has hair cathedrals
> the priest comes down the aisle wearing caterpillar fur.
> In his sermons the toad defeats the knight

In these hair cathedrals (we can picture shaggy root systems reaching down, or buildings constructed from hair, vast subterranean thatchings and hangings) the religion, needless to say, is not Christianity. We are further back than tales in which heroes battle dragons as well; here they fight toads, and are defeated.

All these images of water and underworld are essentially attempts to describe the psyche, and to use the image-making powers that the Father-God or father consciousness has repressed. Many of the images are marvelous, and have real moisture in them; and both "Hair" and "Water Under the Earth" are possessed of lavish sweeps of energy. Yet compared to the way Bly evoked inner mysteries in *Snowy Fields*, these more wildly associative poems seem perhaps a little too much like exercises, willed, overly conscious and aggressive in their approach to the unconscious. In "Tao Te Ching Running" Bly says, "if the fragments in the unconscious would grow big as the beams in hunting lodges,/ . . . then we would find holy books in our beds,/ then the *Tao Te Ching* would come running across the field!" One may like the impulsiveness of the lines and the longing for revelation without feeling that any revelation, or penetration, has occurred in the poem. I find something of the same problem in most of the poems in the first section of *Sleepers*. (Though I would except the "Six Winter Privacy Poems" with which Bly opens the book from this generalization; that sequence of brief poems seems to me to be among Bly's best work, true and haunting evocations of "the other.") The problem is not absent from the long title poem either, but before turning to that we need to look at Bly's single most important Vietnam War poem, looming near the center of the book, "The Teeth-Mother Naked at Last."

"The Teeth Mother" has somewhat the same sort of streaming imagery that we find in "Water Under the Earth" and "Hair," though it is divided into a series of separate dramatic sections. In "The Teeth Mother" the streams of images are also streams of shudders. The poem is a diatribe and a kind of fiery, smoky sermon; it does not seem surprising to learn that Bly "wrote it somewhat with [his] voice ... ." or that he "spoke parts aloud at readings many times before [he] wrote them down." [18] The title, suggesting the nightmare that will be placed before us, would be at home on the sign of a drive-in theater, but it is not merely bizarre or sensational. It is drawn, of course, from Bly's investigations into the mother archetypes. Without some knowledge of its mythological background, a reader will no doubt get little meaning or force from the phrase "The Teeth Mother Naked at Last." The teeth mother comes into view only at the end of the poem, and even here—unlike, say, Yeats' "rough beast"—she is merely named and not actually described:

> . . . the waters underneath part: in one ocean luminous globes
>   float up (in them hairy and ecstatic men—)
> in the other, the teeth mother, naked at last.

But Bly wants us to understand these lines and their ideas, and he virtually explicates the passage, without referring to the poem explicitly, in "I Came Out of the Mother Naked," which follows directly upon "The Teeth Mother." (We are pretty well justified in this case at least in putting aside the disclaimer Bly makes in the essay: ". . . nor should anyone examine my own poems for evidence of [these ideas], for most of my poems were written without benefit of them." [19])

> The increasing strength of poetry, defense of earth, and mother consciousness, implies that after hundreds of years of being motionless, the Great Mother is moving again in the psyche. Every day her face becomes clearer. We are becoming more sensitive, more open to her influence. She is returning, or we are returning to her, just as in leaves floating on a pond you can sometimes make out faces. The pendulum is just now turning away from the high point of father consciousness and starting to sweep down. The pendulum rushes down, the Mothers rush toward us, we can all feel the motion downward, the speed increasing. [20]

While this essay bears some of the marks of being a product of the 1960s, its ideas are far from the simplistic optimism that infects many "new age" theorists. These image-ideas are more complex than that, and Bly says that "the trouble is that a society cannot have one of the mothers without having them all," [21] and opposite the Good and Ecstatic Mothers much celebrated in the sixties (the line "hairy and ecstatic men" read "hairy and ecstatic rock musicians" in an earlier version [22]) stand the Death Mother and the Teeth Mother, "the end of psychic life, the dismembering of the psyche." One sentence more, ". . . the Vietnam War has helped everyone to see how much of the Teeth Mother there is in the United States," [23] provides a final link between the essay and the poem.

One needs the essay, or a knowledge of the ideas behind the essay, to deal adequately with the image of the Teeth Mother; the photograph of a Balinese teeth mother mask included within the essay also helps. But these explanatory materials aside, the poem itself indirectly but powerfully evokes the Teeth Mother before her emergence at the end of the poem. When Bly describes the war, he is describing the borders of her realm. We can hear in the poem masculine power, reasonableness, and resolve, having grown obscene, giving way to insanity and horror:

Excellent Roman knives slip along the ribs.

A stronger man starts to jerk up the strips of flesh.

"Let's hear it again, you believe in the Father, the Son, and the Holy Ghost?"

A long scream unrolls.

More.

"From the political point of view, democratic institutions are being built in Vietnam, wouldn't you agree?"

A green parrot shudders under the fingernails.
Blood jumps in the pocket.
The scream lashes like a tail.

"Let us not be deterred from our task by the voices of dissent . . ."

The whines of the jets
pierce like a long needle.

We have seen before that in his anti-war poetry Bly is not satisfied simply to denounce the war; he wants also to find its root causes. In *The Light* these causes were the pervasive split in American culture and psyche between the inner and outer worlds, and our heritage of "Hatred of Men with Black Hair," fed by a hatred of part of our own beings. In "The Teeth Mother" such explanations are expressed even more emphatically. In fact, they are belabored and exaggerated to an extraordinary degree, and some critics found them not only questionable but downright puerile. As David Cavitch, admiring the poem in general, put it: "What in the name of William Carlos

Williams is Alexander Hamilton doing in those lines where he oversees the massacre at My Lai?"[24] If he had said "What in the name of Ezra Pound . . ." the question would have partly answered itself, for in "The Teeth Mother" Bly focuses much of his attention on the economic origins of the war. Hamilton fares poorly in another passage as well:

> Helicopters flutter overhead. The death-
> bee is coming. Super Sabres
> like knots of neurotic energy sweep
> around and return.
> This is Hamilton's triumph.
> This is the advantage of a centralized bank.
> B-52s come from Guam . . .

Such a passage does not rise much above "glib and clichéd intellectualizing," as Cavitch says, and yet the same line of thought blooms weirdly and powerfully elsewhere in the poem. Section III, which begins with the line, "This is what it's like for a rich country to make war," rephrases the equation between wealth and atrocity relentlessly and in bizarre, wrenching detail, until we are no longer just dealing with an assertion about the economic origin of the war, but experiencing a surreal dredging up of one of the peculiar horrors of the entire Vietnam War phenomenon:

> This is what it's like to have a gross national product.
> It's because the aluminum window shade business is doing so
>   well in the United States that we roll fire over entire villages
> It's because a hospital room in the average American city now
>   costs $90 a day that we bomb hospitals in the North
> It's because the milk trains coming into New Jersey hit the right
>   switches every day that the best Vietnamese men are cut in
>   two by American bullets that follow each other like freight cars
> This is what it's like to send firebombs down from air-condi-
>   tioned cockpits.
> This is what it's like to be told to fire into a reed hut with the
>   automatic weapon.

Another of the "advantages" of wealth is that it makes it possible to distance oneself from the reality of suffering, and as we saw in *The Light* that distancing can have its own terrible results. Section III includes this in its catalogue as well:

> It is because we have so few women sobbing in back rooms,
> because we have so few children's heads torn apart by high-ve-
> locity bullets,
> because we have so few tears falling on our own hands
> that the Super Sabre turns and screams down toward the earth.

Bly concludes the section:

> It's because taxpayers move to the suburbs that we transfer pop-
> ulations.
> The Marines use cigarette lighters to light the thatched roofs of
> huts
> because so many Americans own their own homes.

I am reminded in these juxtapositions of another ambitious attempt to probe the Vietnam nightmare: Francis Ford Coppola's *Apocalypse Now*—specifically its haunting images of officers eating a fine dinner in a mobile home set down in Southeast Asia; of surf boards and Playboy bunnies carried aboard Army helicopters; of a wrecked helicopter suspended in a tree overhanging a jungle river. One of the particularly obscene and mind- and soul-jarring aspects of the Vietnam War was the spectacle of an enormously rich, modern industrial country devastating a nation of peasants; of wealth—whether in the form of sophisticated weaponry or the considerations of a consumer society—gone amok. The connection between wealth and the Vietnam War is obviously more complex than the insistent formula of the poem's litany makes it seem, but within the coarseness of the equation—a coarseness the poem calls attention to and uses for its own imaginative purposes—there lies an idea about American society that we dismiss at our own risk. The passage is powerful because of its relentless rhetoric and grotesque juxtapositions, but also because we sense that its core idea has a bitter truth within it; if those lines are hard to swallow it is not merely because they oversimplify. Bly says in "I Came Out of the Mother Naked," "The culture of affluence opens the psyche to the Teeth Mother and the Death Mother in ways that no one understands." The Vietnam War provided much of the most dramatic reinforcement for this realization, and "the Teeth Mother," at its best, transforms it into a grotesque and powerful poetry of tirade.

At the beginning of Section III are these lines:

> This is what it's like for a rich country to make war
> this is what it's like to bomb huts (afterwards described as "structures")
> this is what it's like to kill marginal farmers (afterwards described as "Communists")

The parenthetical phrases bring us to a second pervasive obscenity of Vietnam: the hypocrisy of official versions of the events and purposes of the war. The poem turns this into another surreally hyperbolic and weirdly effective passage, a litany of lies that occurs in Section II. Black humor is not beyond the range of the rage of "The Teeth Mother."

> Now the Chief Executive enters; the press conference begins:
> First the President lies about the date the Appalachian Mountains rose.
>
> Then he lies about the population of Chicago, then he lies about the weight of the adult eagle, then about the acreage of the Everglades
>
> He lies about the number of fish taken every year in the Arctic, he has private information about which city *is* the capital of Wyoming, he lies about the birthplace of Attila the Hun.
>
> He lies about the composition of the amniotic fluid, and he insists that Luther was never a German, and that only the Protestants sold indulgences,

That Pope Leo X *wanted* to reform the church, but the "liberal
  elements" prevented him,
that the Peasants' War was fomented by Italians from the North.

And the Attorney General lies about the time the sun sets.

The contemporary implications of the references to the Church
and Protestants (i.e., protesters) are clear enough, but many of
the details here seem merely odd and funny. Some are, but as
James Mersmann, whose book *Out of the Vietnam Vortex* contains
a detailed and insightful consideration of Bly's political poetry,
has pointed out, often in Bly's work "what seem arbitrary and
random figures are either intentionally or serendipitously full of
significance":

> . . . in Part II of *The Teeth-Mother* Bly intends us to understand
> that the President lies about everything and anything; but it seems
> strangely significant that he should happen to have him lie about
> the date the mountains rose, the number of fish taken in the Arc-
> tic, the acreage of the Everglades, and the composition of the
> amniotic fluid! [25]

The President is a liar whose distortions extend to life itself at
the most primitive and basic levels.

Bly takes the idea that the President is the enemy of life a
good deal further elsewhere in the poem. The extravaganza of
lies results from, or is symptomatic of, nothing less than a national death wish:

> The ministers lie, the professors lie, the television lies, the priests
>   lie. . . .
> These lies mean that the country wants to die.
>
> . . . .
>
> It's a desire to take death inside,
> to feel it burning inside, pushing out velvety hairs,
> like a clothes brush in the intestines—
> This is the thrill that leads the President on to lie

Mersmann reports that Robert Duncan, another poet who addressed the subject in a direct and major way in his poetry, believes that in such passages Bly "caught the truth behind the Vietnam war."[26] As with "The Teeth Mother" as a whole, each reader will have to decide for himself how much truth there is in this part of Bly's passionate diagnosis. Mersmann emphasizes the relationship of the death wish to a sense of guilt that is peculiarly modern:

> We seek death as expiation of the burden of guilt accumulated from the rape of the frontier and the ecology, from Puritanic morality and discipline, from killing Indians, from a history of violence and socioeconomic inequities—Bly's hysterical images of mutilation seem to spiral out of guilt-frenzy. There are anti-life forces at work throughout the modern world, but Bly senses that they have developed most strongly in America because our "progress" has been more rapid.[27]

The sense of loathing and disillusionment is strong in the poem, coming across not only in violent passages but also in bitter and simple lines like these:

> I know that books are tired of us.
> I *know* they are chaining the Bible to chairs.
> Books don't want to remain in the same room with us anymore.

As the poem moves toward its conclusion, Bly himself speaks for the wish, if not to die, then "to sleep awhile," to pull away from the realities of the war and the anguish that comes in contemplating them. Following a description of children set on fire with American napalm and of the hysteria which is an appropriate reaction to such horror, this passage enters with a chilling and haunted quietness:

> I want to sleep awhile in the rays of the sun slanting over the snow.
> Don't wake me.

Don't tell me how much grief there is in the leaf with its natural oils.

Don't tell me how many children have been born with stumpy hands all those years we lived in St. Augustine's shadow.

Tell me about the dust that falls from the yellow daffodil shaken in the restless winds.

Tell me about the particles of Babylonian thought that still pass through the earthworm every day.

Don't tell me about "the frightening laborers who do not read books."

But the withdrawal is only momentary; the poem does not come to rest there. Bly suddenly shifts tone and pace entirely: "the whole nation starts to whirl," those "luminous globes" containing "hairy and ecstatic men" and the Teeth Mother rise from the ocean, and the poem concludes with an enigmatic injunction:

Let us drive cars
up
the light beams
to the stars . . .

And return to earth crouched inside the drop of sweat
that falls
from the chin of the Protestant tied in the fire.

Enacted here again is the rhythm of rising and falling encountered frequently, in many variations, in Bly's poetry. In this case the images seem to be an attempt to describe the longing to ascend or escape, and the necessity of not doing so. Driving cars up beams of lights expresses a desire to be free of the burdens of earth and conscience in quintessentially American terms, but the final image counteracts it: words like "crouch" and "sweat" tell us more about human destiny; the fetal image of the sweat-drop falling toward the fire suggest what kind of rebirth we can expect, if any. The longings to sleep or to move off into sheer, insubstantial light were both especially strong during the Vietnam period, the first particularly in the conventional culture, the second in much of the counterculture. Sprawling across the page in its lines that spool out and its various sections and subsections, "The Teeth Mother" is a shaggy and powerful assemblage of images, ideas, and rhetoric. Its overriding and unifying intention is to put us inside that falling drop of sweat.

Sleepers was not nearly as widely reviewed as either *Snowy Fields* or *The Light*. David Cavitch's piece in the *New York Times Book Review* represents a mixed response (similar to my own): "[Bly's] shortcomings will annoy a reader because he has written a large-scale investigation of himself as an embodiment of contemporary life and he succeeds in partly implicating us in his conclusions. A poet who attempts less could get away with more." [28] But in general one gets the impression from the reviews and the relative scarcity of them that with *Sleepers* Bly was seen as either having gone off the deep end poetically, or having written one of the major books of contemporary poetry. Those put off by Bly's surrealism and political thrust in *The Light* would certainly not find *Sleepers* any more satisfactory; quite the contrary. Other readers, however, were deeply impressed by the book. Joyce Carol Oates called "The Teeth Mother" a "small masterpiece . . . which will probably be remembered as the finest poem to have grown out of the antiwar movement of the Sixties," and said of the book as a whole that it was "a remarkable collection of poems, in fact one of the most powerful books of any kind I have read recently." [29] Donald Hall considered it the best of Bly's books up to that time and called the title sequence "a great journey poem"; [30] Charles Molesworth, writing a few years later, judged the title poem as "deserving comparison with the best of contemporary poetry." [31]

But if *Sleepers* was not much written about when it appeared, it is quite possible that it will be in the long run. I am thinking especially of the long title poem, which, with its considerable ambitiousness and complexity, has the potential of providing the basis for many articles and dissertations. Like Eliot's "Waste Land," the paradigm of a poem capable of sustaining great quantities of commentary, "Sleepers" reflects the poet's attraction to the study of myth, leaves out discursive links with a vengeance, and contains specific autobiographical references, fragmented and wrapped lightly or heavily in imagery that prevents the personal material from being seen too well. Both speak of personal psychic events in terms of social and historical referents. Also, we may someday have two versions of "Sleepers" to compare and contend with, as we have had with "The Waste Land" since the original version which Pound edited was discovered and published. As of 1981, Bly had grown dissatisfied with certain aspects of the poem: "I have been rewriting it. . . . Some parts of the poem don't communicate at all—they're too high flown and excitable. I relied on the image to do all the work. That's like using a horse to do rice-planting!"[32] (On reading the opinion of the poet himself that parts of the poem "don't communicate at all," the person about to set down a reading of it pauses, scratches his chin—and begins.) But there is another, deeper similarity between "The Waste Land" and "Sleepers": both describe a man's struggle against spiritual desolation.

Among the writers and thinkers from whom Bly has drawn nourishment, intellectual and otherwise, Jung looms large. This influence becomes even greater if we include with Jung as one rich source Jungians such as Neumann, with his investigations into the Mother archetype, and Marie-Louise Von Franz, whose work on fairy tales has interested Bly deeply. Bly started writing "Sleepers" before he had read much Jung, but during the years in which he was at work on it he began studying Jung intensively. In spite of the warning Bly included in "I Came

Out of the Mother Naked" against examining his poems for evidence of this source (though the essay itself ends with a quotation from Jung), an awareness of Bly's Jungian orientation and of Jung's ideas is helpful, perhaps necessary, in reading "Sleepers." The danger of course is that one begins to focus on the influence rather than the poem, to force the poem harder against supposed models or source material than may be warranted, and finally to reduce the experience of reading the poem to a scholarly exercise, as has happened in much that has been written about "The Waste Land." For example, the poem's first line, "The woman chained to the shore stands bewildered as night comes," will suggest to those attuned to myth Andromeda, as she was left chained for the kraken. In Jungian terms, the Andromeda-figure would stand for the anima, the feminine counterpart of the quester Perseus. In saying this, have we discovered something about the poem, or taken a detour away from it? The question of just how far we should go in relating "Sleepers" to Jung and to myth is one of the difficulties the poem presents.

Two detailed analyses of "Sleepers" have been published so far, the first by Michael Atkinson, the second by David Seal (neither of which, by the way, succumbs to the sort of critical dryness I've spoken of). The debate regarding "Sleepers" and Jung has begun. Atkinson believes that reading the poem requires "not just a general sense of the quest but Jung's interpretation of it," and his explication asserts the poem's "implicit and continuous parallelism to Jung's schema of dream imagery in the individuation process." [33] Seal, on the other hand, says that the poem is "only apparently a Jungian drama," because "a substantial part of 'Sleepers' . . . cannot be made sense of by Jung's individuation scheme." It is Seal's idea that Bly "consciously uses Jung, and unconsciously resists [him]." (He suggests, in fact, that Jung appears in the poem, in the person of the old man in the "Meeting the Man Who Warns Me" section.[34])

Personally I don't believe that Bly created "Sleepers" to accord with a Jungian schema. Much of the imagery that is the language of the poem is that which students of myth have catalogued and analyzed, which Bly has used instinctively and distinctively in his poetry all along, and which is the common possession of the human soul everywhere—e.g., the road, the sea, water in general, trees. At times in "Sleepers" such images seem artificial: when Bly begins one section with the line "I was born during the night-sea journey," his remark made in an interview, "the way to ruin a poem is to put in a lot of archetypes,"[35] comes to mind with an odd ring. For the most part, however, the poem's imagery has its own life and seems to spring from the poet's experience and imagination and not merely from his reading. But there is one image in particular that begs a Jungian definition, and that is the shadow, which I referred to earlier in discussing "Where We Must Look for Help" in *Snowy Fields*.

As we have seen in both *Snowy Fields* and *The Light*, Bly begins in his poetry with the sense that we are spiritually fragmented. It is a condition which, although it may be inevitable, he believes we should not accept. This recognition of fragmentation is the starting point in "Sleepers" as well. A sort of inward autobiography, an account of a man in search of himself, the poem begins with fear of a living death: "The woman chained to the shore stands bewildered as night comes/ I don't want to wake up in the weeds, and find the light/ gone out of the body, and the cells dark. . . ." The imagery here reverses that of "Looking into a Face" in *The Light*, where a union or at least a deep intimacy was achieved and the illuminated body was the sign of transfiguration and new life. Once again the interplay of light and dark is complex and crucial in Bly's imagination, and here, we discover as the poem continues, it is paradoxically a loss of shadow that has led to the fear of waking to find the light gone out of the body. This is the fundamental fragmentation described in the opening section of "Sleepers."

This section is titled "The Shadow Goes Away," and early

on we encounter these lines: "The shadow goes away,/ we are left alone in the father's house." Without the basic Jungian designation of the shadow as those aspects of the personality which have been repressed into the unconscious, these lines are obscure; with it, they become much clearer. Part of the poet's psyche has been exiled, leaving him, with a feeling of loneliness and isolation, in a domain of masculine consciousness and authority. Certainly Bly is drawing on Jung in his use of the image of the shadow, but rather than quoting Jung on the concept it is probably more useful to cite one of Bly's own restatements of it. In his essay on Wallace Stevens, Bly uses the concept of the shadow as the basis for his criticism. Near the beginning he describes the exile of the shadow as follows:

> How did the two persons get separated? Evidently we spend the first twenty or twenty-five years of life deciding what should be pushed down into the shadow self, and the next forty years trying to get in touch with that material again. Cultures vary a lot in what they urge their members to exile. In general we can say that "the shadow" represents all that is instinctive in us. Whatever has a tail and lots of hair is in the shadow. People in secular and Puritanical cultures tend to push sexual desire into the shape under our feet, and also fear of death; usually much ecstasy goes with them. Old cave impulses go there, longings to eat the whole world—if we put enough down there, the part left on top of the earth looks quite respectable.[36]

Throughout its various parts "Sleepers" has the dreamlike flow of images that characterizes the book as a whole, but through much of it dream provides not only an associative texture but a setting as well; the poet is slipping back and forth across the border of sleep. The poem has a good deal of the dream journal in it. Early in "The Shadow Goes Away" the poet says, "I fall asleep, and dream I am working in the fields," and he does not wake again until the opening of the next section. Placing us at once in dream is appropriate for establishing the shifting narra-

tive consciousness Bly wants to use here, and it is appropriate
as well for describing the fate of the shadow. The shadow, Jung
tells us, is often encountered in personified form in dreams, in a
figure of the same sex as the dreamer. Here the shadow figure
is identified with a brother who, in the prismatic dream-reality
of the poem, no respecter of either chronology or either/or logic,
is disposed of in several ways in turn.[37] Reference to a coat
"stained with goat's blood" invokes the selling of Joseph into
slavery; in a second version the brother is rejected in a school
yard; then he is given to "the dark people passing." Men tie the
shadow to a tree; it is led away. The "dark people" variation
receives the most development. They become "traveling Sioux,"
who teach the shadow-brother "to wear his hair long,/ to glide
about naked, drinking water from his hands,/ to tether horses,
follow the faint trail through bent grasses. . . ." While the
brother grows closer to the natural and instinctive life, life at
one with the senses, possessed of an animallike grace and alert-
ness, the poet in his conscious personality is meanwhile left in
high school, "alone, asleep in the Law": "I dreamt that I sat in
a big chair,/ and every other second I disappeared." "Alone,
asleep in the Law" is a way of saying, I was only part of a
person, not conscious of what was missing, at rest in collective
patriarchal values. The dream of constantly disappearing sup-
plies one of the poem's more vivid images for the state of being
inwardly split in two. Reading this poem, we understand more
clearly why the moments of nearly instinctive wandering and of
opening to the shadowy scenes and objects of nature in *Snowy
Fields* contained deep joy.

Bly is describing here growing up in a culture which does
not respect the instinctual or primitive side of the psyche and
which encourages, knowingly or unknowingly, inward separa-
tions and disfigurement. "The Shadow Goes Away" is full of
images elaborating this description. Puritan morality ("I see the

birds inside me,/ with massive shoulder, like humpbacked Puritan ministers,/ a headstrong beak ahead"), masculine violence ("I hear the sounds of hoofs . . . coming. . . . Now the men/ move in, smashing and burning. The huts/ of the Shadowy People are turned over, the wood/ utensils broken, straw mats set on fire"), and a mother's wish that her son be both special and respectable ("Looking down, I see dark marks on my shirt./ My mother gave me that shirt, and hoped that her son would be the one man in the world/ who would have a happy marriage, but look at me now—/ I have been divorced five hundred times,/ six hundred times yesterday alone") are all implicated. The section ends with a vision of the Sea of Tranquility despoiled, apparently bombed, and its beaches covered with snakes and transistors. The reptile and technological seem about equally distant—in opposite directions—from feeling and compassion. The devastation seems complete. But from about half-way through the poem, when the poet says of his shadow-brother, "On 66th Street I noticed he was gone./ I sat down and wept," he has been in search of the lost brother. He witnesses the attacks on the Shadowy People, but does not participate in them. When marines offer him money, he turns and leaves. In short, "The Shadow Goes Away" describes not only the exile of the shadow but the advent of awareness of the need to seek it out.

Having dreamed the history of his loss of wholeness, the poet awakes at the beginning of the second section of the sequence, "Meeting the Man Who Warns Me," and finds himself "in the woods, far from the castle." This statement is both symbolic and literal: the poet is lost, wandering, like some hero in a fairy tale, and also actually in the solitude of a forest retreat: "I have been alone for two days, and still everything is cloudy./ The body surrounds me on all sides./ I walk out and return./ Rain dripping from pine boughs, boards soaked on porches,/ gray water awakens, fish slide away underneath." In spite of the poem's title, there are two men that the poet meets. Both confrontations take place in dream. The first goes like this:

> I fall asleep. I meet a man from a milder planet.
> I say to him: "I know Christ is from your planet!"
> He lifts his eyes to me with a fierce light.
> He reaches out and touches me on the tip of my cock,
> and I fall asleep.

This emissary from another world seems disdainful of the poet's blurt about Christ, and his response amounts to telling him to go back to sleep and try again. That he touches him on the cock is an ambiguous detail. It suggests circumcision, and the poet is indeed undergoing a kind of initiation process. But the visitor may also be directing him back to the sensual center of the body, and away from notions of interplanetary salvation. At the same time, he may be symbolically loosening the hold of phallic or masculine consciousness. In light of what follows, the latter possibility seems strongest, for immediately upon falling asleep the poet dreams that "the fathers are dying./ Jehovah is dying, Jesus' father is dying, the hired man is asleep inside the oat straw."

As the domination of the masculine subsides, the poet begins to sense the presence of other visitors: "Who is this that visits us from beneath the earth?" The answer comes in images of water and energy, darkness and light: "I see the dead like great conductors/ carrying electricity under the ground"; "Water shoots into the air from manhole covers"; "Something white calls to us:/ it is the darkness we saw outside the cradle." These are the first moments in "Sleepers" when the poet feels not alienated, torn, or lost, but on the verge of a powerful and ecstatic discovery. "The energy is inside us," he says, and starts toward it. But the second man he meets stops him in his tracks:

> I start toward it, and I meet an old man.
> He looms up in the road, his white hair standing up:

"Who is this who is ascending the red river?
Who is this who is leaving the dark plants?

As the poet aspires to greater consciousness he is challenged.
The suddenly appearing old man is another figure who will gain
instant recognition from students of Jung, though he is perhaps
too thinly and briefly presented here to have much impact for
others. Jung says of the appearance of such a figure in dream:

> In dreams, it is always the father-figure from whom the decisive
> convictions, prohibitions, and wise counsels emanate. . . . Mostly
> . . . it is the figure of a "wise old man" who symbolizes the
> spiritual factor. . . . The archetype of spirit in the shape of a
> man, hobgoblin, or animal always appears in a situation where
> insight, understanding, good advice, determination, planning, etc.
> are needed but cannot be mustered on one's own resources.[38]

Having begun to ascend the red river and leave the dark plants,
the poet is in such a situation, and the role of the old man in
"Sleepers" is to demand of the poet that he give an account of
his own life: "I am here./ Either talk to me about your life, or
turn back." In a way the whole of "Sleepers" could be taken as
a response to such a demand, but the specific response the poet
gives here, after some hesitation, is this statement, both confession and affirmation:

> "I am the dark spirit that lives in the dark.
> Each of my children is under a leaf he chose from all the
>   leaves in the universe.
> When I was alone, for three years, alone,
> I passed under the earth through the night-water,
> I was for three days inside the warm-blooded fish.
> 'Purity of heart is to will one thing.'
> I saw the road. . . ." "Go on! Go on!"
> "A whale bore me back home, we flew through the air. . . .
> Then I was a boy who had never seen the sea!
> It was like a King coming to his own shores.
> I feel the naked touch of the knife,

I feel the wound,
this joy I love is like wounds at sea. . . ."

This takes the poet back in time again, to his first awakening to
the possibility of intense spiritual life, his first glimpse of the
road, and the sacrificial rites of the soul's ongoing death and
rebirth. "Meeting the Man Who Warns Me" ends with this
speech, but the next section, "The Night Journey in the Cooking Pot," picks up where it leaves off. Once again we hear of
the old man, the road, and the journey in the belly of the whale.
The three days inside the whale are associated with the three
years of living alone in New York City Bly experienced in his
twenties. It was then that he first felt the intimations of the
spiritual journey in an irrevocable way. This was a time of
awakening.

I float on solitude as on water . . . there is a road . . .
I felt the road first in New York, in that great room
reading Rilke in the womanless loneliness.
How marvelous the great wings sweeping along the floor,
inwardness, inwardness, inwardness,
the inward path I still walk on,
I felt the wings brushing the floors of the dark,
Trailing longer wings,
The wing marks left in the delicate sand of the corridors,
The face shining far inside the mountain.

The poem continues on an ascending arc through a second
subsection, images flicking up one after another, images of the
hidden inward gift, "the other," near at hand: "For the first time
in months I love the dark./ A joy pierces into me, it arrives like
a runner,/ a radio signal from inside a tree trunk, a smile spreads
over the face, the eyes fall." "Someone is asleep in the back of
my house./ I feel the blood galloping in the body, the baby
whirling in the womb." "Who is it that visits us from beneath
the snow?/ Something shining far down in the ice?" The ecstasy

rises until that other one is referred to with a personal pronoun: "I am not going farther from you,/ I am coming nearer." Finally, it culminates in the conviction that the union within the self is intact, and has always been: "For we are like the branch bent in the water . . ./ Taken out, it is whole, it was always whole. . . ."

This is a beautiful moment, and a treacherous one. The poet has reached here the state that is sometimes referred to as spiritual inflation. For example, in his book *Ego and Archetype*, Edward Edinger, having defined Self as "the central source of life energy, the fountain of our being which is most simply described as God," goes on to describe such inflation as "the state which accompanies the identification of the ego with the Self. . . . a state in which something small (the ego) has arrogated to itself the qualities of something larger (the Self) and hence is blown up beyond the limits of its proper size."[39] Robert Frost, fundamentally a poet of boundaries, pointed out that there is something "that doesn't love a wall." Bly, fundamentally a poet in search of greater wholeness and therefore of what lies beyond existing boundaries, dramatizes here that there is also something that dislikes *an absence* of walls, and the kind of identification/inflation that the poet is experiencing in the rising ecstasy of "The Night Journey in the Cooking Pot." Having overcome the sense of alienation and fragmentation described in "The Shadow Goes Away" and attained this moment of union or near-union, the poet is now brought low again in one brief vignette of deflation after another. The body, capable of ecstasy but an earthly creature and therefore not keen on too much transcendence, is the first to bring him down:

> I see the road ahead,
> and my body cries out, and leaps into the air,
> and throws itself on the floor, knocking over the chairs.
> I think I am the body,

the body rushes in and ties me up,
and then goes through the house. . . .

When one speaks of spiritual things in public, as Bly often does,
the road can easily give way to the ditch: "I am on the road, the
next instant in the ditch, face down on the earth,/ wasting energy talking to idiots." The mind has reached out too far: "The
mind waters run out on the rug./ Pull the mind in,/ pull the arm
in,/ it will be taken off by a telephone post."

The most memorable of these scenes of deflation is one in
which Bly takes a metaphor from the Christmas story to describe the suppression of new spiritual life by the ego. In the
original confession to the old man, the figure of the king was
associated with joyous identity and the discovery of the sea beyond the borders of the kingdom. Here, the king has become
Herod, and is the ego when it has grown conservative and re-
pressive.

The barn doors are open. His first breath touches the manger hay
and the King a hundred miles away
stands up. He calls his ministers.
"Find him.
There cannot be two rulers in one body."
He sends his wise men out along the arteries,
along the winding tunnels, into the mountains,
to kill the child in the old moonlit villages of the brain.

"The Night Journey in the Cooking Pot" ends in anger,
frustration, and dejection. The poet sits on the edge of his bed,
ashamed. "I see what I have betrayed," he says; "What I have
written is not good enough./ Who does it help?" It is a feeling
no doubt known to every writer who has tried to express moments of ecstasy and heightened consciousness in words; it is
also a feeling known to anyone returning to the untransformed,
stubborn world after what seemed a transforming experience of
joy and new awareness. Does the moment of vision do anyone

else any good? Having come down from such a moment, one may feel stupider and more alienated than before.

But perhaps not. It is possible, at any rate, to accept the cycles of union and alienation, of ecstasy and grief, as the natural life of the spirit, until ultimately they become a continuing process or dialogue. That one does not always see the higher (or deeper) reality does not make the moments when one has seen it unreal. This realization itself makes the difference. Henceforward, the cycles are not mere repetition. Moments of vision draw us forward; experience becomes a road, and the road itself becomes a destination. The fourth section, "Water Drawn Up into the Head," expresses this awareness. As the title suggests, a fundamental and nourishing truth that had been unconscious has now been consciously understood. Bly gives us a psalm to the eternal moving energy of the universe and the possibility of entering it. Once having done so, a person does not become "enlightened," but full of longing and ready to praise:

> When the waterholes go, and the fish
>   flop about
> in the caked mud, they can moisten each other faintly.
>   That is good, but best
> is to let them lose themselves in a river.
> So rather than saying that Christ is God or he is not,
> it is better to forget all that
> and lose yourself in the curved energy.
> I entered that energy one day,
> that is why I have lived alone in old places,
> that is why I have knelt in churches, weeping,
> that is why I have become a stranger to my father.
> We have no name for you, so we say:
> he makes grass grow upon the mountains,
> and gives food to the dark cattle of the sea,
> he feeds the young ravens that call on him.

As for the known self, the "I," it is capable of giving pain but also of rejoicing in cycles of death and rebirth. It need not necessarily believe that "there cannot be two rulers in one body"; it can welcome "another being living inside." "Water Drawn Up Into the Head" ends with this passage:

> I have sat here alone for two hours. . . .
> I have sat here alone for two years!
> There is another being living inside me.
> He is looking out of my eyes.
> I hear him
> in the wind through the bare trees.
>
> I met the King coming through the traffic.
> He said, I shall give to you more pain than wounds at sea.
>
> That is why I am so glad in fall.
> I walk out, throw my arms up, and am glad.
> The thick leaves fall,
> falling past their own trunk,
> and the tree goes naked,
> leaving only the other one.

Bly ends "Sleepers" with a coda, "An Extra Joyful Chorus for Those Who Have Read This Far," which sings the self that is open to change and flow as a condition of being. Where much of the rest of "Sleepers" took place in dream, the chorus originates in meditation. Having practiced meditation on his own for a number of years, in 1968 during a trip to Great Britain Bly took formal instruction from the Tibetan meditation teacher Trunpa Rinpoche. In one of the essays in *Leaping Poetry*, Bly included some comments on meditation:

> The West misunderstands "meditation" or sitting because, being obsessed with unity and "identity," it assumes that the purpose of meditation is to achieve unity. On the contrary, the major value of sitting, particularly at the start, is to let the sitter experience the real chaos of the brain. Thoughts shoot in from all three brains in turn, and the sitter does not talk about, but experiences the lack of an 'I'. The lack of an 'I' is a central truth of Buddhism (Taoism expresses it by talking of the presence of a "flow").[40]

This experience of flux, of a chaos which is not destructive but fertile, is described in the Chorus, which opens out into a catalogue of images full of mixed, often contradictory impulses: energy dynamic and potential, animals and light, fire and water, a wild richness. The Mother—moist, nurturing, enveloping, dangerous—and the sword of masculine consciousness are both praised:

> I sit alone late at night.
> I sit with eyes closed, thoughts shoot through me.
> I am not floating, but fighting.
> In the marshes the mysterious mother calls to her moor-bound
>   chicks.
> I love the Mother.
> I am an enemy of the Mother, give me my sword.
> I leap into her mouth full of seaweed.

Read in the proper spirit, the Chorus is a lovely and brilliantly colored chant. Studded with "I's" and "I am's" (in this section Bly does adopt a Whitmanesque parallelism), it is nonetheless not a piece of egotism; it is, if fact, the opposite. The "I" here lets go its claim to a unified, settled identity and accepts the protean, perhaps infinite, aspect of its nature. Within the catalogue occur two lines which express the open self without images: "I am no one at all"; "I am the one whom I have never met." Both are statements which the ego would ordinarily resist. In resisting the first it would be acting within its natural function. It is in resisting the second that it would take on its Herod character. Herod has been overthrown in the Chorus, and it is a cause for celebration.

The eighth section of Whitman's "The Sleepers" begins:

> The sleepers are very beautiful as they lie unclothed,
> They flow hand in hand over the whole earth from east to west
>   as they lie unclothed . . .

Bly could not have been unaware of the Whitmanesque echo with which he ends the Chorus:

> Hands rush toward each other through miles of space.
> All the sleepers in the world join hands.

As he ended his first book with an image of blind men approaching through snow and dusk, and his second with the dumb who shall speak, he closes *Sleepers* with another image of those who inhabit dark worlds, worlds previously hidden to us. Despite the great difference in mood between those two earlier "wounded images" and this one which expresses union, all three have in common that they give homage to the unconscious. All express the conviction that what is asked of us is to meet "the one whom we have never met." At the end of "Sleepers," which began in fear and fragmentation, the poet is not healed, not whole, but he is capable of a compelling and beautiful vision of the union of many selves. In this way among others it is fitting that the poem concludes with lines that nod to Whitman.

Bly makes several explicit references to the *Tao Te Ching* in *Sleepers,* and certainly the key phrase "the curved energy," in "Water Drawn Up Into the Head," is reminiscent of the yin-yang circle. That circle has a perfect balance, a reconciliation of opposites, that seems distant indeed from the densely detailed turbulence of "Sleepers." Yet it expresses a state of being that Bly yearns for throughout "Sleepers," and, as I've suggested before, in his poetry in general. "Sleepers" makes it clearer than ever before that any such wholeness and reconciliation must be dynamic, not frozen or stagnant; it must be a continuous process involving "flowing psychic energy"; a sort of dialogue between the conscious self and "the other one"; it is part of a journey, not an arrival. (And here if one wants to apply a Jungian term, one might refer to this continuous process, this journey, as individuation, in a general rather than a systematic sense.)

The Chorus includes poetry itself as a way in which the soul discovers and carries on its journey:

> Sometimes when I read my own poems late at night,
> I sense myself on a long road,
> I feel the naked thing alone in the universe,
> the hairy body padding in the fields at dusk. . . .

It is a sensation that we are able to share often in Bly's poetry. Those who prefer it in its purer, sharper forms will find poems in Bly's other books—both earlier and later than this one—more satisfying than "Sleepers." But "Sleepers" stands as Bly's most ambitious rendering of the journey as he has experienced it. The poem is both rich and challenging; and so is the sense of the self it describes.

CHAPTER 4

Tiny Poems

> While dreaming, perhaps, the hand
> Of the man who broadcasts the stars like grain
> Made the lost music start once more
> Like the note from a huge harp,
> And the frail wave came to our lips
> In the form of one or two words that had some truth.
> —Antonio Machado
> tr. Charles Reynolds [1]

Since Bly is a poet who creates books that are not miscellaneous gatherings but rather strive for unity of one sort or another, I have thought it best to base the organization of this study on the individual major collections as Bly has conceived and published them. This chapter, however, will depart from that scheme. Thus far I have skipped over with only passing mention a type of poem represented in both *Snowy Fields* and *Sleepers Joining Hands:* the tiny poem, the poem of three or four or half a dozen lines. I have not done so out of a feeling that these poems are minor. On the contrary, they seem to me a distinctive and significant facet of Bly's work, and so I want to give them some specific attention. Far from being merely a novelty or diversion, this form lends itself to some of Bly's talents and themes in special ways, and one finds within this category some of his most memorable and magical poems.

Many of the tiny poems appeared first, or so far have appeared only, in limited editions from small presses. A number of those I'll be referring to, for example, are from an exquisite, hand-decorated pamphlet, now out of print, entitled *The Loon*, from the Ox Head Press of Marshall, Minnesota. A small press publisher himself, Bly has always contributed to and drawn from this alternative publishing network on which the life and liveliness of poetry in America so largely depend. The list of books, booklets, and broadsides that Bly has published through small presses is a long one, and the titles he has brought out through his own Sixties/Seventies Press include a number of collections that have significantly influenced and enriched contemporary American poetry. It seems appropriate to mention small presses in connection with small poems, as both represent life far from the giganticism and commercial standards of mass culture, which increasingly dominate mainstream publishing in the United States along with the rest of the society.

In 1966 Bly edited and published an anthology of tiny poems called *The Sea and the Honeycomb*.² The book shows him at his trenchant best as an editor. It has an idea with some freshness to it—that the very short poem corresponds to the swiftness of brief emotions, emotions largely ignored in a poetic tradition in which the sonnet has been the shortest form respected—and an introduction and selection of poems that make the idea vivid and alive. The territory Bly ranges over for the poems is, characteristically, wide; the selection, unconventional and eclectic. Among the poets are Spanish Arabs of the early Middle Ages, the Japanese haiku masters, classic moderns from several countries, and the young American poet Saint Geraud (Bill Knott), something of a genius in the very short poem. Also characteristically, the book has a strong bias, and here once again the bias is against the rational element in poetry, and in favor of the associative and intuitive. It is particularly biased against the epigram. The epigram, ruled by wit, irony, and denotative statement, is not only disallowed from the anthology, but from poetry as well: the epigram, Bly says, is "not a poem but a versified idea. . . . a commentary on a suppressed poem."[3] The problem, to put it another way, is that the epigram tends to create with rational and witty statement a tight seal which prevents the waters of the unconscious from entering; it is, therefore, from Bly's point of view, an antipoetic form. (It's interesting to note that when rationalists complain about the sort of poetry they dislike they sometimes use the word "damp." When Bly says that a poem has moisture in it, he is paying it a compliment.)

In his introduction Bly uses an analogy to make concrete his sense of the influence of discursive rationalism in a poem:

> Many of the manuscripts we have of early Greek lyric poets like Alcaeus come down from copies made by scholars in Alexandrian libraries. Sometimes a scholar, after he had copied a brief, intense poem of Alcaeus, written several hundred years earlier, would add to it a composition of his own in the same meter, embodying his own thoughts upon reading the poem. Oddly enough today the same poet writes both parts. If he is skillful in rhythm and tone, the link is almost unnoticeable. An epigram is actually a piece written entirely by the Alexandrian scholar. . . .

> An Alexandrian scholar is lurking inside most American poets: the American poet sitting at his desk writes a fine, intense poem of seven or eight lines, then a hand silently appears from somewhere inside his shirt and hastily adds fifteen more lines, telling us what the emotion means, relating it to philosophy, and adding a few moral comments. The invisible scholar is outraged at the idea of anyone writing a brief poem, because he is hardly able to get his chalky hand out of his cloak before the poem is over![4]

Bly's analogies are persistently among the most provocative, telling, and downright interesting moments in contemporary criticism; and if epigrams frequently live by wit, so, in a different form, do Bly's analogies. A second, and a third, complete the introduction's advocacy of the tiny, nonepigrammatic poem:

> *Paradise Lost* is a good example of the long poem. Milton is always there, holding his hand beneath you. He doesn't want you to fall. When angels appear, he suggests the proper attitude to take toward angels. In short, he tells you what to think. He has a huge hand underneath you. In the brief poem, it is all different: the poet takes the reader to the edge of a cliff, as a mother eagle takes its nestling, and then drops him. Readers with a strong imagination enjoy it, and discover they can fly. The others fall down to the rocks where they are killed instantly.
>
> The poet who succeeds in writing a short poem is like a man who has found his way through a stone wall into a valley miles long, where he lives. He walks back up the valley, and opens a door in the wall for an instant to show you where the entrance is. The more imaginative readers are able to slip through in the twenty or thirty seconds it takes to read his poem. Those who expect the poet to give them ideas see only a vague movement on the side of the mountain. Before they have turned all the way around to face the poem, the door is closed.
>
> Readers of recent poetry are used to staggering along under lines swelled with the rhetoric of philosophy courses, experiences under mind-expanding drugs, new criticism—in short, the world of prose. They find it hard at first to concentrate on a short poem, but eventually they learn to find some value in being dropped.[5]

The flying involved in reading tiny poems is a different matter from the flying I referred to in connection with Bly's wildly associative longer poems, such as "Hair" or "An Extra Joyful Chorus." In both cases flying entails associative powers, but in the longer poems the poet carries the reader along with him on broad wings of flowing images and rhetoric; the challenge is not to lose our hold. In the tiny poems, as Bly's metaphor says, it is the reader who must be able to fly on his own.

How much can be accomplished, after all, in a handful of lines that abandon rhyme, the symmetry of set form, and the cutting edge of reason's wit? To some, such poems will seem, no matter whom they are written by, to be works of minimalism and not much more; they will seem to have given up too much— nearly everything. But keeping the Alexandrian scholar out of the poem entirely and relying only on a moment's sliver of seeing and feeling is a discipline that can lead to a freedom and, para- doxically, a great sense of spaciousness. Here is a brief love poem, "Taking the Hands":

> Taking the hands of someone you love,
> You see they are delicate cages . . .
> Tiny birds are singing
> In the secluded prairies
> And in the deep valleys of the hand.
> *(Silence in the Snowy Fields)*

The word "cages" catches a reality of love, yet the birds in those cages sing within expanses of privacy and intimacy. In its five lines the poem follows a smooth arc of associations, from the hands' resemblance to cages, to birds, to the prairies and valleys where they also sing, and from the prairies and valleys back to the hands whose surfaces and creases they, in turn, resemble. The arc becomes a circle so quickly and effortlessly that we ar- rive back at our starting point before we had realized that we had left it. The fragment implies a whole whose borders are known only to the imagination, and the smallest poems some- times contain the widest, freshest spaces.

As we know from haiku and the Imagists, the senses can sometimes be sharpened in the very brief poem. A single sight or sound is focused on, inhabited, as if it were a world. Often such sensory pleasure is central in Bly's tiny poems, as in "Grass":

> The cottonwood leaves
> lie naked on the grass
> still chilled from the night.
> *(The Loon)*

But the objectivity of this poem is not typical. As noted before, objectivity is not high among Bly's poetic values, though he has great ability as sheer describer of the physical world. In the tiny poems as nearly everywhere in his work, subjectivity is invited in, and celebrated along with the world it apprehends. (There will be more to say about description and subjectivity in the following chapter, on *The Morning Glory*, where the blend is often extraordinarily rich.) Somewhere at the other end of the spectrum from "Grass" would be "A Cricket in the Wainscoating":

> That song of his is like a boat with black sails.
> Or a widow under a redwood tree, warning
> passersby that the tree is about to fall.
> Or a bell made of black tin in a Mexican village.
> Or the hair in the ear of a hundred-year-old man!
>
> (*This Tree Will Be Here*
> *for A Thousand Years*)

That "is like" is a slender thread; I think it holds. This is decidedly not the more conventional poetic version of a cricket, chirping on some quiet Wordsworthian hearth, and the poem's appeal lies partly in its impulsiveness and humor. Beyond this, however, the similes do capture in their unexpected associations qualities of the song and its maker. Black seems the right color, tin the right metal, the hair in the ear of a hundred-year-old man the right hair, for the ragged, homely night-song of a tiny, dark, shiny, hidden creature. The sound has a feeling akin to some artifact produced in a Mexican village—certainly not in a factory in Pittsburgh or Japan. The widow at the foot of the redwood is like the cricket at the foot of nature; their cries have the same urgency and smallness. In this poem it is precisely in the balance between oddness and rightness that the poetry lies.

If, as Bly said in the introduction to *The Sea and the Honeycomb*, brief poems have a special relationship to brief emotions, we might examine a couple of his tiny poems from the standpoint of the emotion they carry. The most obvious effect of a poem of this length is the suddenness with which it accomplishes itself, and the attentiveness and quickness with which it credits its reader. Reading such a poem can be very much like experiencing an emotional sensation or awareness which arrives abruptly, and can pass again just as abruptly. But the poem remains on the page and can be reexperienced and lingered over, and beyond the effect of suddenness, what one often discovers in a good very brief poem is a subtle richness. The brief emotion may be powerful through its purity—just a single clear ray of joy, a single black grain of grief—but also through its delicate shading. For example, consider "Marietta, Minnesota":

> Wonderful Saturday nights
> with girls wandering about!
> New farm machinery
> standing quietly in the cool grass.
>
> (*The Loon*)

The youth and aimlessness of the girls, and the strange calm of large, brightly painted machines still and stolid on the grass, make a juxtaposition within which an atmosphere of countless evenings in countless small rural towns is captured. One could write a poem on the same subject in a different mood—it might include some young males leaning against their cars smoking—but here the sexual energy floating in the air is not surly but piquant and joyful. Not much may be happening in those towns, but the poet finds this night beautifully fresh and vivid, like the girls and the silent machines he notices. Yet the poem's mood does have its shadow, which is the knowledge of time implicit in its description of its moment. One can hear in the poem's chord of pleasure a note of sadness. One can hear it even in the word "wonderful"—not that Bly uses it with irony, but simply with the awareness, possibly unconscious just then, that part of what makes brightness moving to us is the fact that it fades. The perfect, unmarked machines will lose their oddly impractical brightness soon enough to time and toil, and something similar will happen to the girls. So there is poignance as well as vitality here; in poems, brief ones perhaps especially, what is not said often accents what is.

Another poem, "Kabekona Lake":

> Lots of men could sleep
> on those fir branches
> swaying near the widow's house!

The first two lines join two images, one realistic, one surreal. Energy flows between them tentatively; the branches and the sleeping men sway together duskily. But when we come to the word "widow," a circuit completes itself, and in an instant we not only understand the association of the first two lines but also feel, in a delicate shock of recognition, a remarkable depth of love, loneliness, and sorrow. The poem's emotion is serious, but Philip Dacey, in reviewing *The Loon*, noted first its "humor, tact, and charm"[6]—and clearly those qualities are present as well. Once again a tiny poem possesses a fine emotional shading, a richness within the space of its fourteen words. (The poem has, incidentally, seventeen syllables, but that is no doubt coincidental. Bly has never been interested in the syllable-count aspect of haiku, but rather in its emotional and imaginative effect. In an interview he remarked: "The Japanese say the haiku is a poem in which there's a tiny explosion inside—and if that's not there— I don't care how many syllables it's got—then it's not a haiku. And that little tiny explosion brings the life to this creature.[7])

Bly ended the essay "I Came Out of the Mother Naked," in *Sleepers Joining Hands*, with the following statement: "I see in my own poems and the poems of so many other poets alive now fundamental attempts to right our own spiritual balance, by encouraging those parts in us that are linked with music, with solitude, water, and trees, the parts that grow when we are far from the centers of ambition."[8] A poem of three or four lines may have a special value in this encouragement; with its quickness, smallness, and sharpness it slips past ambition into the present moment, just as a sudden clear perception can sometimes be an awakening:

WATERING THE HORSE

How strange to think of giving up all ambition!
Suddenly I see with such clear eyes
The white flake of snow
That has just fallen in the horse's mane!

(*Silence in the Snowy Fields*)

One can feel here again the influence of Chinese poetry which I spoke of in discussing *Snowy Fields*—particularly in the theme often expressed by the old Chinese poets, worn out by official duties, beleaguered by tempestuous times: retirement, turning away from the world of affairs to experience a different life, as in this wonderful poem by the Ming poet Yüan Hung-tao, translated by Jonathan Chaves, "On Receiving My Letter of Termination":

The time has come to devote myself to my hiker's stick;
I must have been a Buddhist monk in a former life!
Sick, I see returning home as a kind of pardon.
A stranger here—being fired is like being promoted.
In my cup, thick wine; I get crazy drunk,
eat my fill, then stagger up the green mountain.
The southern sect, the northern sect, I've tried them all;
this hermit has his own school of Zen philosophy.[9]

A difference, of course, is that Yüan's poem describes a turning in a lifetime; Bly's, a turning of consciousness at a certain moment of a single day. Yet in a fundamental way they represent the same movement: a breakthrough into a state of being that is rich through simplicity and immediacy, a breakthrough into "what is." "Watering the Horse" is not a renunciation of ambition; it only says, "How strange to think. . . ." One does not write twenty books without ambition. Yet we need those moments when it all falls away. Ambition per se is not destructive, but that which never allows us to see the flake in the horse's mane takes the universe out of our lives. It is not irrelevant that an animal is close by when such a moment of awareness takes place—the animals are, apparently, masters of being at home in the senses and the present—or that it is a thing as ephemeral as a snowflake that acts as catalyst.

Bly's tiny poems take quick, often affectionate jabs at the preoccupation and clutter of our lives, as in "August Sun":

> Strips of August sun come in through shutters.
> Baskets of unanswered letters
> lie on chairs.
> Some foolish man must live here!

Busyness, one of ambition's lower relatives, is addressed specifically, though inversely, in some of the tiny poems. A number of them celebrate "doing nothing," a kind of anti-discipline which can lead to unusual transformations and satisfactions:

> A DOING NOTHING POEM
>
> After walking about all afternoon
> barefoot,
> I have grown long and transparent. . . .
> . . . like a seaslug
> who has lived along doing nothing
> for eighteen thousand years!
>   (*Jumping Out of Bed*)

Not only is the seaslug devoid of ambition, but evolution itself has seemingly left it behind. But the poem takes pleasure in imagining such an extraordinary, primal leisure. I think of

Whitman, like Bly a poet of the road, saying in Section 27 of "Song of Myself," "If nothing lay more develop'd the quahaug in its callous shell were enough." As human beings we resist that thought, but it is good to keep it in mind for the sake of perspective. Meanwhile, both Bly and Whitman recognize the place of loafing and regression in inviting the soul.

Many of Bly's tiny poems contain animals, partly for reasons mentioned above. He is both delighted and moved by the intentness of nature, of creatures going their own inscrutable ways:

> DUCKS
>
> Two white ducks waddle past my door
> Moving fast:
> They are needed somewhere!
>
> *(Ducks)*

Paradoxically, the poem expresses this very inscrutability by explaining the ducks' motivation, and in distinctly inappropriate human terms. It gives the wrong reason, and thereby somehow manages to get at the truth.

At other times other moods surround a visitation from the animal world:

> ALONE
>
> The river moves silent under the great trees.
> A fish breaks water,
> and then, a few feet farther down, again.
>
> *(The Loon)*

A man feels more alone—yet sometimes, perhaps, less lonely— for being reminded of the animal other, sharing the stream of time with him in a nearly complete separateness. Or possibly I intrude the man where none is intended. Bly may be focusing on the absolute aloneness of a fish jumping in a silent river, with no observor at all to "see" the scene for us, evoking a solitude so great that the human conception of loneliness seems for a moment small and incongruous, out of place in this universe, this calm eternity.

At the same time that he is aware of the otherness of animals, Bly reaches out across the gap between them and the human. Perfectly poised and deeply penetrating, the following poem seems to me among the best of Bly's tiny poems:

> THE LOON
>
> From far out in the center of the naked lake
> the loon's cry rose . . .
> it was the cry of someone who owned very little.
>
> *(The Loon)*

The words "center" and "naked" stretch out the line, but in their effect they move us toward the recognition, made explicit in the final line, of an essential state of being—the voice of a creature, of the thing itself, life simplified and clarified, coming suddenly across the water. Such a response to the cry of loons may have been one reason why Thoreau was fascinated by them, though in "Brute Neighbors," where he gives literature's best-known account of an encounter between man and loon, he emphasizes rather the unpredictable energy of the bird, appearing and disappearing and laughing in the waters of the pond. In the poem the bird, and the natural world of which it is a part, is again distant from us, "far out"—yet why is it that the cry of the loon goes so directly to the heart? Why does it seem, in fact, to rise in the heart and in the mind at the same instant it rises from the lake? There is no explanation for that, but we can note that Bly shares with Thoreau an exceptional ability to translate into words the language they both hear the natural world speaking to the human soul.

Because they are different from us, animals are associated

in our minds with what is hidden from us as we remain sitting in the small room of ordinary human consciousness:

FALL

> The spider disappears over the side
> of the yellow book, like
> a door into a room never used.
>
> *(The Loon)*

The sense of other rooms, of the hidden "other," is a sustaining mystery in Bly's poetry. We have seen it in the landscapes of *Snowy Fields*, in the visionary glimpses at the end of *The Light*, and in the spiritual record of "Sleepers Joining Hands." But here again the tiny poem seems especially well-suited for describing the experience, as for example in this one, in which the presence of that "someone" who moves in the music of Bach is felt:

LISTENING TO BACH

> There is someone inside this music
> who is not well described by the names
> of Jesus, or Jehovah, or the Lord of Hosts!
>
> ("Six Winter Privacy Poems,"
> *Sleepers Joining Hands*)

At times "the other" makes itself known not through an animal or inspired music, but in an intuitive knowledge of another self besides the "I." One of the finest renderings in poetry of the other who both is and is not oneself comes in this poem by Juan Ramon Jimenez, which Bly has translated, "I Am Not I":

> I am not I.
>   I am this one
> walking beside me whom I do not see,
> whom at times I manage to visit,
> and whom at other times I forget;
> who remains calm and silent while I talk,
> and forgives, gently, when I hate,

> who walks where I am not,
> who will remain standing when I die.[10]

Here is a similar poem by Bly which, in its own way, is just as fine:

> When I woke, new snow had fallen.
> I am alone, yet someone else is with me,
> drinking coffee, looking out at the snow.
>   ("Six Winter Privacy Poems,"
>   *Sleepers Joining Hands*)

"Drinking coffee, looking out at the snow": these details communicate the shadowy presence with utmost calm and suggestiveness; it is *physically* there. Again, as in the Bach poem, "someone." As Jimenez says, we sometimes visit, or are visited by, someone beyond us, *this one;* and sometimes that someone is forgotten. For Bly, the possibility of the visit is the possibility of ecstasy, of vision, of new life. The visitor may be many things. It would be hard to exaggerate the importance of the visitor in his poetry.

The soul of the tiny poem is its suggestiveness, spareness, and swiftness. It lets go everything but the moment of perception, emotion, and intuition, and by doing so it achieves both clarity and mystery. I have tried to move quickly in this survey of Bly's tiny poems, but writing about them one does feel somewhat like the Alexandrian scholar, with his chalky white hand. Having noted a few of their primary effects and recurrent themes, I would like to end this chapter by taking a liberty, and allowing the reader one, by quoting two more tiny poems—the first of which appeared in *Poetry* magazine,[11] the second from "Six Winter Privacy Poems"—without comment.

THE MOOSE

The Arctic moose drinks at the tundra's edge,
swirling the watercress with his mouth.

How fresh the water is, the coolness of the far North.
A light wind moves through the deep firs.

My shack has two rooms; I use one.
The lamplight falls on my chair and table
and I fly into one of my own poems—
I can't tell you where—
as if I appeared where I am now,
in a wet field, snow falling.

CHAPTER 5

The Morning Glory

"And what, O my master, would become
of me, if I should ever attain with
my mind to that, where no creature is?
Must I not cry out, 'I am undone!' "
—The Disciple, in Jacob Boehme's
"Of the Supersensual Life"

When Bly included in *Snowy Fields* in 1963 two prose poems, he made a beginning movement toward a form, or genre, which was rare in American poetry. Eliot's *Collected Poems* has one prose poem; Sandburg's line stretches out into prose frequently, and that of Jeffers, Ginsberg, and others who have used the long Whitmanesque line stretch in that direction too. Karl Shapiro published a book of prose poems in 1958; Kenneth Patchen had written some. But with such scattered exceptions, the prose poem, in spite of its hundred-year tradition in French and other European languages, hardly existed in American literature until the late 1960s. By the 1970s prose poems were being written by scores of poets of all levels of reknown, and its proliferation could have been taken as the final step in the rebellion against formalism which had been in progress by then for well over a decade.

And by the 1970s the prose poem had established itself in Bly's work as one of his dominant modes of expression. His work in the genre is certainly among the most interesting prose poetry written by an American so far, and in his first collection of prose poems, *The Morning Glory*, he created a truly joyous and invigorating book.

Why write poetry in prose? Obviously some things are lost—though the flattened music and predominance of open form of recent American poetry made the jump to the prose poem less dramatic than it might otherwise have been. Different poets will have different reasons for turning to it. In Bly's case there are at least three factors that can be pointed to as ways in which the prose poem has suited his needs and inclinations.

The first is the use of colloquial language. As noted earlier, Bly's adherence to a plain diction has been steady. Though the imagery in his work is sometimes dense or enigmatic, and the transitions disorienting, in the words themselves Bly hews to plain American language consistently. Running from Wordsworth and Whitman through Frost and Williams, the pursuit of the common, plain-spoken tongue in poetry has a powerful tradition, and in contemporary American poetry it has found itself in the position of the orthodoxy, as firmly and widely established as the use of rhyme was a century ago. While the movement toward language as spoken need not necessarily culminate in the abandonment of the line, or even meter or rhyme, as Frost demonstrated as well as anyone could require, the connection between the colloquial and the prose poem is nonetheless a real one. As Russell Edson has said, "Natural speech is prose." [1] For the most part, that is true.

For most poets committed to the colloquial, the use of common spoken language is part of the search for one's own individual voice as well. This is certainly the case with Bly. He has said, "it wasn't until *This Body Is Made of Camphor and Gopherwood* [his second book of prose poems], after ten years' work with prose poems, that I felt my own pitches enter."[2] Others felt those pitches entering earlier. Writing in 1971 of the smaller collection which grew into the full-length *Morning Glory*, Galway Kinnell had said, "For the first time in his poetry, Bly in *The Morning Glory* speaks to us—and for us—in his own voice."[3] In *The Morning Glory* Bly's voice becomes warmer, more open, more fully—and likably—human than it had been before. The impression of purity that *Snowy Fields* created in the mind was in part the result of an austerity, in tone and in what was and was not allowed into the poems. For example, reading *Snowy Fields* and Bly's early work in general, one would not know that this poet had any humor in him. In *The Morning Glory* Bly's sharp and generous sense of humor has been invited in. Whether one prefers the more open voice—both more casual and more rhetorical—of *The Morning Glory* to the subtle artifice of spareness in *Snowy Fields* is, of course, another question. Something has been gained, but something has been lost as well. Happily, we have both, and need not choose one or the other.

For a second way in which the prose poem lent itself to Bly's poetic purposes, we can look back to a well-known statement by one of the pioneers of the genre, Baudelaire: "Which of us, in his ambitious moments, has not dreamed of the miracle of a poetic prose, musical, without rhyme and without rhythm, supple enough and rugged enough to adapt itself to the lyrical impulses of the soul, the undulations of the psyche, the prickings of consciousness."[4] This passage is quoted by Michael Benedikt in his introduction to *The Prose Poem: An International Anthology*, in which he also cites Bly's "Looking for Dragon Smoke," an essay which he says "bids fair to become as central to our time as 'Tradition and the Individual Talent' was to Eliot's."[5] To think of Baudelaire's statement in connection with Bly's ideas on association is clearly appropriate, and it is even moreso to relate it to Bly's prose poems. Bly himself has not specifically linked the prose poem and association in his essays, he makes no special claim for it in this regard, but in terms of following "the lyrical impulses of the soul, the undulations of the psyche, the prickings of consciousness"—in terms of spirited and surprising association—he is nowhere more successful than in some of the prose poems of *The Morning Glory*.

Perhaps the first thing a reader coming to *The Morning Glory* will notice is that in it Bly's imagination is a well-spring of metaphor. Sometimes the metaphors and similes are quick, individual strokes, as when, looking into a hollow stump, he comments, "Its Siamese temple walls are all brown and ancient." More often such strokes accumulate and give the poem a bold, detailed, intricate texture. One paragraph in "A Poem in Tennessee," for instance, gives us in rapid succession, among other comparisons, the carcass of an animal on a lakeshore which resembles "a rotted glove, with the hand still inside"; a muskrat that "swims past like a commuter"; and a swirl in the water from an oar stroke which becomes "a sculpture disappearing again into the stone." Sometimes the metaphors are carried further, with impulsiveness, accuracy, and surprise. A great blue heron: "He turns his head and then walks away . . . like some old Hittite empire, all the brutality forgotten, only the rare vases left, and the elegant necks of the women" ("Sunday Morning in Tomales Bay"). The goalie in a hockey game: "The goalie has gone out to mid-ice, and now sails sadly back to his own box, slowly, he looks prehistoric with his rhinoceros legs, he looks as if he's going to become extinct, and he's just taking his time" ("The Hockey Poem"). Seaweed floating in a tide pool: "On the surface the noduled seaweed, lying like hands, slowly drawing back and forth, as the healer sings wildly, shouting to Jesus and his dead mother" ("Looking into a Tide Pool"). We can notice in these last three examples metaphor reaching a good way beyond physical resemblances. When the heron is linked, suddenly, almost casually, to the ancient world, or the goalie is linked to a primitive animal or the seaweed to religious ecstasy, energy flows from one world to another. The syllables may not sing, but the imagination does. In one way there are probably too many comparisons in *The Morning Glory*, yet it is partly this abundance that gives the poems their liveliness and color.

The phrase "beyond physical resemblances" might be misleading, however, if it gives the impression that Bly slights the physical actuality of things. On the contrary, careful attention to the physical world is a crucial element in *The Morning Glory*—of both its pleasure and its meaning. The third way in which the prose poem has been especially useful to Bly is that it has afforded him a space in which to practice the discipline of observation, to describe things in detail. Often in these poems we feel we are watching an artist sketching. As the lavish use of metaphor just noted indicates, the poems are not objective, and neither do they stop with the description of a thing. Yet a major, distinctive part of them is this careful description, the effort to focus—to use a phrase of Mary Oliver's—"the rich lens of attention."[6] Whether the prose poem per se is any friendlier to detailed observation than other kinds of poems is debatable. In general, the prose poems written in the past ten or fifteen years have, it seems to me, been more given to mind-play and storytelling than observation. But in Bly's case at any rate the prose poem has been the medium specially suited for the detailed seeing which he feels is a countermeasure against abstraction and "plural consciousness":

> I think that the prose poem appears whenever poetry gets too abstract. The prose poem helps bring the poet back to the physical world.
> We see many poems in magazines today with a sort of *mental* physical world. Such poems contain "flowers," "trees," "people,"

"children" . . . but the *body* doesn't actually perceive in that way. The body never sees "children playing" in a playground. The body sees first one child with a blue cap, then it sees a child with a yellow cap, then it sees a child with a snowsuit . . . the body sees detail after detail. An instant later the mind enters and says: "That is children playing." . . .

When a poem contains a lot of plural nouns you know perception has been wiped out. . . .

For me the prose poem is an exercise in moving against "plural consciousness." In the prose poem we see the world is actually made up of one leaf at a time, one Lutheran at a time, one apartment door at a time.[7]

Criticizing Charles Olson, Bly once said: "It's a problem with intuitive types. There are no cows; a cow is a symbol for some part of his psyche. There are no horses; every horse is a symbol of part of his psyche."[8] It is probably apparent by now to readers of this study that Bly himself is "an intuitive type." Reading Bly's complaint about this type, one may think back again to the horses, barns, and lakes of *Snowy Fields*, and ponder. Whatever one decides about the generalization vis-à-vis those clear, resonant images, one way of seeing *The Morning Glory* is as an attempt by an intuitive type to develop "the primitive method of perception," to sharpen the senses, to perceive the physical universe as it is, detail by detail. The attempt to see things as they actually, physically are enriches *The Morning Glory*—but so does Bly's inability to stay with it for very long. That is, what makes *The Morning Glory* remarkable and deeply alive is its marriage of intense observation and an irrepressible subjectivity and intuitiveness.

An implicit acknowledgment of this lively marriage is made in the introductory note Bly wrote for the book:

There is an old occult saying: whoever wants to see the invisible has to penetrate more deeply into the visible. All through Taoist and "curving lines" thought, there is an idea that our disasters come from letting nothing live for itself, from the longing we have to pull everything, even friends, in to ourselves, and let nothing alone. If we examine a pine carefully, we see how independent it is of us. When we first sense that a pine tree really doesn't need us, that it has a physical life and a moral life and a spiritual life that is complete without us, we feel alienated and depressed. The second time we feel it, we feel joyful. As Basho says in his wonderful poem:

> The morning glory—
> another thing
> that will never be my friend.

The idea of granting beings of nature "a moral life and a spiritual life" will seem strange, sentimental, or outrageous to many. Bly of course knows this, and would probably consider each reaction a different symptom of the narrowness of the assumptions that predominate, among intellectuals and nonintellectuals alike, in our culture, recent investigations into the capacity for feeling among animals and plants notwithstanding. Obviously feeling, whether sensory or emotional, is still a good way off from "moral life"; we might well ask what a pine or a horse could do that would be immoral and, failing to find anything, refrain from using the term moral at all. Bly says no more about that particular issue, though he does go on to deal with the proposition of consciousness in the natural world at some length in the 1980 anthology *News of the Universe*. But the point here is that in the introductory note to *The Morning Glory* Bly reveals the crucial contradiction or paradox under which the book is written. It is symptomatic that in pointing out how independent natural beings are of us, he immediately endows them with prerequisites of humanness: moral and spiritual life. They would not need to have either of these to be worthy of our fascination and respect.

I have mentioned the place of contradictory impulses in Bly's thought and work before, and here we see them coming together in a distinctive way as the generative field out of which the book springs. Bly wants to resist the drive to "pull everything . . . in to ourselves." At the same time, he is a poet who in describing the natural world relates it constantly to human life. He describes seawater flowing out across stones and says, "it is the gentleness of William Carlos Williams after his strokes" ("Sea Water Pouring Back over Stones"). Logs of driftwood floating in toward the shore relate directly for him to "the donkey the disciples will find standing beside the white wall" ("Sea Water Pouring Back over Stones"); both appear as a sort of inexplicable gift. This contradiction, paradox, or crosscurrent results when a strongly intuitive poet, one drawn to the vision of inner and outer correspondences of Jacob Boehme and other seers, one who says that "inside the human being watching the waterfall there is an inner waterfall,"[9] strives to sharpen his seeing of what is concretely before his eyes and his sensitivity to the independence of the nonhuman world. Another statement of Basho's which Bly likes to quote is pertinent: "The trouble with most poetry is that it is either subjective or objective."[10] The poems in *The Morning Glory* try to overcome that problem. From the standpoint of those who would like to deny that the natural world has "spiritual life," he gets into trouble of his own. But in his solution to the problem Basho speaks of—which is to bring both objective and subjective elements strongly into the poems—two kinds of vision press against and flow into one another, making a blend that is both fresh and moving, provided one is not too deeply attached to objectivity.

The close detail and eccentric metaphors of these poems call to mind Marianne Moore perhaps more than any other American poet. And this statement of Moore's, made in reference to Williams, could well be used to characterize the effect of *The Morning Glory:* "The 'ability to be drunk with a sudden realization of value in things others never notice' can metamorphose our detestable reasonableness and offset a whole planetary system of deadness."[11] The writer whose work *The Morning Glory* seems to bear the strongest kinship to, however, is the contemporary French poet Francis Ponge. Bly admires Ponge's prose poems on objects greatly, and finds in them a kind of observation which beautifully eludes the subjective/objective categories. He says, "Ponge doesn't try to be cool, distant, or objective, nor 'let the object speak for itself.' His poems are funny, his vocabulary immense, his personality full of quirks, and yet the poem remains somewhere in the place where the senses join the objects."[12] Ponge, along with the Rilke of *Neue Gedichte*, is for Bly the master of close observation of objects in poetry. But he reports that it was not out of Ponge's or Rilke's example that he began writing "object poems." *The Morning Glory* is dedicated to his daughter Mary, "who brought me a gift." The gift was a caterpillar, but also the prose poem and the careful observation Bly associates with it:

> The first prose poem I wrote tried to describe a caterpillar that [my daughter] brought me when she was three years old. . . .
> It was the first time that I'd really looked at a caterpillar. Usually I look in my mind when I write. My daughter brought it to me and said it was beautiful, though that was questionable. So I decided to describe it.[13]

That the earliest poem in *The Morning Glory* is about a caterpillar is appropriate; the book is remarkable for the number and variety of animals that inhabit it. In addition to the caterpillar and the heron and muskrat mentioned above, we meet here seals, sea gulls, ducks, octopuses, turtles, lobsters, elephants, ants, cows, dogs, a mole, a slug, a porcupine, a salamander—and others. About half the poems deal with animals in a direct way, and nearly all of the rest refer to them less directly in one way or another. Even in poems specifically about human beings, animals enter at once: a poem about Robert Creeley compares him to a crow, and one about Andrei Voznesensky starts by saying that he "has a curious look like a wood animal, one that often lives not far from marshes, near places where the deer sink in up to their knees." The book is a sort of bestiary. We have seen animals before in Bly's poetry—they are plentiful throughout—and I made a few fragmentary comments regarding them in discussing the tiny poems. Animals are much in evidence in Bly's more decidedly surreal poetry, and there too they bring a strong and distinct animal energy into the poems. *The Morning Glory*, however, where animals are presented most realistically and a turtle is a turtle before it takes on totemic significance, seems the right place to base a consideration of the importance of animals for Bly,[14] and this consideration can in turn afford a way of reaching an understanding of the thrust of the book as a whole.

(One ought to acknowledge somewhere in a discussion of this sort the presumption of drawing a line between humans and the nonhuman animals as if there were really just two kingdoms, and everything on the nonhuman side could justifiably be lumped together. The soul or consciousness of a seal is no doubt as different from that of a crab, and the crab's as different from that of sea weed, as the human being's is from that of the seal. As to whales and dolphins, we have only preliminary glimmerings of what goes on inside them. We sense that we possess a unique spark, but the fundamental reason we draw that single heavy line is at base only that we are human and all the others are something else.)

We might ask at the outset whether there necessarily need be "reasons" for being drawn to animals. Can't one simply be attracted (or repelled) for their own massive or delicate, beautiful or grotesque, sakes? Given the nature of human psychology, at least that in which imagination is not extinct, that is too simple. Words like "beautiful" and "grotesque" already indicate that something more is going on, and we cannot help using them, or feeling what they stand for, when we look at animals. Can't one simply appreciate them for their self-sufficient animalness? Even in saying that, we touch on one way that they speak to us.

Commenting on Whitman's role in the evolution of poetry, Bly once wrote, "He said goodbye to the libraries, invited animals into his poems, and let his form out of school." [15] When Whitman looked to the animals in "Song of Myself" he began, "I think I could turn and live with the animals,/ they are so placid and self-contained." The passage these lines occur in (Section 32) is one that Bly has anthologized, recites occasionally in his readings, and quotes from (not quite accurately) in one of the poems in *The Morning Glory*. Certainly the "self-contained" quality we sense in animals, sensed elsewhere in the natural world as well, and also in children, is one reason for the fascination we feel for them. For us, past the age of eight or ten, it is a quality not easy to come by.

In "Looking into a Tide Pool" Bly notices "the tiny white shell people on the bottom, asking nothing, not even directions!" It is a fine statement; in its comic way it catches the truth cleanly. They do not need "directions" because they are ineffably where they are in a complete way human beings can only vaguely imagine. The sense that the animals require nothing of us, not even the fact of our existence, is a source of wonder and pleasure to Bly, and it comes across frequently in *The Morning Glory*. Human consciousness is excitable, both dynamic and unstable, and the animals, though they have their own kinds of agitation, possess a steadiness that we lack. In some way, they seem to be better at the simple, absolute act of living on the earth than we are; they seem to have a wholeness that we have lost. (Seem. Always "seem" in this business of looking across the distance to the other creatures—though Bly himself does not always observe this distance.) Even a porcupine that has been scared part way up a tree trunk by the poet's approach and is unable to decide whether to go further up, for all its apparent slow-wittedness and confusion, contains something beautiful and stolid. Here is a squat, fantastic creature of the earth, free of the longings for transcendence, for "the immaterial sky":

> He waited, occasionally looking at me over his half-turned shoulder. I stepped over and looked into his eye. The eye was black, with little spontaneity, above an expressionless nose. The porcupine knew little about climbing: he was nervous, and the claws kept slipping on the gray poplar bark. His body felt no excitement anyway to be headed up, higher, toward the immaterial sky—he couldn't remember any stories he had heard. But he hung on.

Over and over in *The Morning Glory* Bly implies by his own attention that it is a good thing for the human mind to contemplate such as these. The poem does not end there; characteristically it moves on toward another kind of mystery.

> Sun already down. The white needle-fur stands out, something pre-Roman, by the elegant bark. And the wind through miles of empty forest is a third thing, like a drop of blood on a black cross.

A drop of blood on a cross contains a world of experience and significance at a great remove from the porcupine's world—though it is significant that the aspect of the Passion invoked here is the sacrifice of the body, and not the later victory over the grave. The human mind has again leaped beyond nature, but it has had the reticence not to place one world over another. It only places them side by side.

In general the animals that are encountered in *The Morning Glory* seem unimpressed by the intruding human presence. Their responses range from wariness—"a wild cat runs away from his inspection of a wet gopher hole as I come near"—to toleration, and on to a certain interest. In "Sunday Morning in Tomales Bay" the poet and some others are drifting about in a boat, unable to see well because of fog. He sees a blue heron, at first mistaken for "a machine far away, a derrick." Then they encounter sea lions, perfectly at home in the water, as they "gaze at the godless in their wooden boat." They are "neither arrogant nor surprised." Throughout the poem the impression gathers that human beings, while possibly worthy of a sea lion's attention, are basically somewhat awkward visitors not just in this foggy bay but among the natural life of the planet as well. We cannot see very well, we cannot swim long in the cold water, we float around tentatively on the surface while the sea lions slip about "somewhere in the water underneath us." The tone is a long way from the misanthropy Robinson Jeffers sometimes felt as he observed similar scenes a little further up the coast, but nevertheless the humans seem like newcomers, as the gaze of the sea lions around the boat suggests: "The whiskered heads peer over at us attentively, like angels called in to look at a baby."

The detailed description which Bly is practicing in these poems lends itself to communicating the self-contained quality of animals. "Finding a Salamander on Inverness Ridge," in the characteristic way of Bly's object poems, is partly close observation and partly meditation. It begins: "Walking. Afternoon. The war still going on, I stoop down to pick up a salamander." The reference to the war adds a peculiar note to the poem, one that is not entirely forgotten in the quiet intensity of the description which follows: "This one is new to me—the upper part of his eyeball light green . . . strange bullfrog eyes. The belly brilliant orange, color of airplane gasoline on fire, the back a heavy-duty rubber black, with goose pimples from permanent cold." The salamander itself is referred to once as "this war." In the background of the poet's awareness is Vietnam, in the foreground this small, vivid, intent, mute creature held in his hand.

Between the two a tension exists, out of which the poem's final metaphor emerges:

> But he is patient, this war, he can be held between a thumb and forefinger for many minutes, and the front paws hold on to your thumb resignedly—perhaps for hours. Perhaps it could be held quietly this way for days until it died, the green eyes still opening and closing. When I roll my hand over, I see the long orange-black tail hanging into the cathedral of the open palm, circling back and forth, rolling and unrolling like a snake, or some rudder on an immensely long boat, a rudder that can't be seen by those on board, who walk up and down, looking over the handrail.

When the tail is seen as a rudder the poem makes a sharp shift from a single salamander to a sense of the natural world underneath the human world, unseen but powerful, determining a course that the people on deck pay no attention to yet depend on. Even a war, long and terrible in human terms, is something that happens on the ship, not beneath the surface. The detachment and patience of the salamander are astonishing, not only nonhuman but beyond-human as well. He seems almost outside of time, and in a way he is. He and his tribe have followed their ways steadily since millions of years before man staged his first war. This is not by way of consolation, but it does give a subtle and profound sense of perspective.

The dimension of timelessness is evoked again in one of the best of the object poems, "The Large Starfish." The poet climbs down cliffs to the tide pools below. He carries inside him an anticipation: "Now the ecstasy of low tide, kneeling down, alone." But he comes on a starfish in one of the pools, and it is again a close, fascinated seeing that he is drawn into:

> In six inches of clear water I notice a purple starfish—with nineteen arms! It is a delicate purple, the color of old carbon paper, or an attic dress . . . at the webs between fingers sometimes a more intense sunset red glows through. The fingers are relaxed

. . . some curled up at the tips . . . with delicate rods . . .
apparently globes . . . on top of each, as at World's Fairs, waving about. The starfish slowly moves up the groin of the rock
. . . then back down . . . many of its arms rolled up now, la-
zily, like a puppy on its back. One arm is especially active . . .
and curves up over its own body as if a dinosaur were looking
behind him.

Such observation is a form of praise, and it also has interesting
effects on the consciousness of the observer. Ordinarily we think
of "experiencing eternity" in terms of those who have crossed to
some other shore, saints and mystics, but it may in fact not be
entirely out of our reach. When Bly reports, quite casually, that
the starfish's active arm rises "as if a dinosaur were looking behind him," the poem bridges, in that instant, eons. With regard
to the starfish, and the rocks and seawater it inhabits, it could
just as well be a dinosaur as a man that happens along. Once
again we are looking at a creature whose ancient race has been
coeval with both. It is not accidental that many of the animals
in these poems are ancient ones. Given the proper attitude of
attention on the part of the human observer, they can take us
out into stretches of time so vast they open onto eternity.

The poem ends with a sort of self-negation. (We may hear
in it an echo of a poem by another poet interested in the physical world and its relationship to consciousness, Wallace Stevens'
"The Snow Man.")

I put him back in . . . he unfolds—I had forgotten how purple
he was—and slides down into his rock groin, the snail-like feelers
waving as if nothing had happened, and nothing has.

Nothing has happened: the starfish is back in its pool; things are
as they were before and, except for the presence of a human
being, as they have been for millions of years; soon the tide will
come in again. . . . In another way, though, something has
happened. Through observation of a creature a certain self-for-

getfulness has occurred; a man has dwelled closely on a natural thing "out there," and so to some extent has gone outside himself. Such forgetfulness is one of the ways in which consciousness reaches out beyond its ordinary ego-bounds. In another poem of the shore, "A Rock Inlet on the Pacific," an even greater absence of self-consciousness is sensed, and the thought is strangely exhilarating: "The sloshing water is too wild for seaweed, but limpets understand—and it goes on for centuries, and no one gets tired of it . . . there is no one to *get* tired!" And the expectation of "The ecstasy of low tide" with which "The Large Starfish" began? The root of the word "ecstasy" connects it with displacement and "going out," and in the clear-eyed, alert contemplation of a primitive animal, the poet's anticipation has, in a special way, been met.

All of the animals in the poems I have been discussing—the porcupine, the sea lions and the heron, the salamander, the starfish—possess in one way or another the quality of being curiously self-contained, at one with what they are. One of the explanations that is sometimes given for this quality in animals is that they do not have the consciousness of their own mortality distracting them from living their lives in the present upon the earth. That idea is presented in one of the supreme poems on animals, Rilke's eighth Duino Elegy: ". . . we alone *see* death; the free animal/ has its destruction always behind it/ and before it God, so when it moves, it moves/ into eternity, like a running spring."[16] But at times it seems clear that animals do know they will die. One such time is described in *The Morning Glory* in "The Dead Seal near McClure's Beach," and in its slow dying— it has been poisoned by an oil spill—the seal has a fierce dignity which is of a piece with the gaze of the sea lions in the Tomales Bay poem, "neither arrogant nor surprised." *The Morning Glory* does not make generalizations on the question of animals' consciousness of death. It works instead from actual encounters.

When the rotting carcass was seen on the lakeshore in Tennessee, Bly noted that it was "sending out reminders." The two presences of death and animals mingle in many of the poems in *The Morning Glory*, and it is clear that in their dying lies another way in which the animals pull the mind into contemplation of them. If we often feel that we can witness a deep dimension of being alive in animals, there is also the sense that we can learn something from their dying. Some of the poems, such as "The Dead Seal . . . ," "Looking at a Dead Wren in My Hand," "The Hunter," and "A Hollow Tree," are outright elegies. The animal elegy runs a special risk of sentimentality, and the risk is no doubt compounded in Bly's case by his propensity for the pathetic fallacy—a term which it is not at all clear he would accept. Sometimes, as when he says, "I hunch down among friendly sand grains. . . . And the sand grains love us, for they love whatever lives without force" ("Walking among Limantour Dunes"), "pathetic fallacy" does seem the appropriate epithet. Elsewhere, however, Bly is able to speak of the nonhuman world in human terms in ways that are not only convincing but extremely moving. A poem that is especially remarkable in this regard is "The Hunter."

The poet, walking once again along a rocky shore, meets a Japanese man collecting octopuses. The encounter is friendly, informal. The hunter is casual about his catch, and his casualness makes a counterpoint to the poet's intrigued reaction.

> He sits down. I get up and walk over. May I see them? He opens the plastic bag. I turn on the flashlight. Something wet, fantastic, womblike horse-intestine-like. May I take hold of one? His voice smiles. Why not? I reach in. Dry things stick to my hands, like burrs from burdocks, compelling, pleading, dry, poor, in debt. You boil them, then sauté them. I look and cannot find the eyes. He is a cook. He ate them in Japan.

Two attitudes are represented here. On the one hand, the poet, curious, excited, sympathetic; on the other, the hunter—taciturn, practical, crisp. The contrast is reflected in the structure and tone of the sentences. Those describing the poet's reactions turn into vivid emotional catalogues; the rest, brief and clipped, reflect the hunter: "He is a cook. He ate them in Japan." Neither attitude, we sense, is wrong; the poem merely juxtaposes them, suggesting two kinds of consciousness which might in fact coexist within a single mind.

But the third character involved in this small drama, the octopus, is not left out, and Bly manages to imagine what, after reading this poem, we may no longer wish to resist calling its grief:

> So the octopus is gone now from the mussel-ridden shelf with the low roof, the pool where he waited under the thin moon, but the sea never came back, no one came home, the door never opened. Now he is taken away in the plastic bag, not understood, illiterate.

The seemless shift from "the sea never came back" to "no one came home, the door never opened" makes arguments about the pathetic fallacy seem irrelevant. "Taken away in a plastic bag" is just as sad as it is objective. "Not understood" undercuts plainly and delicately the act of empathetic imagining which has just taken place. And best of all is the word "illiterate," heretofore strictly a human designation. Used in this unexpected context, the word is as telling as it is strange and specific. It is a way of expressing the animals' distance from us, and of suggesting that in their own deaths all things are, finally, alone, incommunicado. It is a dark way of saying "self-contained." It is a way of saying as well that human consciousness, which knows itself through language, is not all of consciousness. What do we know of the consciousness of an octopus? Nothing. It is all speculation. In this poem Bly has speculated marvelously.

Bly achieves his richest evocation of the simple fact of creatures dying in "A Hollow Tree." He has commented that "we often feel in a prose poem a man or woman talking in a low voice to someone he is sure is listening." [17] The excited tone that characterizes many of Bly's prose poems makes that statement seem incongruous, but in this poem we can see, or hear, what he had in mind when he made it. Everything in the poem—its incident, its voice, its quiet eloquence—arises with utmost naturalness.

A HOLLOW TREE

> I bend over an old hollow cottonwood stump, still standing, waist high, and look inside. Early spring. Its Siamese temple walls are all brown and ancient. The walls have been worked on by the intricate ones. Inside the hollow walls there is privacy and secrecy, dim light. And yet some creature has died here.
>
> On the temple floor feathers, gray feathers, many of them with a fluted white tip. Many feathers. In the silence many feathers.

Utmost naturalness. That is the effect the poem creates, yet it is an extremely shapely, and unobtrusively shaped, naturalness. Most of Bly's prose poems are more notable for their movement, their notations of process, their descriptive and imaginative richness, than for their shapeliness and perfect wording, but there are in *The Morning Glory* certain poems which are exceptions to this generalization. "A Hollow Tree" is probably the most striking example, and I would mention also poems such as "Looking at a Dead Wren in My Hand" and "A Turtle." These poems tend to be less lavish in their details, and they give up the open-ended feeling which is often marvelous in *The Morning Glory;* instead they leave an impression in the mind which is rounded, complete. In "A Hollow Tree" it is the hushed incantation of the final brief paragraph, with its repetition of the words "feathers" (augmented by the sounds of "floor" and "fluted") and "many," which closes the circle.

"A Hollow Tree" describes an experience of felt knowledge. There is here again the sense of ritual that Bly caught often in *Snowy Fields*. He suggested in his comments on "the primitive method of perception" quoted earlier that the body could see things individually an instant before the mind comes in and generalizes about them. In "A Hollow Tree" the body is in fact slightly quicker in perception than the mind, but in a different way. The simple act of bending over and looking down has a significance here, which the body is involved in before the mind realizes it. When the mind notices that the inside of the stump resembles temple walls, the body has already assumed an attitude of reverence and sensed that the stump is a kind of altar. A mood gathers quickly; we are in the presence of a mystery.

The dusky emptiness within also sends a message. The silence inside the stump is the sound that surrounds the dying of animals—though the bird itself (killed by a skunk or an owl?) may have shrieked briefly. Only the human being coming across this place is moved to elegy. The bird is gone, and its absence, within the silence of the stump, is a door a human being goes through, a door that opens out onto the mortality of the things of the world, including himself. The mood is not melancholy, nor is it precisely grief. A different emotion arises, and we feel it in the repetitions of the last paragraph. In addition to the surrounding silence, the poem evokes mysterious natural patterns: in the walls worked by "the intricate ones," in the "fluted white tips" of the feathers, in spring returning. Subtly, these interwoven images create the sense that the dying too is part of such a pattern, the ultimate response to which must be, neither melancholy nor grief, but a profound assent.

Sometimes grief is the right word to describe the emotion evoked through the contemplation of an animal's death. In "The Dead Seal Near McClure's Beach" there is the grief of sharing responsibility for the death: "This is the oil. Here on its back is the oil that heats our houses so efficiently." In "Looking at a Dead Wren in My Hand" there is the grief connected with the delicacy and transience of life: "Forgive the hours spent listening to radios, and the words of gratitude I did not say to teachers." In both cases the poet is struck by the fact that his grief is not needed by the animal. At the end of "The Dead Seal" Bly says, "You don't want to be touched by me. I climb the cliff and go home the other way." The last sentence of the wren poem is, "The black spot on your head is your mourning cap." While mourning for a dead or dying creature is fitting, it is we, not they, who require it.

The Morning Glory uses words like "buoyant," "affectionate," "cheerful," and "triumphant" very freely. They make the poems themselves too buoyant at times—inflated, lighter than water—and to my mind the book could be strengthened by the excision of ten or fifteen such words. It should also be noted that in it we do not see nature in her bloodier and more brutal aspects. But in spite of these things *The Morning Glory* is firmly and beautifully connected to the earth, and it is largely because of its sane respect for animals, in their living and in their dying, that this is so. In the first poem in the book, "A Bird's Nest Made of White Reed Fiber," Bly looks at the small, animal-created object and says, "It is something made and then forgotten, like our own lives that we will entirely forget in the grave, when we are floating, nearing the shore where we will be reborn, ecstatic and black." The intuition concerning the ambiguous rebirth does not reappear in *The Morning Glory* after that, but the sense of our lives as something made, and someday to be "forgotten," is felt throughout the book, almost always through the intercession of the animals.

The self-contained, "at one" aspect of animals, and the reminders they deliver concerning death, sometimes give way to a third thing. Some of the poems in *The Morning Glory* go a step further into what we might call earthly visions. It is not necessary that an animal be present for this kind of experience to take place—the poet's own animal, the body, can be enough—but in Bly's case being near some other creature seems to help. I don't mean to fence off too neatly a separate category for this kind of poem. The quality of the imagination in Bly's object poems gives them all a certain visionary quality, if sharpness and freshness of seeing is considered visionary—and a good case can be made that it should be. William Carlos Williams probably wouldn't have been interested in being called a visionary, but as compared to the ordinary citizens of Rutherford and Paterson he certainly was one. And metaphor itself entails a kind of vision, implying as it does not only the imagination's capacity for transformation but a far-reaching web of relationships in the world as well. But in *The Morning Glory* we get more than sharp, rich perception of physical details. The solid, earthly scenes propel the poet's consciousness to unknown, or forgotten, places.

The brief poem "A Turtle" might be viewed as transitional—an object poem in which a visionary current can be felt. It is felt first, vaguely, in the opening sentence: "The orange stripes on his head shoot forward into the future." Then the turtle is carefully observed, described in the striking and accurate metaphors and similes characteristic of *The Morning Glory:* "The slim head stretches forward, the turtle is pushing with all its might, caught now on the edge of my palm. The claws—five on the front, four on the back—are curiously long and elegant, cold, curved, pale, like a lieutenant's sword. The yellow stripes on the neck and head remind you of racing cars." But then, as the poet turns the turtle over and looks at its underplate, a remarkable change takes place. It is here that sensory vision transforms into the second kind of vision:

> The bottom plate is a pale, washed-out rose color from being
> dragged over the world—the imagination is simplified there,
> without too much passion, businesslike, like the underside of a
> space-ship.

In the last simile, presented calmly, "without too much passion," the mind reaches suddenly and simultaneously in opposite directions: into the long amphibian past and into the future;
down to a creature that moves across the earth slowly, low to
the ground, and out toward unknown space. That an otherworldly strangeness is discovered in an animal as ancient and
lowly as a turtle is in keeping with Bly's general sense of the
physical and the spiritual, the ordinary and the mysterious, that
has been emerging steadily since the first page of *Snowy Fields*.

The shift from the creaturely to the visionary is at times
extremely abrupt, as in "On the Rocks at Maui," where the
of a crab climbing a rock prompts a sort of fit of identification
and transformation. It is a lively and impulsive piece, but in
other poems the imagination moves more smoothly and with
greater penetration. We can take three poems to stand for the
kind of visionary effect I have been referring to: "At a Fish
Hatchery in Story, Wyoming"; "Sitting on Some Rocks in Shaw
Cove, California"; and "Walking on the Sussex Coast." In each
an arc is made from an actual scene in the present into a visionary dimension and then back to the present again. To put it
another way, the poems contain a kind of diastole and systole of
consciousness. Also, all three poems contain in one form or another a birth, and this is indicative of their thrust: the psyche
finds new life through the earth and the imagination.

In "At a Fish Hatchery" the poet is watching fingerling trout
being scooped into tubs. As the fish fall through the air they
glitter and twist in the sun and, in the poem's first transformation, they are seen as energy itself.

> They are immense reserves of pure energy, like snowbanks, like
> mountains, like millions of hands . . . and when they do fall,
> they leave behind pure strokes in the air, vanishing into the
> washtub of fish, that contains so much, like the white stones
> dropped by glaciers, and washed by chilly streams . . .

The glaciers and glacial streams become a link from the light
and energy of the fish to the distant past, and a second transformation or leap takes place:

> . . . or the furs wrapped around old shoulders in the back of
> caves, where the skins have been chewed by women with lumi-
> nous faces, who glow because their child has come into the uni-
> verse . . .

The thought of a birth thousands of years ago, uniting the new-
born and the ancient in a single image, takes us beyond time.
By holding inside it both the glittering stream of fingerlings and
the people in caves "who glow because their child has come into
the universe," the poem creates a vision of life itself pouring or
struggling forth always and everywhere.

But the poem does not end there. Bly adds this:

> . . . and now lies on their naked breast, which gleams in the
> risen light like a fish.

We circle back to the image which was the starting point of the
poem's arc of vision. The association of the breast and the fish
through the imagery of light—identified with life throughout the
poem—makes a particularly graceful and resonant return. Beginning with the radiance of fish shining in sunlight, we are
pulled into the past, and as we come back to the present again
through the final simile a subtle momentum through time is felt.
So a vision of the past based in the present implies also the
future. It is as if we could feel the stream of life flowing and
continuing to flow.

In "Sleepers Joining Hands" we encountered the line,

"fragments of the mother lie open in all low places." Like *Snowy Fields*, *The Morning Glory* lets us feel what that statement only tells us. The book takes us often to low places—tide pools, the hollow stump, puddles, the floors of barns, crevices in rocks— and in the cave Bly's thoughts went to in "At a Fish Hatchery" we were clearly inside a dark space where new life is born and nourished. In "Sitting on Some Rocks in Shaw Cove, California," the setting is literally a cave—a cliff-hollow. Here there are fossils, remnants of life long gone, so the place is a kind of tomb. There are also "furry shells"—primitive, silent beings living here still in the ceaseless ebb and flow of the ocean. Life past and life present are both here, and so is life not yet born. The generations of shell-people will continue to come, but the cliff-hollow is also a womb-like place for the consciousness of the man sitting there. As the poet sits on the rocks—the body tucked, folded—once again, as in "A Hollow Tree," it is likely that the mind understands this significance via the body's sensing of it. In any case, thoughts of birth come quickly:

> The sea breathes and breathes under the new moon. Suddenly it rises, hurrying into the long crevices in the rock shelves, it rises like a woman's belly, as if nine months had passed in a second; rising like milk to the tiny veins . . .

The body begins to feel intensely alive, with its own inner motion and new life: "I have the sensation that half an inch under my skin there are nomad bands, stringy-legged men with firesticks and wide-eyed babies." Intuition, too, has been awakened, and it offers one of those statements guaranteed to aggravate some and—what shall I say?—*interest* others: "The rocks with their backs turned to me have something spiritual in them." This is followed by the statement, "On these rocks I am not afraid of death; death is like the sound of the motor in an airplane as we fly, the sound so steady and comforting." The total

effect of these parts is to let us sense the energies of life moving—being born, living, dying, being born—within the physical
universe and time, much as we experienced it in "At a Fish
Hatchery" The effect is, to put it simply, that of sensing that
the universe is alive. Having touched these transpersonal energies, the individual consciousness is capable of perceiving its own
life in a new way. The rest of the poem should demonstrate the
arc in the vision I have referred to, and the return.

> And I still haven't found the woman I loved in some former life—
> how could I, when I have loved only once on this rock, though
> twice in the moon, and three times in the rising water. Two
> children a thousand miles away leap toward me, shouting, arms
> in the air. A bird with long wings comes flying toward me in the
> dusk, pumping just over the darkening waves. He has flown
> around the planet, it has taken him centuries. He returns to me
> the lean-legged runner laughing as he runs through the stringy
> grasses, and gives back to me my buttons, and the soft sleeves of
> my sweater.

This passage, it seems to me, exemplifies "the lyrical impulses of the soul" in prose. The woman from "some other life"
is an expression of the spiritual longing that draws a man forward. So are the children, though they may also be the poet's
actual children suddenly leaping into his thoughts: it would be
perfectly appropriate to say that they are both. When the bird
enters, it too appears like a long-lost, visionary presence, like
something out of a fairy tale. But the bird is also a creature
actual and present, and as he flaps slowly above the moving
water, consciousness centers again on the vitality of the body.
The final image of the buttons and sleeves of a sweater is at first
glance a strangely anticlimactic conclusion, but its mundaneness
does not in fact undercut the vision of the poem—at least not
any more than is fitting. It is simply a return to the ordinary,
sensual reality of the body. This is where the poem's arc of

consciousness originated, and it is the appropriate place for it to come to rest.

In "Walking on the Sussex Coast" a stone barn takes the place of the imagined cave of "At a Fish Hatchery" and the actual cliff-hollow of "Sitting on Some Rocks at Shaw Cove." Looking at the muddy ground around the barn, Bly says, "The hoof marks in the muck outside the door mean only that the hoofs are glad to be going out, it is not an ominous sign." In that sentence we feel again the attempt to stay on the level of things themselves, to let a hoof-print or pine "live for itself." But when the body feels a vibrancy from taking in such sights as the muddy yard and the barn floor "fresh and yellow from tumbled bales," intuition also grows alert. It keeps watching for "signs." Bly says, "I stand a long time looking at the barn floor." Then he notices "A portable wooden gate [that] leans against the stone wall; it is calm, like an altar, some slivers missing." After noticing those cracks in the wood, he imagines a different kind of split:

> Maybe at night we split up into different beings, and one of them comes back here, to stand inside this barn, with only one eye, loved by the other cows, or at least recognized by the brown patches on my sides. How good to flop down here, our sides touching other cows, protected from seawind by stone walls that will later become the color of night. We know that at dawn we can look out the door and see the green hills again!

A door opened, dawn's light, the green hills—it all describes a consciousness that has been nourished and refreshed and opened. Once again a visionary moment, fostered by surroundings rich with associations of both animals and the womb, leads to its own kind of rebirth.

As much in evidence in *The Morning Glory* as animals is water. It is a very wet book. There are lakes, waterfalls, puddles, and rain, but most of all, the ocean. The book is divided into three parts, and the middle section, called the Point Reyes Poems, grew out of a stay near that California seashore area in 1970–71. All but one of the poems in that group are shore or coast poems, and a number of others in the first section are as well. It was only appropriate that Bly, a Midwestern poet who even two thousand miles inland felt the presence of some invisible sea, as he did repeatedly in the "regionalist" poems of *Snowy Fields*, should get himself to the ocean and write some of his best poetry about it. At the shore two worlds literally meet, and Bly is always interested in exploring such meeting places. And of course water itself excites Bly's imagination. In addition to being the home of sea lions and octopuses, it speaks to the soul.

The visit to the California coast is not the only travel represented in *The Morning Glory*. It is in fact a sort of travel book, ranging from Hawaii to Norway, specifying along the way locations such as Reelfoot Lake, Tennessee; the Isleta Pueblo, New Mexico; Kansas City; Vancouver; Los Angeles. Mentioning the names of specific places is a gesture to remind the reader, and perhaps the writer as well, that the emotions and intuitions of the poems grow from places that can be found on a map—i.e., it is another way of making the connection between the inner man and the earth. It suggests at the same time that inner states are as real as the states of Tennessee, California, or Minnesota.

But after all the traveling represented in it, *The Morning Glory* in its last several poems returns to the home-ground of Minnesota. Once again a rhythm of going out and returning is felt. Corresponding to this return is a growing sense of acceptance. These poems communicate a gratefulness at the fact of being alive which is solid and moving. The closing poems also enact something of a seasonal progression. "A Caterpillar on the Desk," "August Rain," and "Grass from Two Years" take place in late summer, when the months of intense growth and heat subtly give way to the waning that is to come. As summer turns to fall, a man feels a change inside him as well:

It is the first of September. The leaf shadows are less ferocious on the notebook cover. A man accepts his failures more easily— or perhaps summer's insanity is gone? A man notices ordinary earth, scorned in July, with affection, as he settles down to his daily work, to use stamps.

("A Caterpillar on the Desk")

After a month and a half without rain, at last, in late August, darkness comes at three in the afternoon, a cheerful thunder begins, and then the rain . . . [ellipses mine] The rain deepens. It rolls off the porch roof, making a great puddle near me. The bubbles slide toward the puddle edge, become crowded, and disappear. The black earth turns blacker, it absorbs the rain needles without a sound. The sky is low, everything silent, as when parents are angry. . . . What has failed and been forgiven—the leaves from last year unable to go on, lying near the foundation, dry under the porch, retreat farther into the shadow, they give off a faint hum, as of birds' eggs, or the tail of a dog.

The older we get the more we fail, but the more we fail the more we feel a part of the dead straw of the universe, the corners of barns with cowdung twenty years old, the chairs fallen back on their heads in deserted houses, the belts left hanging over the chairback after the bachelor has died in the ambulance on the way to the city. These objects also belong to us, they ride us as the child holding on to the dog's fur, these appear in our dreams, they are more and more near us, coming in slowly from the wainscoting, they make our trunks heavy, accumulating between trips, they lie against the ship's side, and will nudge the hole open that lets the water in at last.

("August Rain")

There is an absence of existential anguish here that some readers will feel an evasion and others will find a blessing. The second group will include those who believe that what man shares with the animals and the life of the planet is as great as what separates us from them, and that it is possible, at times at least, to experience consciously that which we have in common. The poems do not tell us what failures have had to be accepted, and one wonders if the lonely bachelor would have given the same account of failure, yet "August Rain," and *The Morning Glory* itself, builds to an eloquence and sense of reconciliation that is hard to deny. Reconciliation with the "ordinary earth," like celebration of the animals who live and die on it, is a key theme and longing throughout *The Morning Glory*.

Following the late summer poems, the final two poems in the book take place on Christmas Eve and New Year's Eve, our midwinter birth festivals. They describe religious observations of two different sorts. The first takes place at a midnight church service, the second in a barn.

In "Christmas Eve Service at Midnight at St. Michael's" the birth of Christ and the pleasures of the celebration must make room also for death. Bly's only brother had been killed in a car crash six months before the evening described here, and thoughts of this death suffuse the poem. Even small details connote the precariousness of human life: the sidewalk the poet and his family walk on is icy, the night is cold, the houses "frail" and surrounded by the darkness. As the family gathers near the Christmas tree there is weeping, the brother's absence fresh again at such a celebration. The family then goes to the midnight service, and the poem becomes a moving account of the power of ritual. For many, this power has leaked out of the church's rites and symbols. This is not the case here, however; "Christmas Eve Service at Midnight at St. Michael's" is one of the rather small number of modern poems which honors that power, and conveys it intact.

> Just after midnight, [the priest] turns to face us, lifts up the dry wafer, and breaks it—a clear and terrifying sound. He holds

up the two halves . . . frightening . . . for like so many acts, it is permanent. With his arms spread, the cross clear on his white chasuble, he tells us that Christ intended to leave his body behind . . . it is confusing . . . we take our bodies with us when we go. I see oceans dark and lifting near flights of stairs, oceans lifting and torn over which the invisible birds drift like husks over November roads . . . The cups are put down. The ocean has been stirred and calmed. A large man is flying over the water with wings spread, a wound on his chest.

The confusion raised by the priest's statement about Christ's body is of course related to the poet's thoughts of his brother's death, and those thoughts also make the sound of the breaking of the wafer "clear and terrifying"; he feels a significance in that act perhaps more strongly than ever before: "like so many acts, it is permanent." The confusion is not resolved; it subsides, under the power of ritual devoutly performed and experienced. Ritual is not intended to solve mysteries. It only gives them forms, and thereby makes them not only bearable but even nourishing.

Whether the priest was right about Christ and the body is a question that we are left with, but the book's final poem, "Opening the Door of a Barn I Thought Was Empty on New Year's Eve," returns to the body alive upon the earth, and returns as well to animals. Certain elements of ritual—the unconscious kind this time—are also present. Dusk, a barn, opening a door—all carry a significance beyond themselves which the body and the psyche, given the proper sensitivity, can feel. The sensitivity needed is of the kind that first enabled Bly to write the poems in *Snowy Fields*, and which remains strong in *The Morning Glory*. "Whoever wants to see the invisible has to penetrate more deeply into the visible."

And whoever wants to feel the flow of life on this planet does well to go among animals. As the title begins to explain, the poem describes an unexpected encounter. Instead of an empty barn, the poet finds massive mammal life milling quietly about inside:

> I got there by dusk. The west shot up a red beam. I open the double barn doors and go in. Sounds of breathing! Thirty steers are wandering around, the partitions gone. Creatures heavy, shaggy, slowly moving in the dying light. Bodies with no St. Teresas look straight at me.

The last sentence there is a fine one, but if the steers know nothing of the intensity of religious ecstasy, they nonetheless possess a kind of light.

> These breathing ones do not demand eternal life, they ask only to eat the crushed corn, and the hay, coarse as rivers, and cross the rivers, and sometimes feel an affection run along the heavy nerves. They have the wonder and bewilderment of the whale, with too much flesh, the body with the lamp lit inside, fluttering on a windy night.

It is not a beacon or halo, but rather the lamp of the life of the heavy body itself. The poem may be wrong in its guess as to what it is that runs along the steers' nerves, but what is most important here, and most beautiful, is the final image. At its conclusion *The Morning Glory* takes us to the brute flesh of the animals and finds a delicate, stubborn light there.

In an interview Bly once remarked that "what is precious in poetry is the inwardness and the love of animals,"[18] and one senses that the conjunction of those two elements is not just coincidental. Turning the statement around in the mind a while, one can see within it, "what is precious is the soul and the body." Bly wants to set soul and body on terms of equal value, celebrating both. Speaking of them like this, as if they could be well separated by us, is of course clumsy. The division seems especially awkward, arbitrary and mental, in comparison to Bly's poems, for while he uses it at times himself, he is a poet whose ability to describe the life of the soul-in-the-body, not separated, is one of his key gifts. Marvin Bell has said of Bly, "Because of [him], the imagination is more and more physical." [19] This is true because of Bly's insistence on the image as the primary means of expression in poetry, but also because of his robust, vivid, fine responsiveness to the physical world itself. Of all Bly's books, it is *The Morning Glory* in which sheer physical vitality is clearest and strongest. *The Morning Glory* is a book of the body: the body among earth, rocks, water, other bodies (only occasionally human). Because the world's body is honored so well, the human body which takes it in is also honored. The physical senses are wonderfully alive, and life flows directly from them to other senses—intuition, imagination. In one poem (the one in which he cites Whitman's celebration of animals: "November Day at McClure's") Bly comments, "Inside us there is some secret." He might have said "soul." In *The Morning Glory* Bly catches again and again the presence of the secret, and the presence of the body carrying it forward. The poem concludes, "We are following a narrow ledge around a mountain, we are sailing on skeletal eerie craft over the buoyant ocean."

But Bly's statement about "inwardness and the love of animals" contains more than my reworking of it, as it also says, what is precious is what is inside the human being, and what is "out there," among "the wild things of the universe." Between these two Bly conducts another healing celebration, simultaneous and organic with the celebration of body and soul. It is not just inside *us* that secrets exist. Body-soul. Human-animal. These dynamics, these continuities, are important throughout Bly's work; they are the heartbeat of *The Morning Glory*.

CHAPTER 6

This Body Is Made
of Camphor and Gopherwood

If they tried rhomboids,
Cones, waving lines, ellipses—
As, for example, the ellipse of the half moon—
Rationalists would wear sombreros.
                    —Wallace Stevens,
               "Six Significant Landscapes"

The cistern contains: the fountain overflows.
                    —William Blake,
          "The Marriage of Heaven and Hell"

And how can the soul walk without its body?
          —"When the Wheel Does Not Move"

Talking in 1978 about the sameness and cautiousness he saw in much current American poetry, Bly said: "Perhaps poetry is developing a protective camouflage of brown and gray feathers. A poetry shelf has fewer and fewer peacocks with long tails, like Robinson Jeffers. Probably this heavy breeding is nice. And it's possible that hawks don't see some gray birds and don't attack them."[1] Each of the books I have discussed in this study so far had a striking originality. *Sleepers Joining Hands* had been the most notable peacock of Bly's books, but in his second collection of prose poems, *This Body Is Made of Camphor and Gopherwood*, published the year before Bly made the statement quoted above, he produced a book which in some ways went beyond it. It is a flamboyant book—gaudy, excited, tender, didactic. Its title is partly drawn from The Song of Solomon ("My beloved is unto me as a cluster of camphire in the vineyards of En-gedi." 1:14), and the idiosyncratic, richly colored, aromatic style Bly adopts here resembles that poem more than it does almost anything in contemporary poetry. One has to admire the audacity of the project. Unfortunately, however, it resulted in a rather high proportion of affected writing.

The offbeat title itself is certainly the opposite of camouflage. Philip Dacey, the most effective hawk with regard to *Gopherwood*, went right at it, calling his review "This Book Is Made of Turkey Soup and Star Music." Dacey takes Bly to task on a number of points; for example, the question of artifice:

> Although Bly, a classic literary demagogue, rails against artifice in poetry . . . many of the prose poems in this book are more artificial—pieces clearly contrived in a language one is not likely to hear outside the poem—than virtually any of, say, Frost's poems in blank verse. Frost and countless others achieve the natural or a semblance of it through the artificial; Bly wishes to bypass the latter and ends up smack in the middle of it.[2]

The imagery in *Gopherwood* is alternately brilliant and baroque. Exuberance turns at times to bathos, and tenderness to sentimentality. But probably the most bothersome aspect of the book is the one Jonathan Chaves put his finger on (Dacey and others mentioned it as well) when he said that in *Gopherwood* Bly has written in "the consistently strident voice of the preacher, asserting rather than revealing."[3]

The last three words are the most important there. Bly has

of course adopted the preacher's voice before in his poetry, sometimes with powerful effect. In *Gopherwood*, he raises and lowers his voice, but in either case he seems to protest too much. I noted in discussing *The Morning Glory* that Bly said that it was in writing *Gopherwood* that he first "felt [his] own pitches enter."[4] Whatever he felt, however, the suggestion that the voice in *Gopherwood* represents a poetic advance, an advance into greater authenticity, seems to me ill-conceived. In poetry, prose, public speech, and conversation, Bly has better, more convincing pitches than those which dominate this book.

There is another ecstatic text in addition to the Song of Solomon that should be mentioned in connection with *Gopherwood*. In 1965 Bly received as a gift from James Wright a copy of *One Hundred Poems of Kabir*, translated by Rabindranath Tagore and Evelyn Underhill.[5] He did not read the book until three or four years later, but when he did he was powerfully attracted to the spirit he found in the poems of the fifteenth-century Indian poet, and he began reworking the Tagore-Underhill translations, done fifty years earlier, into contemporary American English. These revised versions were published in various pamphlets and broadsides, and then were gathered in 1977 as *The Kabir Book: Forty-Four of the Ecstatic Poems of Kabir*. It is a marvelous collection—wise, crackling with energy and humor, full of spiritual hectoring and encouragement, bracing, and utterly fresh. Not many readers would have been able to feel all this life through the rather musty Tagore-Underhill versions, and it is one of Bly's great contributions to American poetry that he was able to do so, and then to express it in absolutely unpretentious, clear contemporary language. (Bly later did similar work with poems of the thirteenth-century Sufi, Rumi, and the sixteenth-century woman poet of India, Mirabai.)

One suspects, however, that the work on Kabir may be partly responsible for the inflation and affectation that we encounter in *Gopherwood*. We can see evidence of this influence not only in the determined effort to write "ecstatic poetry," but also in certain mannerisms Bly uses in *Gopherwood*. Here is one of the Kabir versions:

> Oh friend, I love you, think this over
> carefully! If you are in love,
> then why are you asleep?
> If you have found him,
> give yourself to him, take him.
> Why do you lose track of him again and again?
> If you are about to fall into heavy sleep anyway,
> why waste time smoothing the bed
> and arranging the pillows?
> Kabir will tell you the truth: this is what love is like:
> suppose you had to cut your head off
> and give it to someone else,
> what difference would that make?[6]

That urgent opening sounds a note we hear often in *Gopherwood*, though the Kabir poem achieves a light and sure touch compared to which most of the *Gopherwood* poems seem rather forced. The repeated address to a "friend," the excited didacticism, and the use of rhetorical questions are also shared by the two books, as are certain images. In each case, what works wonderfully in the Kabir poems works far less well in *Gopherwood*.

> Friend, this body is made of camphor and gopherwood. So for two days I gathered ecstasies from my own body, I rose up and down, surrounded only by bare wood and bare air and some gray cloud, and what was inside me came so close to me, and I lived and died!
>
> ("The Pail")

> Is this world animal or vegetable? Others love us, the cabbages love the earth, the earth is fond of the heavens—a new age comes close through the dark, an elephant's trunk waves in the darkness, so much is passing away, so many disciplines already

gone, but the energy in the double flower does not falter, the
wings fold up around the sitting man's face. And these cucumber
leaves are my body, and my thighs, and my toes stretched out in
the wind. . . . Well, waterer, how will you get through this
night without water?

("Wings Folding Up")

We seem to have a case here of a brilliant act of (re)translation
being a dangerous influence on the translator's original work.

As its title announces, *Gopherwood* is a celebration of the
body. The title invokes not only the sensuousness of The Song
of Solomon but the ark and the animals of the Noah story: "Make
the ark of gopher wood" (Genesis 6:14). *The Morning Glory* was
also a book of the body, but the prose poem feels distinctly different in the two books. Beyond (or perhaps behind) the didacticism of *Gopherwood* there is another difference. *The Morning Glory*
was written in the language of the body, and from the body's
perspective: the human body was not mentioned often, but we
were strongly aware of it moving among the places and animals
it encountered and observed. In *Gopherwood* the body is mentioned constantly, but even when Bly takes us into the interior
of the body, into a country where both cells and dreams are
viewed close up, it is less perceiver than perceived. There is a
glittering and fragrant sensuousness about much of *Gopherwood*,
but it does not honor the senses in the solid way *The Morning
Glory* did. Attentive, detailed, sustained description has for the
most part disappeared; distinct physical settings are mostly gone
as well. Only one poem, "Snowed In," could be called an "object poem." There are animals, but they are less plentiful and
far less substantial than they were in *The Morning Glory*. As praise
of the body, *The Morning Glory* is a finer, subtler, more convincing, and simply more physical book than *Gopherwood*.

Bly was not trying, however, to repeat what he had done
in *The Morning Glory*. He was attempting something new and

difficult. For all its images, there is a paradoxical abstractness about *Gopherwood:* a celebration of the body, it is not so much a book of the solid, alert flesh and the senses as of energy. The flamboyance of *Gopherwood* does not derive solely from the poetry. Its twenty poems are accompanied by twenty exquisitely detailed, naturally arabesque drawings of snail shells, by Gendron Jensen. The drawings are remarkable in themselves, but there is more: when the pages of the book are flipped, the drawings become an animation, the snail shell rising, turning over, coming to rest again on its other side. It seems a good bet that this feature of *Gopherwood* represents a first in the history of poetry. But the drawings are not merely decorative, and the animation is not just a novelty. The rising and falling snail shell is a form in motion, and with its graceful swirls and ridges it is also motion caught in a form. It therefore reflects the fundamental attempt of the poems, which is to describe energy itself experienced through the form in which we live, the body.

The prose poem is a rectangular shape on the page, but like the drawings, the poems in *Gopherwood* contain many swirls. There are motions of many kinds, but especially motions described by words like "whirling," "circling," "waves," "roll," and "revolve." In a poem about his children, "Coming in for Supper," Bly says, "How amazed I am, after working hard in the afternoon, that when I sit down at the table, with my elbows touching the elbows of my children, so much love flows out and around in circles." Water images again abound, and the water is usually moving. There are images of spouts and fountains, waves crashing and rushing around boulders, river whirlpools "that draw in green cottonwoods from collapsed earth banks"; even a garden hose lies "curled near the rhubarb." The book is dedicated, at the request of Gendron Jensen, to "All the waters of the world."

All the whirls and curves of *Gopherwood* recall the "curved energy" Bly spoke of in "Sleepers Joining Hands": "So rather than saying that Christ is God or he is not,/ it is better to forget all that/ and lose yourself in the curved energy." What he is talking about there and what he is dealing with in *Gopherwood* is essentially the same curved, circling energy, the elemental energy of being and creation. The vision of whirling energy is almost enough to supersede the terminology which has been so fundamental to him:

> Then what is asked of us? To stop sacrificing one energy for another. They are not different energies anyway, not "male" or "female," but whirls of different speeds as they revolve. We must learn to worship both, and give up the idea of one god . . .
> ("Walking to the Next Farm")

But while Bly says it is time "to worship both," "male" and "female," fast and slow, yang and yin, oppositions remain. Contrasted with the moving energy are structures which resist the natural flow. In "Snowed In," a blossom and a snowstorm are seen as "two oceans living at a level of instinct surer than mine":

> . . . one cold, one warm, but neither wants to go up geometrically floor after floor, even to hold up a wild-haired roof, with copper dragons, through whose tough nose rain water will pour. . . .
> So the snow and the orangey blossoms are both the same flow, that starts out close to the soil, close to the floor, and needs no commandments, no civilization, no drawing rooms lifted on the labor of the claw hammer, but is at home when one or two are present, it is also inside the block of wood, and in the burnt bone that sketched the elk by smoky light.

Bly does not dismiss geometric structures and the commandments and civilization they imply, but he does cast a satiric eye in their direction. In "Walking Swiftly" he remarks, "We live in wooden buildings made of two-by-fours, making the landscape nervous for a hundred miles." This statement no doubt owes a debt to a passage in *Black Elk Speaks*, which Bly quoted in the "I Came Out of the Mother Naked" essay in *Sleepers*. Black Elk, an old Oglala Sioux holy man forced to live in a reservation house said:

It is a bad way to live, for there can be no power in a square.

You have noticed that everything an Indian does is in a circle, and that is because the Power of the World always works in circles, and everything tries to be round. In the old days when we were a strong and happy people, all our power came to us from the sacred hoop of the nation, and so long as the hoop was unbroken, the people flourished. The flowering tree at the living center of the hoop, and the circle of the four quarters nourished it. . . . Everything the Power of the World does is done in a circle. The sky is round, and I have heard that the earth is round like a ball, and so are all the stars. The wind, in its greatest power, whirls. Birds make their nests in circles, for theirs is the same religion as ours. . . . Our teepees were round like the nests of birds, and these were always set in a circle, the nation's hoop, a nest of many nests, where the great Spirit meant for us to hatch our children.

But the Wasichus have put us in these square boxes. Our power is gone and we are dying, for the power is not in us any more.[7]

The poem's comment about the landscape's nervousness is comic where Black Elk's statement has tragic weight, but both derive from a sense that the rectangular houses stand for a way of life at odds with the natural flow of the world's energies. Bly is not suggesting that living in round houses would help us, but he does say that it is possible and important for us to know the curved energies, to enter them and allow them to enter us. Sometimes the energy flows smoothly, calmly, as at the end of "Snowed In," where we find this scene: "A man and a woman sit quietly near each other. In the snowstorm millions of years come close behind us, nothing is lost, nothing rejected, our bodies are equal to the snow in energy." Elsewhere, at other times, it is fierce; geometric containers and commandments are inadequate to it not because they are too artificial or harsh, but because the flow is too powerful for them. This wild energy, hot, longing to find its outlet, is evoked at the end of "Walking Swiftly":

> The heat inside the human body grows, it does not know where to throw itself—for a while it knots into will, heavy, burning, sweet, then into generosity, that longs to take on the burdens of others, then into mad love that lasts forever. The artist walks swiftly to his studio, and carves oceanic waves into the dragon's mane.

In "Sleepers" Bly said of the source of the curved energies of creation, or the energies themselves, "we have no name for you." In *Gopherwood* he says something else. The final poem in the book, "The Cry Going Out over Pastures," is a love poem, and love has already been conceived of in previous poems as a flow of energy. It ends with this passage:

> There is death but also this closeness, this joy when the bee rises into the air above his hive to find the sun, to become the son, and the traveler moves through exile and loss, through murkiness and failure, to touch the earth again of his own kingdom and kiss the ground. . . .
>   What shall I say of this? I say, praise to the first man who wrote down this joy clearly, for we cannot remain in love with what we cannot name. . . .

All poetry is a kind of naming, but *Gopherwood* is an attempt to name energy and flow themselves, and the joy of experiencing them. The language of the poems is kinetic not only because of the excited moods of the poet but also because of the nature of their ultimate subject. The kinesthesia extends even to the poems' punctuation. As in *The Morning Glory*, Bly's favorite punctuation in *Gopherwood* is the ellipsis. (Unless otherwise noted with brackets, all the ellipses in my quotations from prose poems are Bly's.) In *The Morning Glory* the ellipses were usually expressive of the dance between eye and imagination. In *Gopherwood* their main effect is to emulate continuing flow, to resist closure. The prose poem in *Gopherwood* represents a kind of action writing which tries to describe, discuss, and praise various currents of energy. The animated snail shell drawings are one way of depicting spirals and motion; the poems attempt to do the same thing in words.

Just as "we cannot remain in love with what we cannot name," just as the flux of experience needs to be articulated into language, so the flowing energy is not experienced without some vessel, some form through which to know it. And so we come again to the body, "this body [. . .] made of energy compacted and whirling" ("We Love This Body"), "so beautifully carved inside, with the curves of the inner ear, and the husk so rough, knuckle-brown" ("The Origin of the Praise of God"). Essentially *Gopherwood* is about incarnation, but what orthodox Christian doctrine presents as a unique occurrence in history, it sees as a universal and continual process. We know the arcs of the curved energy of creation through the ark of the body. *Gopherwood*, then, is another stage or variation—the most explicit and insistent—of Bly's honoring of the body and redefining of its relationship to the spirit.

I have mentioned The Song of Solomon and Kabir, but a work from which Bly must have taken special inspiration—and encouragement—in writing *Gopherwood* is Blake's "Marriage of Heaven and Hell," which he has called "surely one of the greatest works of English literature."[8] If *Gopherwood* often sounds like a sermon, Bly might have taken this famous passage for his text:

> 1. Man has no Body distinct from his Soul; for that call'd Body is a portion of Soul discern'd by the five Senses, the chief inlets of Soul in this age.
> 2. Energy is the only life, and is from the Body; and Reason is the bound or outward circumference of Energy.
> 3. Energy is Eternal Delight.

Bly's conception differs somewhat from Blake's; instead of saying that "Energy . . . is from the Body," he says that we experience transhuman energies *through* the body. But Blake and Bly are fighting the same fight, singing the same hymn, and Blake's brilliant redefinitions are certainly a crucial antecedent for Bly's enterprise in *Gopherwood* and elsewhere. (Both also give themselves up to the paradox of having to separate body and soul in order to talk about their union.) Among the many "Proverbs of Hell" that could aptly serve as epigraphs for *Gopherwood* is this one: "Eternity is in love with the productions of time." The production of time to which a human being owes the most fundamental debt of praise is the body. As Whitman (one would be remiss not to mention him too somewhere in discussing *Gopherwood*) said, "I too had been struck from the float forever held in solution,/ I too had receiv'd identity by my body."[9]

Charles Molesworth, the critic who has been most receptive to *Gopherwood*, sees the revaluation of the body as the key element of Bly's religious sense and affirmation:

> [This is] what is distinctive about Bly's religion: he has made the body equivalent to the Western-Christian-Protestant "soul," an entity of nearly unspeakable longings that has its true abode in the vast beyond and that can realize its essence only in the momentary gestures of escape and ecstasy.

> What I think Bly's poetry enacts, especially in the strengths and weaknesses of *Camphor*, is the persistent desire of American poets simultaneously to celebrate the body and to incorporate the universal energies, thus making them available to all. How to domesticate the sublime? Bly's answer seems to be to deify the *truly* immediate, that is, the data of consciousness understood not as thought, but as bodily sensation.[10]

The body has been referred to often as a temple by those trying to redress the slanders and slights committed against it by religion and philosophy. *Gopherwood* goes further. The body is not just a temple, but also a kind of priest, or shaman, or wise uncle. It has an intelligence, a secret knowledge, of its own.

"Walking Swiftly," which opens the book, begins, "When I wake, I hear sheep eating apple peels just outside the screen. The trees are heavy, soaked, cold and hushed, the sun just rising." The sentences are sensuous, and they signal the awakening of and to the body. But in general, in *Gopherwood* Bly is less interested in the five senses than in others that lie beyond them in the body. We get one example of this in "Finding the Father." The theme of the lost father is one that Bly touched on in "Sleepers Joining Hand," and would focus on strongly in subsequent work; we will come to this theme shortly, in chapter 7. What I want to call attention to here, however, is not the lost father but the role the body plays in finding him in this poem. When an unidentified stranger appears to take us "through the blowing and rainy streets, to the dark house," it is the body, personified in this poem and elsewhere in *Gopherwood* as if it were a distinct character, that makes the necessary decision: "We will go there, the body says." Here we see part of the body's wisdom dramatized. It is the body which has the gut-sense, right-instinct, or longing required to make us set out to find the lost father, who is also "lonely in his whole body, waiting for you."

The poem that deals with the intelligence of the body most explicitly—and in a nearly expository mode—is "Falling into Holes in Our Sentences." Emerson mentions in "Self-Reliance" that when we hold an artificial smile for any length of time the body sends a message about the depth of our sincerity in the form of tension in the muscles of the face. "Falling into Holes" takes up the same line of thought but carries it considerably further. In it Bly says, "every longing another person had that we failed to see the body returns to us as a squinting of the eyes when we talk." The body is sensitive to what the conscious mind misses, or succeeds in ignoring: "Each step we take in conversation with our friends, moving slowly or flying, the body watches us, calling us into what is possible, into what is not said, into the shuckheap of ruined arrowheads, or the old man with two fingers gone." The phrase "what is possible" is not used here in the idealistic sense; it refers rather to those realities which conversation, for a variety of reasons, is not likely to absorb very well. The images of the arrowheads and the old man suggest loss, pain, struggle, and failure, experienced over long stretches of time. The body, the poem asserts, possesses a stubborn knowledge of these things which the part of us that makes conversation loses sight of easily. Our sentences are full of holes, holes made by politeness, repression, the desire to be loved, idealism, arrogance, and abstraction, including the unavoidable abstraction of language itself. The poem gives a series of instances of such holes, and of the ways the body devises to deliver messages when we have stepped into those holes.

"Falling Into Holes" sees the body as both guardian—"This body holds its protective walls around us, it watches us whenever we walk out"—and as a sort of alchemist: "the ruthless body performing its magic, transforming each of our confrontations into energy, changing our scholarly labors over white-haired books into certainty and healing power, and our cruelties into an old man with missing fingers." As this last statement says, the energy derived from confrontations is in turn transformed into other manifestations. The squinting of the eyes is the simplest example the poem gives of these manifestations. Others include accidents—"We talk all morning of the confusion of others, and in daylight the car slides off the road"—and meaningful coincidences: "we console each other, and opening a *National Geographic* see an old woman lying with her mouth open." They include also dreams—"I give advice in public as if I were adult, that night in a dream I see a policeman holding a gun to the head of a frightened girl, who is blindfolded"—and consequences that reach from one generation to the next: "Overly sane afternoons in a room in our twenties come back to us in the form

of a son who is mad." In all these instances there is a relationship between events in which cause and effect is to one degree
or another hidden. Bly does not presume to explain these shadowy phenomena, but he is sure that the body is intimately involved in the transmission or transformation. The poem pro-
poses a law of compensation: the body "calls us," whether we
comprehend its messages or not, "into what is not said."

When Bly includes in this law accidents which are not really
accidental and coincidences which are not simply coincidental,
not to mention dreams, he is talking about occurrences which
would ordinarily be discussed in terms of the unconscious, not
the body. The direction of Bly's thought here is interesting. Explaining once to a group of students how repressed suffering
comes back in other forms, Bly put the idea this way:

> We have ecstatic nerve endings, we have pain nerve endings. You
> try to use only the ecstatic ones and I guarantee you you'll end
> up as a lump. If you don't use your suffering nerve endings, life
> will force you to do it. It'll give you a husband who'll beat the
> hell out of you. And that'll be real pain. If you open yourself to
> suffering, the suffering will come through and maybe change into
> joy shortly afterward. If you try to block the suffering out and
> say, "I don't want to suffer, if I have to suffer to be a poet, I
> don't want to be a poet," that means I don't want to be a human
> being. Advertising urges you to say that.
>   Then the suffering waits around in the unconscious, and it
> says, "You don't want me, huh? Okay, dad, you don't like me,
> what do you think I am? Slap! That's for you. Slap! Cancer?
> Would you like that? Slap! I can't hear you. Huh? You want a
> wife who'll bitch at you all the time, I'll give you that." I'm se-
> rious, these things exist in the unconscious and you can't fool
> with them. You can push them away all you want to and they'll
> come right back.[11]

When the term "the unconscious" is used, it is ordinarily assumed that the word "mind" follows it, whether it is actually

stated or not. But in "Falling Into Holes" Bly isn't talking about the unconscious *mind*—or if he is, he is locating it in the body— the body whose eyes squint, that opens a magazine and drives a car; it is even, according to the poem, the body that sends us dreams. To put it another way, what is usually thought of as the unconscious mind is an intelligence or knowledge unconscious to the mind but conscious to and in the body. More than just semantics are involved here. Where he uses "the unconscious" and "life" in the statement above, in "Falling Into Holes" Bly substitutes "the body." The body is not the unconscious, but it is on intimate terms with it. They sit together at the table of instinct, and the poem suggests that they have other meeting places as well. It implies a model in which the body stands between the ego and the unconscious. The body listens to the unconscious whether the conscious mind wants to or not. This model may help to understand what took place in *Snowy Fields* and *The Morning Glory* when simple physical actions and experiences took on ritual significance, when they became encounters with a mystery, and the body was involved in the encounter before the conscious mind knew what was happening. The body can be celebrated for other reasons, and it is in Bly's poetry, but in this intimate connection between the body and the unconscious lies one crucial reason for his concentration on the body, and his praise of it, in *Gopherwood* and throughout his work.

Bly also ascribes the religious impulse to the body, and like other anti-Puritans before him he specifically links the religious and the erotic. Many times in his poetry Bly has used images and even fairly elaborate scenes to describe what is felt within the body, as for example in "Waking from Sleep" in *Snowy Fields*, where sensations and emotions were expressed through images of a harbor coming to life in the early morning: "Inside the veins there are navies setting forth,/ Tiny explosions at the water lines,/ And seagulls weaving in the wind of the salty blood." Such internal scenes are set before us again in *Gopherwood* in "The Origin of the Praise of God," with the difference that here they are not only metaphorical but microscopic as well. The effect is a little bizarre. Keep in mind that what is being described in the following passage is, simply, "walking near another person":

> As we walk we enter the magnetic fields of other bodies, and every smell we take in the communities of protozoa see, and a being inside leaps up toward it, as a horse rears at the starting gate. When we come near each other, we are drawn down into the sweetest pools of slowly circling energies, slowly circling smells. And the protozoa know there are odors the shape of oranges, of tornadoes, of octopuses. . . .

As two people draw truly close, in love and sex, the excitement of the cells takes on religious intensity:

> So the space between two people diminishes, it grows less and less, no one to weep, they merge at last. The sound that pours from the fingertips awakens clouds of cells far inside the body, and beings unknown to us start out in a pilgrimage to their Saviour, to their holy place. Their holy place is a small black stone, that they remember from Protozoic times, when it was rolled away from a door . . . and it was after that they found their friends, who helped them to digest the hard grains of this world. . . .

"The Origin of the Praise of God" is dedicated to Lewis Thomas, and to his book *The Lives of a Cell*.[12] Thomas—scientist, essayist, "biology watcher"—has a particular genius for communicating the drama, coherence, and mystery of "lower" life forms, and for suggesting continuities between "low" and "high," large and small. The poem too wants to describe the lives of cells, to envision events taking place in infinitesimal worlds within the body, though its colorful personifications and flurries of synesthesia do not succeed in doing so as well as Thomas's calm, sharp prose.

The image of the protozoa on pilgrimage is a strange one—
but then again, what takes place in the world visible only through
a microscope does have a surreal quality all its own. "The Origin of the Praise of God" represents the most extreme reach of
Bly's attempt to describe the movements of the spirit-in-the-body.
He inserts within this prose poem a small poem in lines:

> The sunlight lays itself down before the protozoa,
> the night opens itself out behind it,
> and inside its own energy it lives!

Between the light and the darkness stands the single living cell.
Here Bly stops just short—one cell short—of seeing the pure
energies themselves. The body is made up of these cells and it
too stands on a border where light meets darkness. It is the border on which Bly has seen man standing throughout his work,
envisioned in his poem on the most elemental level. Where else,
the poem asks, would our spiritual lives originate but far inside
the country of the body?: "My friend, this body is made of bone
and excited protozoa . . . and it is with my body that I love the
fields. How do I know what I feel but what the body tells me?"
Out of the spirit in the body rises the kinds of intelligence we
saw in "Finding the Father" and "Falling into Holes in Our Sentences." Out of the cells that make up the body rise man's spiritual ecstasies, longings, and songs:

> From the dance of the cells praise sentences rise to the throat of
> the man praying and singing alone in his room. He lets his arms
> climb above his head, and says, "Now do you still say you can-
> not choose the Road?"

If energy rising from the very cells of the body brings us to
praise and a sense of the Road, energy clogged inside it has the
opposite effect. This is the subject of "When the Wheel Does
Not Move." As the title suggests, when energy is blocked we
may feel as if life has ground to a halt. The energy in question

here is sexual, and the basic news the poem brings is not startling: desire that finds no outlet is a misery. Energy, in this case, is not Eternal Delight. Although extraordinary possibilities of diverting the pent-up flow into other channels are suggested by the examples of some saints and artists, this poem is concerned with the more common result: frustration and unhappiness. Bly goes beyond simple frustration, however, seeing the blocked eros both as spiritual barrier and the cause of a fundamental alienation from the stream of life.

> There is a dense energy that pools in the abdomen and wants to move and does not! It lies there fierce and nomadic, blocking the road, preventing anyone else from going by.
> When the sperm wants to move and does not, then it is as if the earth were not made for me at all, and I cannot walk with the cricket voyaging over his Gobi of wood chips; he is too free for me. I hear a howling in the air.

In poems such as "The Origin of the Praise of God" and "When the Wheel Does Not Move," as in all of *Gopherwood*, Bly is attempting to describe the body-energy-spirit nexus with immediacy and intensity, and he achieves, for all the poems' high-flown effects, an undeniable dynamism. We can feel energy flowing, rushing, swarming, knotting, whirling. A poem that contains a strong sense of motion and which describes the meeting of energy and flesh specifically is "Galloping Horses." The poem courts allegory. Horses and riders race across a plain and encounter obstacles: a line of fire, a stream, a crevice—"space stretched out sideways." Fire, water, air—the horses have met and swept past three of the ancient elements of creation. The fourth, earth, in the poem becomes flesh, appearing in the form of a garden full of animals:

> And the horses slow, they become confused among so many gentle animals, the riders look to the side and behind them, turning in their saddles to see the large animals peacefully grazing behind.

Bly capitalizes the word "Garden": what he is describing is not just *a* garden, but *the* garden. But instead of a fall from innocence and grace, we witness here a return to the Peaceable Kingdom. The arrival in the earthly garden of the body is disorienting to the saddled and driven horses of energy—we might translate them as aggressive or masculine will—and surprising to their riders. Sometimes when the racing horses slow, and wander bewildered or amazed among the mute, animal flesh of the body, it is as if we were again, for a time, unfallen, in The Garden once more.

"Galloping Horses," like a number of the poems in *Gopherwood*, has a dreamlike quality. Some deal with sleep and dream explicitly. "The Sleeper" offers a dream and a brief commentary upon it: the sleeper within the dream is offered a dulcimer but does not play it because he is "all withdrawn into himself"; the poem gives us the dreamer as the self-absorbed man in his purest form. "A Dream of What Is Missing" describes a dream that the poet might have had after spending an evening reading in Jung's *Psychological Types:* the poem is a sort of paraphrase of Jung's idea that there are four functions of consciousness—thinking, feeling, intuition, and sensation—and that greater wholeness comes through development of the weaker functions. The most resonant of the dream poems is "Snow Falling on Snow," which ends with this delicate and mysterious transcription:

> . . . thin feet come down the mountainside, hooves clatter over the wooden bridges, walk along the stone walls, and then pause, and look in at an orchard, where a fount of water is rising in the air. . . . Men are lying asleep all around its base, each with his sword lying under him. And the orchard-keeper, where is he?

The mood here is entirely different from that of "Galloping Horses," but once again horses and riders arrive at a garden, or orchard, and stop and look at its strange and peaceful beauty. We might take this dream as another arrival at the body. The fountain in the orchard suggests the peace that can sometimes be found in the body when the swords of "masculine consciousness," instruments of both quest and the sharp strokes of differentiation, are laid down for a time; it suggests also the psychic waters welling up in a dream within the sleeping body. And the missing orchard-keeper? If this reading of the dream is correct, he then would be the invisible one we know through his works, which include our bodies and the images that come to us in dreams.

Readers of *Gopherwood* will of course wonder about the identity of the "friend" Bly addresses directly in several of the poems. On one level the friend is the reader himself. But *Gopherwood* is part sermon but also part hymn of praise, and on this second level the friend is someone else. Charles Molesworth says of him, "the friend is not merely a rhetorical crutch . . . but the very deity made companionable. In other words, the friend is the savior, or us, or the savior-in-us, less a social force than a private, inner healer." [13] Another way of putting it would be to say that the friend is the unseen orchard-keeper, the mysterious maker whose life and art are witnessed through the orchard and the fountain he keeps.

The tradition of praise of the body is an ancient and fundamental one in poetry. It is a tradition that has flowered again among the poets of Bly's generation. A number of them have told us, in one way or another, that ours is a culture which, for all its unprecedented materialism, is far from possessing a true sense of the sacredness of matter and of the "portion of the Soul discern'd by the five Senses," the body. Denise Levertov, John Logan, Galway Kinnell, and Gary Snyder might be singled out as poets of that generation whose work has been especially strong in its praise of the body. At times the praise is explicit; more often it is implicit, expressed in the sensuousness of their description, their language, and of their very intelligence.

Bly belongs among this group and this tradition. In its ambition of praising the body *Gopherwood* is uncompromising and deeply characteristic of Bly. At times the praise has real radiance. In "Going Out to Check the Ewes" he writes:

> . . . . I get up, morning is here. The stars still out; black winter sky looms over the unborn lambs. The barn is cold before dawn, the gates slow. . . .
> This body longs for itself far out at sea, it floats in the black heavens, it is a brilliant being, locked in the prison of human dullness. . . .

The lights and darks are fine there, as is the sound, the play of o's, l's, m's, and b's, and the way the slow barn gates link with those of the prison. Two passages, one realistic, one visionary, come together to communicate the darkly shining life of the body. As the gates in the barn open in the dark, starry morning, we know that the doors of the prison of human dullness can be opened as well.

It is one of Bly's special gifts in his poetry that he is able to open just those doors—to give a deep sense of being alive, not dull, in a body in the world. But although *Gopherwood* is the book in which he celebrates the body most explicitly and concertedly, for the most part it is not here that he best demonstrates this gift. Sermon, treatise, and hymn to the body as "brilliant being," as ark of energies, as possessor of mysterious wisdom and common sense, as garden, *Gopherwood* is a unique and unguarded performance. But it seems to me Bly's least successful book. In the face of language and emotion that are often too insistent and overwrought, the body itself seems not at ease enough simply to walk across a field or along a shore; only sporadically in these poems, I think, does the body find its elemental freedom and tongue.

CHAPTER 7

This Tree Will Be Here for a Thousand Years and The Man in the Black Coat Turns

> My father's labor who sees? It
> is in a pasture somewhere not yet
> found by a walker.
> —"Finding an Old Ant Mansion"

When an interviewer asked him, in 1971, "Why did you leave the *Snowy Fields?*" Bly replied: "I write what you call 'snowy fields' poems without pause, maybe eight or nine a year. They gradually come along."[1] In 1975 he published with the Unicorn Press a group of twenty poems with rural subject matter and a spare style under the title *Old Man Rubbing His Eyes*. In 1979 he added to that group twenty-four more poems in the same mode and brought out with Harper & Row *This Tree Will Be Here For a Thousand Years*. In an introductory note he suggested that "These poems . . . form a volume to be added to *Snowy Fields;* the two books make one book."[2] Those who find, as I do, the unity of *Snowy Fields* to be one of its key powers will want to resist that suggestion. To combine the two books would not only disrupt that unity but would dilute the impact of *Snowy Fields* as well. *Tree* is a noticeably slighter book. Its poems are often lovely, and sometimes more than that, but it does not strike as deep or true as *Snowy Fields*. Something is missing. I think that something is primarily the sense of things "obeying what is beneath them" ("Night," *Snowy Fields*). That is, Bly has not been as successful in tapping the unconscious sources as he was in *Snowy Fields*. Also, the motif of the journey is not present here, and the Minnesota landscape is neither as solid nor as resonant in *Tree* as it was in the first book. Though *Tree* is another collection of spare, rural poems, it seems unlikely that it would have had *Snowy Fields'* unique and powerful impact on American poetry if it had been published in its place in 1962.

Tree provided the occasion for probably the most vitriolic review that Bly has received—something of a landmark in the career of a poet with a special gift for evoking polarized reactions. The review, written by Eliot Weinberger for *The Nation*, was not limited to *Tree* but attacked Bly's work and influence as a whole.[3] Beyond the fact that it represents one extreme of opinion, Weinberger's piece is also worth noting in that it can serve as a kind of primer of how Bly's work is likely to be oversimplified and distorted by those hostile to his ends, means, or personality. To say that Bly has "dismissed most of the North American masters (Pound, Williams, Eliot, et al.)," or that he believes simply that masculine energy is destructive, is only to express understandable but superficial impressions. Weinberger does identify aspects of Bly's work that are problematical: e.g., his attempt to reclaim the exclamatory; his radical trust in association; his way of speaking of the natural world in human terms. But Bly's weaknesses and strengths often lie close together. If his exclamatory impulse sometimes has led to melodrama, it has also brought the freshness and life of open joy and anger into his work, valuable especially in a poetic landscape in which careful modulation and understatement remain the dominant tendencies. If his trust in association sometimes results in skeins of images that seem manic or arbitrary, his work with images and association has helped to give his poetry an extraordinary psychic and sensory richness, embodying consistently a simple truth: the rational intelligence is not the only intelligence. And if Bly sometimes assumes too much oneness in his contemplation of the nonhuman universe, the absence of the assumption that man exists apart from nature, cut off at the end of the process that produced him and surrounded by dead matter and irrelevant "lower animals," has allowed him to write, throughout his poetry, a unique and marvelous meditation on the mysteriously circling and interpenetrating worlds of earth, plants, animals, and man. Weinberger sees none of this complexity, or at least does not acknowledge it.

Hayden Carruth, who in reading *The Light Around the Body* found himself "wishing it were poetry," and who dismissed the ideas Bly puts forth in his introduction to *Tree* about the possibility of finding a union between human consciousness and a consciousness in the nonhuman world as "Swedenborgian nonsense, very dangerous," nevertheless went on in his review to say this:

> Bly writes against my grain, yet in some poems he catches me, and I am not off my guard. "Sometimes when you put your hand into a hollow tree/ you touch the dark places between the stars." Not many of Bly's readers have done that, I imagine, but I am a country poet, like him, and I *have* done it. I'm damned if he isn't right. I pull back. Sometimes it is good, better than good, to guard oneself and still be caught.[4]

(Weinberger, it happens, also refers to these lines. To him, however, they are "a remark that might be charming if uttered by a 6-year-old.")

Such intuitive moments as the one Carruth cites are perhaps the principal reward of *Tree*. Often they appear within the religious references that Bly is very much at ease with here, and uses gracefully and with a delicate humor. In "Fishing on a Lake at Night" he describes a light left on in a boathouse, seen from out on the lake: "And the light/ simply comes, bearing no gifts,/ as if the camels had arrived without the Wise Men." In "Fall Poem" a few physical details—wisps of grass, the eyes of a rooster, boards left out in the weather—give him a sense that in the sharpened atmosphere of autumn some revelation is at hand. He says, "Something is about to happen!/ Christ will return!," and then adds, laconically, not exactly disappointed, "But each fall it goes by without happening." Both of these passages express well Bly's sense of the steadiness of the natural world, sufficient unto itself, indifferent to human longings and meanings but not irrelevant to them. In "A Walk" Bly sketches a tree, a shoot a rabbit has chewed, a grove of pines ("somber,/ made for winter, they knew it would come"), and then thinks of the cows in the barn:

> And the cows inside the barn, caring nothing for all this,
> their noses in the incense hay,
> half-drunk, dusk comes as it was promised
> to them by *their* savior.

As he did many times in *The Morning Glory*, Bly once again expresses our distance from the animals, yet in doing so he brings us closer to them. It is as if he understands the significance of Christ being born among animals but can't spell it out in so many words, or doesn't want to. Instead he lets the reader feel that understanding in poem after poem.

If one thinks of *Tree*, as Bly suggested, as a sort of annex to *Snowy Fields*, it seems a paler, lighter sequel to a strikingly original book. Actually, if we wish to see it in relation to Bly's other work, *Tree* is interesting more for some of its differences from *Snowy Fields* than its resemblances, and for the signs it contains of developments that were still to come. First and most significant is the way in which death appears in these poems. Death was evoked repeatedly in *Snowy Fields*, but except in "At the Funeral of Great-Aunt Mary" it was more or less impersonal, and it was likely to appear as "the sea of death" plunged into in solitude ("Return to Solitude") or "the death we love," a powerful transforming force but one that is pervasive rather than particular ("With Pale Women in Maryland"). In *Snowy Fields*, published when Bly was thirty-six, death was as much metaphor as mortality. In *The Morning Glory* he wrote of the deaths of animals and dealt, in "Christmas Eve Service at Midnight at St. Michael's," with the death of his only brother. In the poems collected in *Tree* we again see death becoming more literal and more personal. Bly turns toward his own death, and the deaths of people near him. This turning would be crucial in bringing him into a new phase in his poetry.

Thoughts of death arise in many of the poems in *Tree*. In "Writing Again" Bly gives an impressionistic description of writing "of moral things," and then ends abruptly with these lines: "Well that is how I have spent this day./ And what good will it do me in the grave?" A tiny poem, "Roads," is an elegy in images, perhaps written for the poet's brother. In "Passing an Orchard by Train" he thinks of the vulnerability of human beings—"One slight bruise and we die!" (he may have been thinking of *The Death of Ivan Ilich*)—and suddenly feels moved to tell a stranger walking down the aisle that he forgives him, and to ask for the stranger's forgiveness in return. The poem is pared very thin, but the pattern is a basic one: the awareness of mortality is the first step toward compassion and reconciliation. In "Prayer Service in an English Church" the sight of an hallucinatory "ghostly knot" in a page of the psalm book, the priest's call for the savior to come again, and the singing of old people standing nearby, combine to create a reverie which leads to a sudden and piercing vision of "the last day . . . / the whispers we will make from the darkening pillow . . ." And in "A Long Walk Before the Snows Began,"[5] the poet wanders across winter fields, the dead cornstalks "knocked flat." He sees the tracks of animals who have walked in these same places, and feels a connection between them and himself: "I am walking with an immense deer./ He passed three days ago." These intimations of time finally precipitate another sudden, vivid vision of death:

> It must be that I will die one day!
> I see my body lying stretched out.
> A woman whose face I cannot see stands near my body.
> A column of smoke rises from Vonderharr's field.

It may have been that column of smoke that was the catalyst which drew the imagined scene out of the mood of the walk. The poet may have felt in it an association with the funeral pyre, sensed that in its looming silence, still in the distance but within sight now, the smoke was like death itself. However that may be, the use of the specific name Vonderharr is a marvelous touch here. With its heavy, sonorous, earthbound quality, it counterpoints the image of the narrow, rising smoke, which resembles a column but also a road. One can feel in the juxtaposition of the name and the image the double knowledge we live with: that our lives, which carry particular names and identities, are as real and substantial as the earth we walk on, but will someday disappear like smoke.

To thoughts and premonitions of death another element is added. Bly's growing consciousness of death does not derive solely from the fact that he himself is growing older. The death of his brother must have had a strong effect on him, and it becomes evident in two poems in *Tree* that the advancing age of his parents has affected him as well. In "Driving My Parents Home at Christmas" he observes his mother and father as they sit with him in the car, and says, "their frailty hesitates on the edge of a mountainside." He is struck not only by the frailty but also the distance of old age: "I call over the cliff,/ only snow answers." Those who live on that mountainside inhabit another place, partly hidden by the quiet, white falling of the snow; those who have not yet arrived there can only call out across the space between. The mother and father, meanwhile, sit close to one another, "as if pressed together by snow." When the poet watches them go into their house and "disappear," it is clear that he is very much aware that they will soon disappear through a different door.

A four-line poem called "Late Moon" expresses the awareness of death in connection with a parent more obliquely. Like many of Bly's tiny poems, it describes a glimpse of hidden knowledge or feeling, the moment held within a spare configuration of images. The poet observes the waning moon, "half of it dark now, in the west that eats it away," casting its light over his father's farm. The juxtaposition contains a dimly-lit awareness that the father will die; the phrase "eats it away" suggests that he may already be afflicted. (Bly confirms the premonitory nature of the phrase. He dates the poem from 1973; his father was diagnosed as having cancer of the lung in 1974.) Then follows a statement that seems an irrelevancy, interesting but arbitrary: "The earth has rocks in it that hum at early dawn." The poem would, I think, be purer and sharper without this line. Yet it is not merely an odd, floating detail, and is connected to the rest of the poem by certain threads of association. The rocks, buried in the earth, make a link to death, the knowledge of which sometimes comes starkly and unmistakably, but more often exists inside us as a kind of background hum. (In "Sitting on Some Rocks in Shaw Cove, California," in *The Morning Glory*, Bly compared death to "the sound of the motor in an airplane as we fly, the sound so steady and comforting.") In the first three lines of "Late Moon" the poet is noticing that hum. Thoughts and feelings are nearby, but still submerged, indistinct.

Like "Driving My Parents Home at Christmas," "Late Moon" contains a doorway. In "Late Moon," however, the poet does not watch someone going through the door but rather has an unexpected encounter there: "As I turn to go in, I see my shadow reach for the latch." The suddenly appearing image of the shadow will jump out at the reader aware of Bly's study of Jung and his use of the shadow in "Sleepers Joining Hands." But of course the shadow's association with death is at least as old in the psyche as its association with a hidden part of the personality, elaborated upon by Jung. Both of these associations are at work in the poem. As a son realizes, with new depth and immediacy, that his father will die, his sense of his own mortality deepens as well: it is elders, and parents especially, who stand between us and death. At the same time the son will likely feel a closeness to his father he had not known before, and in that opening of feeling he encounters a part of himself which had been hidden to him.

The turning described in "Late Moon" can be taken to stand for Bly's turning toward the new phase I've mentioned. In this tiny poem mortality and the father loom together within the poet's consciousness, and bring him to a door. The shadow he meets there is not only the shadow of death but the shadow of his relationship with his father. After twenty years of celebration of the feminine, it was this relationship that would become the focus of his next book, published in 1981, *The Man In the Black Coat Turns*. Thinking of the resonant landscapes of *Snowy Fields* and the more acute consciousness of mortality in poems scattered throughout *Tree*, we can make a generalization: if it was Mother Nature that helped Bly on his journey toward the feminine, the Mother, it was Father Time that brought him to the father.

But when Bly wrote about the feminine and the Mother, it was psychic forces he was dealing with. He was finding ways of talking about kinds of consciousness; individualized, flesh and blood women were even scarcer in his work than men. But in *Black Coat* it is not just *the Father* but *his father* that he focuses on. In discussing *The Light Around the Body* I said that Bly's attention in his poetry has been weak in "the middle ground"— the ground of ordinary human lives and fundamental human relationships. He had been a poet of fields, lakes, and trees, and of what they can draw forth from the man among them in solitude. He had been a poet of the political, historical, and psychic life of his country; of the soul's journey; of animals, ordinary objects, and the body. But he had not, before he was about fifty years old, dealt much with the ground of human relationship. In *Black Coat* he makes a concerted effort to do so. He still reaches out beyond the personal and the particular: *Black Coat* is in large part an extended meditation on the masculine soul, on wounds that are not only his or his father's but are shared by many men; it is the irrepressible nature of Bly's mind to do so. But at the center of this meditation stands the distinct and memorable figure of the poet's own father.

Before examining this figure, however, there are some other aspects of *Black Coat* that should be commented on. The first is its mood and emotional weight. The book contains just twenty-four poems, but it has the feel of a substantial, major collection. This is due not to the fact that many of the poems are somewhat longer than had been usual for Bly, but to their seriousness and emotional density. In tone *Black Coat* is Bly's most somber book since *The Light*. A sober and reflective mood prevails, and except in a few cases, the kinetic and dazzling effects of Bly's more excitable style, and the ecstasies which sometimes seem aggressive, have been avoided. In *Gopherwood* a fountain bubbled over; here the waters flow quietly. In one poem, "My Father's Wedding," Bly says of himself, "I learned to walk swiftly, easily,/ no trace of a limp./ I even leaped a little." We have seen that ecstasy and grief make up one of the principal dialectics at work throughout Bly's poetry; as he wrote in "Wanting to Experience All Things," in *The Light*, "The heart leaps/ Almost up to the sky! But laments/ And filaments pull us back into the darkness." In *Black Coat* it is the downward motion of the spirit that Bly is dealing with, and honoring. The gravity is not that of anguish and moral outrage, as during a Vietnam War, but of a quiet, steady awareness that human lives and ties are so easily and often broken. The book's title comes from a line in its opening poem, "Snowbanks North of the House," which is a catalogue of breakdowns, losses, and failures human life is heir to: it serves as a sort of invocation of grief. And the heightened consciousness or mortality which I've spoken of is strong in the book, and lends its weight as well.

If Bly is not "leaping" in terms of emotion in *Black Coat*, the same can be said for his use of association. There are poems here—"Kennedy's Inauguration," "What the Fox Agreed to Do," "A Sacrifice in the Orchard"—written in Bly's wilder surrealistic, leaping style, but leaping does not seem the right term for the poems that are most characteristic of *Black Coat*. There are striking disjunctures in the flow of thought, but there is also the contemplative tone and at times a discursive manner that make the shifts feel more like juxtapositions than leaps. In such poems as "The Prodigal Son," "The Grief of Men," "Fifty Males Sitting Together," and "Crazy Carlson's Meadow," distinct sets of images are poised against one another, and the meaning of the poem lies largely in the interplay among them. These poems are configurations of parts that form a unity, but not the sort of unity that yields readily to paraphrase. In them, Bly achieves a remarkable richness of idea and emotion.

At the same time that Bly has calmed and darkened his

tone, and added tension to his associative style, he has also started
to work more deliberately with the formal aspect of the poem
than he had in any of his previous books. The middle section of
Black Coat is made up of prose poems, but many of the other
poems have been shaped with obvious care into regular stanzas.
The stanzas are of Bly's own devising, roughly syllabic; he still
does not acquiesce to forms handed down by tradition. The jacket
note tells us that "some of the poems . . . began as prose poems,
then were recast into continuous lines, then recast a third time
into stanzas"—a slow, highly conscious process, particularly for
a poet who had asserted earlier that "in the true poem, both the
form and the content arise from the same place; they have the
same swiftness and darkness." But as I mentioned earlier in connection with *Sleepers Joining Hands*, as the 1980s began Bly was
making a different sort of statement in his essays:

> I have been thinking that we have not been very faithful servants
> of art. . . . By "we" I mean the poets of my generation. We have
> been lively and fierce servants, but was it of art? Or was it of art
> but not the work of art?[6]

> . . . we think of the flow of creativity after reading Whitman
> rather than the shape and weight of a jar. . . . All artists love
> art, but we miss sometimes in Whitman reminders of what a
> triumph the intensely worked poem can be. . . .[7]

In the poems in regular stanzas in *Black Coat* we see Bly laboring
to become more of a servant, as he puts it, of the work of art,
of "the intensely worked poem"; laboring to become more of a
maker. He would no longer say, as he did in 1962, "Impersonal
poets construct; great poets merely are sensitive."[8]

One other aspect should be noted: *Black Coat* is considerably allusive. There are important biblical references, and figures
such as Heraclitus, Pythagoras, and Descartes, Osiris and Odin,
make brief but significant appearances. Bly's allusiveness is not

nearly as extreme as Eliot's or Pound's, but it springs from a common desire: to recover the past and make it useful. The source most in evidence in *Black Coat* is the fairy tale. Bly entered the study of fairy tales through Jung, beginning in the early 1970s, and it has been a major phase of his activities since. He has lectured widely on the subject, sometimes includes the telling of a story in his readings, and in 1981 he began work on a book-length study of classic fairy tales as they apply to men— a project clearly related to the themes of *Black Coat*. To Bly the fairy tale represents an especially useful past. Let me quote a passage from Padraic Colum's introduction to *The Complete Grimm's Fairy Tales:*

> We have another past besides the past that history tells us about, a past which is in us, in individuals, more livingly than the recorded past. It is a past in which men slowly arrived at self-consciousness while building up the community, the arts and the laws. Today we have advanced poets and novelists who are trying to find means to suggest the unrecorded past in our memories and in our attitudes and so give their work another dimension. Well, it is this long past, the past that merges with the time when men were comradely with the animals and personalized the powers of nature that comes to us in these and other traditional stories. With it certain things are restored to our imagination.[9]

The recorded and the unrecorded past are both strong presences in *Black Coat*, and the evolution of human consciousness has been a major theme in Bly's work since cave references first appeared in some of his earliest poems.

Having made these general comments about *Black Coat*, we can turn again to the subject of the father. Bly's father had appeared fleetingly in Bly's earlier work. In addition to the references in *Tree*, he was mentioned in "Sleepers Joining Hands." There was a glimpse of "the chaff blowing about my father's feet," and these ominous lines: "I fall into my own hands,/ fences break down under horses,/ cities starve, whole towns of singing women carrying to the burial fields/ the look I saw on my father's face." Most revealing is a simple statement that occurs within the "Water Drawn Up Into the Head" section. As he tells of having entered "the curved energy," Bly says, "That is why I have become a stranger to my father." So we begin with the knowledge that some fundamental estrangement has afflicted the relationship between Bly and his father.

Then in *Gopherwood* there was the poem called "Finding the Father," in which the father was a man "whom we have never met," who was lost in a snowstorm on the night of his child's birth, lost his memory, and has lived a life of wandering and work at lowly jobs ever since. When he is at last found again, this is how he appears: "He sits there behind the door . . . the eyebrows so heavy, the forehead so light . . . lonely in his whole body, waiting for you." The father here is a mythic presence, partly drawn from the world of fairy tales, partly from some good 1940s movie. He is drawn also, however, from the poet's own father, as can be recognized when we turn to the portrait Bly draws of him in *Black Coat*. What we recognize is a heaviness that is connected with both strength and vulnerability, and a sense of distance and loneliness that belongs to the son as well as to the father.

There is another antecedent to the *Black Coat* portrait, however, which is of special importance—which is in fact an invaluable companion piece to this book and to Bly's poetry in general. In 1976 the University of Minnesota Press published a collection of autobiographical essays called *Growing Up In Minnesota: Ten Writers Remember Their Childhoods*.[10] Bly's contribution was "Being a Lutheran Boy-God in Minnesota," a piece which can stand among the best of his writing. It celebrates the life on the farms of an earlier day, praising the farm culture especially for the respect it accorded physical work—the loss of which Bly sees as a key breakdown in modern culture. The descriptions Bly gives of farm work scant the drudgery, but they have great vividness and exhilaration: certain passages do for the remembrance of work something comparable to what Dylan Thomas did for memories of childhood leisure in "Fern Hill." Woven through the essay are two character sketches: Bly's description of himself, which includes discussion of the psychological type he refers to as "the boy-god";[11] and a portrait of his father, who emerges not as a god but as a decidedly heroic figure, the carrier of noble and adult values.

"Being a Lutheran Boy-God in Minnesota" does not merely supplement *Black Coat;* it complements it. The essay is joyous where the poems are somber and meditative, and this contrast is especially noticeable in their portrayals of the father. In the essay the father comes across as a man of great strength and integrity—in short, of wholeness. In the poems, while he is still heroic, we hear also of his "invisible limp," his isolation, and some of the pain and distance that are part of the relationship between father and son. In one poem, "Fifty Males Sitting Together," we hear of a husband and father who comes home late and drunk; in another, "My Father's Wedding," the father is associated with pig noses, dog teeth, and "doing what you want." The essay is radiant; the poems bring out more of the dark. There is a fascinating interplay of images between the two. In the essay the father's silences and stubbornness are seen as independence, staunchness:

> At church he kept his arms crossed over his chest. He had the sturdiest respect, grained and unplaned, for some men and women; when others were mentioned, you were astounded to find out how little he thought of them. A brooding secretly lifted the short sentences he said. And he stubbornly refused to be carried away on easy judgments that serve to bind a company together and resemble stones bouncing over the surface of the water. He preferred weight, even if the stone sank all the way to the bottom.[12]

That final image finds a strange variant in the final stanza of "A
Meditation on Philosophy":

> Last night I dreamt that my father
> was an enormous turtle—the eyes open—
> lying on the basement floor.
> The weight of his shell kept him from moving.
> His jaw hung down—it was large and fleshly.

In "Snowbanks North of the House," "the man in the black
coat," who "turns, and goes back down the hill," is the climactic
figure in the poem's catalogue of images of loss and separation.
In the essay we first see the father "wearing a large black coat
stand[ing] near the windmill." [13] A few sentences later Bly says
that his father's intense and decisive nature "did not bring him
more company, but did carry the burdens higher up the mountain." The essay opens with the image of an old milk wagon that
had been used by an uncle, who had suffered "some disaster";
the wagon "stood there floating, pale, deserted by human
beings." [14] In "The Grief of Men" we hear of an uncle who was
shattered by his wife's death in childbirth, and at the beginning
of "My Father's Wedding" the poet, "lonely for [his] father,"
sees a dead branch and says, "it was the log/ that lay near my
uncle's old milk wagon."

   This stitching of cross-references accents the complexity of
the feelings about the father expressed in the poems. In the essay Bly tells the story of an incident in which a hired man was
saved from an unjust prison sentence through his father's de-
cency and concern. This incident taught Bly "that the indignation of the solitary man is the stone pin that connects this world
to the next"; and he says simply, "To be able to respect your
father is such a beautiful thing!" [15] That respect remains when
Bly comes to write the poems in *Black Coat*. But in them there
is also a considerable amount of pain that clearly goes a long

way back in the relationship. It is the pain of distance and of a
longing for reconciliation. The key poems for this theme are
"My Father's Wedding" and "The Prodigal Son."

"My Father's Wedding" begins with a straightforward
statement of loneliness for the father. It then shifts to four discursive stanzas on the need to acknowledge the crippled and the
primitive aspects of ourselves. Bly accuses himself of having failed
to make such an acknowledgment: "I grew up without dogs'
teeth,/ showed a whole body,/ left only clear tracks in sand."
This revelation is an important one, but I think it belongs in
another poem. In these stanzas Bly expounds colorfully on certain psychological ideas pertinent to his father and himself, but
"My Father's Wedding" could exist very well without them, and
it is hard not to feel that this discursive digression damages the
poem's dramatic and emotional effect. Once Bly returns to the
father and describes the wedding scene, in the sixth stanza, his
words take on great power, and we only regret that it took so
long to arrive again at the organic body of the poem.

The poem carries as a subtitle the date "1924": in short, the
scene it describes takes place two years before the person describing it was born. But it is an imagined scene in more than
that, for what the poem portrays is a reality that existed beyond
or inside the wedding that took place in the visible world on
that day in 1924. The "invisible limps" the earlier stanzas talked
about are here plainly visible, as is an invisible bride who steps
forward before the actual bride and whom the father in fact
marries. The poem's rendering of the scene is beautifully drawn;
it is like a dream powerful enough to be remembered for a lifetime. It is also eloquent, particularly where it comments directly
on the father:

> On my father's wedding day,
> no one was there
> to hold him. Noble loneliness

held him. Since he never asked for pity
his friends thought he
was whole. Walking alone, he could carry it.

. . . .

. . . He already had
his barklike skin then,
made rough especially to repel the sympathy
he longed for, didn't need, and wouldn't accept.

The invisible bride is not only a strange figure but an ominous one. In her left breast she carries "the three drops/ that wound and kill." The inspiration for this image is apparently the fairy tale "Faithful John." [16] Bly does not borrow the image merely because it is striking; the story has relevance to the poem. Faithful John is just what his name says he is: loyal, steadfast, willing to make sacrifices. In this he bears a fundamental resemblance to the picture of the father we have seen emerging. Faithful John is a king's servant, and he helps his master to gain what he desires and to avoid disaster a number of times. Finally, at the king's wedding the bride collapses, and would die, but Faithful John quickly carries her to her room and sucks three drops from her breast. As a result the bride recovers, but Faithful John is turned to stone.

The bridegroom in the poem, however, has no one to stand in for him to suck out the poison. His solitariness is emphasized throughout: he is his own Faithful John. Though the poem says that "he already had/ his barklike skin then," it seems reasonable to see the allusion to the story as suggesting that the father is a man whose strength, solidity, and independence turn him, not to stone, but to wood. In this poem and elsewhere, Bly consistently associates his father with trees and wood in one form or another. "My Father's Wedding" begins, it will be recalled, with that association: "Today, lonely for my father, I saw/ a log, or branch,/ long, bent, ragged, bark gone." As an image of a man's

character, wood contains both praise—"He had the sturdiest respect, grained and unplaned, for some men and women"—and
something other than praise.

The ceremony is performed: the minister or justice of the
peace—another man in black—"speaks the sentence." "Sentence" refers of course to "I now pronounce you . . . ," but it
unmistakably suggests as well a man being sentenced to a pun-
ishment. Long confinement and hard labor are not irrelevant associations with regard to marriage, either literal marriage or the
inward marriage that is the true subject here. What does it mean
to be married to the invisible bride? It was drops of blood that
Faithful John sucked out of the bride's breast. Swallowing blood
and being turned to stone, or wood, suggests feeling held inside,
feeling swallowed. We know from the "Boy-God" essay that the
father "had a gift for deep feeling," and we know from the poem
that he longed for sympathy but would not accept it. The feeling is there, but certain kinds of feeling are not expressed: his
own pain he keeps to himself. When the service is over, the son
holds his father in his arms "for the first time and the last." The
ache of loneliness and alienation of many years, the ache of the
longing for tenderness and intimacy, is contained in that embrace. The father is a man of strength and dignity, and of deep
feeling, but he and his son will never embrace again.

Bly is describing in this poem the situation of "the strong
male" whose strength involves stoic loneliness. He regards such
a man with compassion and respect, and not only because the
person described is his own father. But the father-son relationship is central to the poem, and he expresses what it is like to
be the son of such a man, first in that single embrace which
takes place in the invisible world, and then in the stark yet rich
image with which he ends the poem. Here is the poem's final
stanza:

After that he was alone
and I was alone.
No friends came; he invited none.
His two-story house he turned
into a forest,
where both he and I are the hunters.

The ambiguity of the last three lines is purposeful. The image contains terror; that forest is clearly a place where Oedipal rituals might be enacted, like the forest in Hawthorne's "Reuben Bourne," one hunter unconsciously stalking another. But the imagery of forest and hunters carries other suggestions as well. If a house that is turned into a forest is not entirely safe or comfortable, neither is it barren. In another poem ("For My Son Noah, Ten Years Old"), which describes moments of a kind of tenderness and openness between father and son that apparently were lacking in his relationship with his own father, Bly says, "what is primitive is not to be shot out into the night and the dark." A man with less fierceness, less strength and feeling, would not be capable of turning a house into a forest. This father kept something primitive alive. The son feels a darkness in the father that is both frightening and vital. We can assume from the poem's emphasis on loneliness and walking alone that these are solitary hunters, yet associations of initiation are also present. The image of hunters is rich in associations, including violence, seeking, hunger, loneliness, and strength. Bly wants us to feel all of these associations, for the relationship he is describing involves all of these elements. "My Father's Wedding" is emotionally complex, but one does not smooth over the complexity or pain of the poem in saying that, ultimately, it is a love poem.

The same can be said of "The Prodigal Son," another poem which deals directly with separation from the father and the longing for reconciliation. This poem is an outstanding example of the associative method I spoke of earlier, in which the disjunctures of thought feel more like juxtapositions than leaps. The title refers us immediately to the well-known parable of Jesus (Luke 15:11–32), but Bly adds to this basic reference other elements which complicate and personalize the poem's meditation on fathers and sons.

As the poem opens we see the Prodigal Son "kneeling in the husks." In terms of the parable, he has already left his father and squandered his inheritance, and has been reduced to the life of a swineherd. He longs to return: when he folds his hands in penitence, he has a vision of "father beyond father beyond father." The swine, meanwhile, continue to feed in the sunlight, unconcerned about human exile and remorse. Then a different scene is set before us: an old man and his son in the midst of a wild argument, the son physically dragging the father across the room. The old man cries out, "Don't drag me any farther than that crack on the floor—/ I only dragged my father that far!" The mood here is a far different thing from the hush that surrounds the Prodigal Son and the swine, but the passage brings in more than new emotion. The old man's cry adds two ideas as well: that the conflict or alienation between father and son is enacted in every generation, and that there are limits or boundaries that must not be violated in the struggle. The selfishness of the Prodigal Son and the anger of the son dragging his father across the floor are both great, but there is a deeper bond that can survive them. Once broken, however, it may never heal.

We do not find out whether that son dragged his father beyond the crack, but the rest of the poem takes place where reconciliation and healing are still possible. The Prodigal Son in the parable was reunited with his father, and in the poem we see him yearning to return. When he was kneeling among the husks he thought of a dying man who cried out, "Don't let me die, Doctor!" This sounds a note that is heard also in the cry of the old man being dragged—a note of urgency and vulnerability. There is an echo of this note as well in the poem's final stanza, where the poem turns to another father, the poet's own: "My father is seventy-five years old./ How difficult it is,/ bending the head, looking into the water." Time is running out. The length of the father's lifetime is another boundary that must be observed, his death a crack in the floor beyond which no reconciliation takes place. Once again, the awareness of mortality is connected with a longing for reconciliation and the return to the father. When Bly says, "How difficult it is . . . ," he is expressing the difficulty of that return. At the same time, looking into the water is looking into the psyche. At an earlier stage the son—Bly, or any other son—would not have thought that the inward search would involve a return to his father. Now he realizes that the journey into his own life and the return to the father are deeply intertwined.

When "The Prodigal Son" was first published, in *The New Republic*,[17] its final line read: "What we cannot solve is expressed by the swine." What we cannot solve is probably death itself, which might well be expressed by such mortal earthly creatures as pigs, which do in fact have ancient associations with death. But we can feel Bly groping here, reaching for a meaning he is not yet sure of himself. It is as if he knew that the swine had a further role to play, but he did not know fully what the role was. That feeling of reaching to grasp emotions and insights that are both complex and only newly emerging into consciousness is present in a number of poems in *Black Coat*—and it is not necessarily an undesirable effect at all. But that line was a weak ending, and in *Black Coat* Bly has replaced it with a line that is far sharper and stronger: "Under the water there's a door the pigs have gone through." I believe that to understand it we should refer to another story from the New Testament, linked to the poem through the image of swine disappearing in water.

The story is that of Jesus' curing of the demoniacs, recorded in Matthew 8:28–32. The demoniacs are cured when Jesus makes the demons that possess them leave their bodies and go into a herd of swine feeding in the distance. When this happens the pigs go mad and rush off a cliff into the sea. The mysterious image of the poem's last line makes a strong echo of this story. Like the story, the poem concerns a casting out of demons—but not the demons of insanity. In a sense, the heedlessness and selfishness of the Prodigal Son and the anger of the fight between the shouting son and father are both forms of possession. In these terms, "The Prodigal Son" deals with the casting out of the demons of self-absorption, antagonism, and alienation. At this point a glance back at "Being a Lutheran Boy-God in Minnesota" becomes useful.

In characterizing boy-gods Bly says, "They are boys, and yet they feel somehow eternal, out of the stream of life, they float above it." The boy-god "is just not sensitive enough to any heavy object outside himself," including human beings. Bly says of his own boy-godness, "This embodied itself in a sense that I was 'special,' and so in a general lack of compassion for others. If someone were suffering, or in a rage, I would feel myself pull away, into some safe area, where I did not 'descend' to those emotions. . . ." He adds, "How high I was all through high school! What a terrible longing to come down!"[18] Much of Bly's poetry can be read as a record of a long effort to "come down." The attention to "low places" and the ordinary earth of his native place in *Snowy Fields*, his conscious work on "objects outside himself" in *The Morning Glory*, his praise of grief in *The Light* and *Black Coat*, all reflect that effort. In my opinion his poetry is strongest where the effort is most evident.

If I am correct in seeing "The Prodigal Son" as a poem about a kind of exorcism, the "demons" in question are tendencies related to the boy-god. The healing, or descent, entails acknowledgment of one's own poverty and grief ("The Prodigal Son is kneeling in the husks") and an intimate recognition of mortality that connects one to the flow of living and dying ("My father is seventy-five years old"). When these things occur the demons of arrogance and detachment begin to leave.

Animals have been important to Bly throughout his poetry for the purity and wholeness of their earthly existence, and it is appropriate that they appear again now. The pigs, creatures that live and die, that feed in the sunlight and go through the door, are the antithesis of the boy-god, who feels "somehow eternal, out of the stream of life." In "The Prodigal Son," as in the story of the demoniacs, it is these animals who carry away the demons. But as we have seen in "My Father's Wedding," and as we see in other poems in *Black Coat* and in the "Boy-God" essay, the father too, in his human heaviness and mortality, is the opposite of one who "floats above it." "He preferred weight, even if the stone sank all the way to the bottom." So while "The Prodigal Son" is about the possibility of reconciliation with the father, it is not only the healing of the relationship that is involved. For Bly, contemplation of his father is involved with an effort to heal a wound within his own soul as well.

The metaphor of the exorcism should not be taken to suggest that the reconciliation and healing that are yearned for, and worked toward, in *Black Coat* take place quickly or magically. Throughout the book it is perseverance and long labor that are affirmed, largely through the character of the father. That a man should write a prodigal son poem, a poem about casting out boy-god demons, in middle age is not surprising, for the healings described may take a long time, and no doubt usually do. An awareness of the long journey toward wholeness is present in the poem that immediately precedes "The Prodigal Son," "For My Son Noah, Ten Years Old," though there it is felt in the tenderness the poet feels in a relationship that has not yet been seriously torn. The ten-year-old boy is also still basically whole. He sits "coloring a man with fire coming out of his hair." A composed wildness and spontaneity is still possible to him; "what is primitive" has not yet been exiled from his personality, not "shot out into the night and the dark." The poet treasures the wholeness of the son, and the wholeness they share: "So I am proud only of those days that pass in *undivided* tenderness . . ."; ". . . we sit at a table, with small tea carefully poured./ So we pass our time *together*, calm and delighted" (italics mine). The poet's experience of exile and separation described in "My Father's Wedding" and "The Prodigal Son" stands behind the quiet gratitude of those lines.

In "My Father's Wedding" and "The Prodigal Son" Bly writes as a son. In "For My Son Noah, Ten Years Old," he writes as a father, though his own father is in a way present there too, in the imagery of wood in the opening stanza: "The lumber pile does not grow younger, nor the two-by-fours lose their darkness, but the old tree goes on, the barn stands without help so many years." In other poems his contemplation of the male soul is not linked explicitly to his own father-son relationships. In his earlier poetry Bly had described the male soul (e.g., "A Man Writes to a Part of Himself") or the masculine principle (e.g., "The Busy Man Speaks") damaged by being cut off from the feminine. Now he describes something else: a loss of feeling is still involved, but now it is feeling wedded to conviction, purpose, intensity, and sacrifice. In "A Meditation on Philosophy" he comments, "After Heraclitus dies,/ the males sink down to apathy,/ to not-suffering./ When you shout at them, they don't reply./ They turn their face toward the crib wall, and die." In "Fifty Males Sitting Together" he gives another description of the boy-god, and says, "He lives thousands of years ago. He does not *know*/ what he should give, as herds slowly/ pass the cave mouth,/ what the world *wants* from him. . . . / . . . how far he lives/ from working men!" And in "Crazy Carlson's Meadow," a meadow cleared through the labor of a solitary man and now left to go back to woods brings the poet into thoughts of Christ, who "broke off/ his journey toward the Father,/ and leaned back into the mother's fearful tree." Even Christ is incomplete. He "fell off then, and the horse galloped away/ into the wind without/ [him], and disappeared/ into the blue sky. [His] horse never reached [his] father's house." Bly ends "Crazy Carlson's Meadow" by pointing toward another god who suffered on a tree—Odin:

> Now each young man wanders in the sky alone,
> ignoring the absent
> moon, not knowing
> where ground is, longing once more for the learning
> of the fierce male who hung for nine days only
> on the windy tree.
> Beneath his feet
> there is darkness; inside the folds of darkness words hidden.

The poem is the statement of a man who is a Christian—Bly specifically refers to Christ as "my master," as if to acknowledge this—but for whom the old pagan gods have great reality. Moreover, he sees them as carriers of vital energies. The story alluded to in the final stanza is that of Odin's sacrifice on the world-tree Yggdrasil, carried out in order to gain the wisdom of the runes, wisdom which he would share with gods and men. In the *Elder Edda* Odin says:

> I know that I hung
> on the windswept tree
> for nine full nights,
> wounded with a spear
> and given to Odin,
> myself to myself;
> on that tree
> of which none know
> from what roots it rises.

They did not comfort me with bread,
and not with the drinking horn;
I peered downward,
I grasped the "runes,"
screeching I grasped them;
I fell back from there.[19]

Both Christ and Odin offer themselves up, but Odin performs
the sacrifice upon himself: Christ's sacrifice was passive, Odin's
active. Christ's agony on the tree won atonement, Odin's won
wisdom. Rightly or wrongly, the aspects of Christ that come
across most strongly to most Christians are his mercy and purity; he is seen as an ultimate victory over strife and struggle.
The tone surrounding Odin, "All-father," is different. He is a
warrior doomed to defeat, possessor of divine wisdom who hun-
gers for greater wisdom, the god weighted with the responsibility of holding off the inevitable day when heaven and earth will
be destroyed. When Bly says that each young man "longs for
the learning/ of the fierce male," he is saying that a need is felt
not only for wisdom, for spirit, but for the intensity and strength
necessary to gain them. Bly's own attraction to Odin is not irrelevant here; he too has felt that longing. Odin, in addition to
being a warrior-god and a seeker after wisdom, is also the god
of poetry. It is interesting to note that it was an image of Odin
that Bly chose in 1958 as the emblem for his fledgeling magazine, the address of which was given as Odin House, Madison,
Minnesota.

The loss of intense, active feeling which is also a loss of
purpose and direction is one of several griefs drawn together in
"The Grief of Men," a poem in which the poet's father appears
again and which is one of Bly's most moving meditations on "the
masculine condition." It begins with an anecdote. A Buddhist
writes a message, signs it "Buddha," and sends it to himself.
The note says, "Busyness has caught you, you have slowed and

stopped./ If you start toward me, I/ will surely come/ to meet you." When the man reads the note he weeps. The message itself makes up nearly all of the poem's second stanza, but in the last line we shift to the poet himself, who is "exhausted by work and travel." As the juxtaposition indicates, the poet knows that his situation and the Buddhist's are the same. He too has been caught up in getting and doing, and now he walks alone, near water and animals.

He hears "the coot call his darkening call,/ and the dog's doubt far back in his throat." He thinks of a porcupine, which no one sees, moving through bushes. The porcupine is anonymous, unnoticed, with no world of "busyness" to distract him from his road. Then the poem moves off again, to thoughts of "men [who] have died on high slopes, as others watch," who "look around, and do not see/ those they love most." We may think here of Bly's instinctive use of the image of the mountain in the "Boy-God" essay to express his sense of human life and purpose: a man of deep feeling and serious action helps to "carry the burdens higher up the mountain."[20] The porcupine, the natural creature, is free of the dangers of the busyness that catches human beings, but in its freedom neither does it experience the "high slopes" of lonely human struggle and aspiration: the men on those slopes "call out/ The sound the porcupine does not make." What is experienced there is another grief added to the "slowing and stopping" described by the Buddhist and the separation of the human and the natural world.

Then the poet observes or thinks of "fresh waters [that] wash past the tidal sands,/ wash past clear/ bars and are gone." In another poem in *Black Coat*, "Mourning Pablo Neruda," the flow of water becomes a symbol for the flow of human life toward death. Here it has the same association, and the poem moves directly from the image of the water to the story of the death of a woman, the poet's aunt, in childbirth. She had been warned by her doctor against having any more children, but she and her husband "wanted a child." Though Bly says that his aunt was "inwardly near [him]," his purpose here is not to elegize her, but to deal with "the grief of men." He shifts his focus to the husband, who is crazed with sorrow at his wife's death, throws himself against the wall, and has to be restrained. The poem ends with these lines: "Men come to hold him down./ My father is there,/ sits by the bed long night after night."

This last grief that the poem sets in constellation with the human griefs evoked earlier is distinctively male. In some ways men are outside "the stream of life" more than women. In the act of giving birth a woman participates in that stream in the most immediate and fundamental way, and even if she should die in childbirth that still remains true. She is the one within whom new life grows, and, in this case, the one who loses her own life. The man, meanwhile, stands apart, a helpless observer, and when his wife dies he bears not only the sorrow of her death but also an inevitable guilt: "They wanted a child"; she died. The grief this man experiences is overwhelming, and now it is another man who comes and keeps vigil through the long nights.

The poem gives, then, a complex intellectual and emotional definition of the abstraction Bly uses for his title. The grief that it defines includes fatigue, failure, loneliness, and responsibility. The poem's total definition is greater, and more moving, than the sum of its individual parts. It creates from several thoughts one thought. A man, thinking of the road of the spirit, recognizes that he is at a standstill. A man, walking among the natural world, is aware of a distinctively human plight. A man is shattered by the death of his wife; it is as if a part of his own being is taken from him. Against this complex of griefs is set the steadfastness of another man, the widower's brother-in-law and brother in more than that. And this steadfastness itself, this burden of responsibility and care, represents another grief added to those already invoked.

Bly's contemplation of fathers and sons, of the male soul and the grief of men, is at the heart of *Black Coat*, but it is also a part of a larger meditation—one that amounts to a search for values. "The Grief of Men" moves from busyness and exhaustion to long nights of vigilence, from isolation and loss to brotherly concern. The poet's father, as he is presented in the poems and in the companion essay, is a carrier of values. He is a man who limps, but his limp is a sign not just that he is partly crippled but also that he is a bearer of burdens: "Since he never asked for pity/ his friends thought he/ was whole. Walking alone, he could carry it." He accepts loneliness, feels deeply, accepts sacrifice, knows "what the world *wants* from him." When Bly deals with the boy-god, either implicitly in the poems or explicitly in the essay, he is dealing with a condition in which values are unsubstantial and self-centered, and relationship to the world is at best unclear. Bly links the condition to the young male, but I would like to set it in a broader perspective. Distance from nature; a strange blend of arrogance and abstraction; self-absorption; lack of purpose and intensity; lack of identification with life beyond one's own life—piece by piece a picture emerges of a condition which belongs not just to some young males but to the modern soul-life itself. (And of course it is also somewhat arbitrary to identify it with the modern age. The condition that I am referring to has no doubt existed for a very long time— perhaps as long as human beings have existed—though it has surely become aggravated and more widespread in recent history.) Bly says that the boy-god tends to be cheerful. Take away this cheerfulness from the state of being "out of the stream of life" and it becomes easier to see that what is being described is a condition of alienation. Not social alienation of the more obvious sort—though that can be a related phenomenon—but a condition in which one's life is not felt as part of some larger entity or meaningful pattern, and therefore lacks both bearings and depth. Some "float above" the stream; many others, while they do not float, exist equally outside it. Various words in addition to alienation are associated with this condition: words such as despair, drifting, nihilism, ennui, malaise, cynicism.

When Bly says in "Eleven O'Clock at Night," a mellow psalm in prose to the mundane and the inevitable, "Now more and more I long for what I cannot escape from," he expresses in a low-key and fatalistic way the desire to feel himself as part of the stream of life. Elsewhere he expresses it more sharply and richly. I would like to look now at four more poems, in which Bly responds in various ways to the profound alienation which leaves a human being outside the stream of life, and outside his own life as well.

The first of these is another poem to a father—in this case a poetic father, Pablo Neruda. The poem is titled simply "Mourning Pablo Neruda." The use of the phrase "stream of life" in such close proximity to a discussion of this poem seems a bit heavy-handed, for Bly elegizes Neruda specifically in terms of water. But there is nothing heavy-handed about the poem; on the contrary, it is remarkable for its delicacy and grace—even its indirection. Bly adopts the brief, ragged line of Neruda's *Odas Elementales* for this poem, but otherwise no reference is made, except in the title, to Neruda or his art. This is appropriate, for it wants to praise not the achievements or qualities of an individual, but a life that has been useful, has run its course, and now, simply, mysteriously, in the way of all lives, "is/ gone."

Bly had associated Neruda with water before. In the introductory essay to his Neruda translations, "Refusing to Be Theocritus," he had imagined him as "a deep-sea crab, all claws and shell . . . able to breathe in the heavy substances that lie beneath the daylight consciousness."[21] There he describes the psychic quality of Neruda's dense surrealist poems, but in "Mourning Pablo Neruda" the water is different. It is carried in buckets, used to water young trees in August; it is drinking water carried in a jar; and finally, it is water flowing in rivers to the sea. Neruda was a huge figure—prolific, passionate, embroiled in political struggles, possessed of a rich and astonishing imagination—but the poem begins, not with oceans or jungle rivers, but with the statement, "Water is practical." Later it says, "water doesn't intend/ to give, it gives/ anyway," capturing the sense that a life's gifts are not simply a matter of conscious willing, that the value of the gifts a person gives in his life—the degree to which the life "is practical"—is not something that is known by him. For example, the poet writing does not know what value his poem will have to the unknown person reading it.

There is sadness in the lines

> . . . the dead remain inside
> us, as water
> remains
> inside granite—
> hardly at all—
> for their job is to
> go
> away,
> and not come back,
> even when we ask them . . .

—but not bitterness, such as Keats or Hardy sometimes expressed thinking of the likely oblivion of death. Ultimate anonymity belongs to all human beings, even great poets. But what does that matter, the poem seems to say, if the life has been of use? Implicit throughout the poem is the idea of purpose deeper than individual identity. Even the dead have "a job." Water flows from place to place, "always closer/ to where/ it has to be," and as it moves it is practical, nourishing. To Bly, Neruda's life had this sort of deep, disinterested usefulness. In "Refusing to Be Theocritus" he said, "Neruda wishes to help humanity, and tells the truth for that reason,"[22] and clearly in his poetry Neruda had been a source of great nourishment to Bly himself. Bly mentions none of this in "Mourning Pablo Neruda," but the poem's affirmation is clear: it praises life that gives itself to life, like water that is drunk by roots and men as it flows steadily toward "the Gulf."

Perhaps the first time we realize that our lives are not truly our own, that we belong to something beyond us and would willingly die for someone else, with no trace of the romantic but out of pure instinct, is when we have children. In the poem he placed last in *Black Coat*, "Kneeling Down to Look into a Culvert," Bly links thoughts of his children with a readiness to die. Out walking alone, he stops to peer into a steel culvert. What he sees is mysterious, somehow otherworldly, a mixture of shadows, water, and distant light: "The other end seems far away./ One cone of light floats in the shadowed water." There is a fine accuracy in this description, but as he looks into the culvert's "shadowy insides" the intuitive breaks through. Gazing at the floating light, he says, "This is how our children will look when we are dead." The perspective here is the inverse of that in the Neruda poem. Rather than thinking out toward the dead and gone, Bly now imagines looking back toward the distant, luminous world of the living after he has died.

He walks on and comes to a lake. "I have seen this lake before," he says, ". . . it is a lake/ I return to each time my children are grown." At this point his thoughts suddenly dilate: "I have fathered so many children and returned/ to that lake." The poem shifts to that dimension where the meditation of a particular father thinking of his children and himself and time takes place in all time. Then, in one of the stranger and more wonderful transformations in his poetry, Bly imagines himself as another being entirely: "I am a water-serpent, throwing water drops/ off my head. My gray loops trail behind me." He imagines a life of aboriginal freedom: "How long I stay there alone! For a thousand years/ I am alone, with no duties, living as I live." This sense of timelessness and freedom is broken when "one morning a feathery head pokes from the water." The encounter is not refused, no attempt is made to escape: "I fight—it's time—it's right—and am torn to pieces fighting."

The father is torn to pieces; the older creature is killed by the newer one. In his review of *Black Coat*, Donald Wesling called "Kneeling Down to Look Into a Culvert" "a successful poem in the rather rare genre of the archetypal memory, original because it shows the perspective of the parent who will be replaced." [23] The poem is also original in the *way* it renders that perspective. The mood surrounding the culvert, the intuition concerning the mysterious cone of light, and the instinctive return to the lake prepare the way, but it is the surprising and surprisingly beautiful transformation into the serpent and the events that follow that make the poem's expression of the parent's consciousness uniquely bold and moving. The last line captures it well. There are moments when we recognize that life demands that we offer ourselves up, and we feel ready to do so with no sense of injustice, but with something closer to joy. With luck, a parent experiences this. In the poem, the father, one of his children grown, senses that a part of his life is gone, complete, and he goes out alone to experience imaginatively an instinctive ritual of living and dying.

"Kneeling Down to Look Into a Culvert" follows immediately on "Crazy Carlson's Meadow," with its concluding stanza on Odin, and perhaps it is because of this that I notice that the image of the swimming snake resembles a Viking ship. The spirit of the last line also has something in common with the Vikings, who believed that "fearlessness is better than a faint-heart for any man who puts his nose out of doors. The length of my life and day of my death were fated long ago." [24] I do not suggest that Bly is making conscious references here—though Bly is deeply interested in his old Scandinavian roots, and though the unconscious does set up strange hidden links in poems. All I mean to suggest with this perhaps overly subjective association is that the man who wrote the poem shares something with the ancient Viking affirmation. He understands that feeling deeply a part of the on-going life involves going beyond the stage where one's own life is of paramount importance.

The motif of sacrifice is strong in *Black Coat*, particularly so in the poems that end the book. There is the readiness to die in "Kneeling Down to Look Into a Culvert," and the references to Christ's and Odin's sacrifices in "Crazy Carlson's Meadow." In the poem that precedes these, "Fifty Males Sitting Together," we find the description, cited earlier, of one who does not know what it means to offer himself up—"He does not *know*/ what he should give . . . / . . . what the world *wants* from him"—and so does not really participate in the world. Once again Bly takes his meditation far back in time. He imagines a boy or a young man sitting at the mouth of a cave, watching herds move slowly by, unsure of his purpose, as if in a dream. There has been a hunt, or a sacrifice—the two are closely related—but the boy is not involved: "Blood rises from dark/ neck-holes./ But how far he lives/ from working men!" The living and dying go on around him, but not through him. The blood speaks: it asks, "Whose head has been cut off? The question is mysterious, but it implies that self-absorption and detachment are related to fear of the sacrifice, fear that one's own head might be the one cut off. The boy is like the dreaming man in "The Sleeper," in *Gopher-wood*, in that he "is all withdrawn into himself. He thinks the sound of a shutting door is a tooth falling from his head, or his head rolling on the ground." He is unlike Odin on the windy tree, or the water-serpent who says, "it's time—it's right." (He is also far from the spirit and knowledge of the Kabir poem quoted earlier: "Kabir will tell you the truth: this is what love is like:/ suppose you had to cut your head off/ and give it to someone else,/ what difference would that make?") The boy at the maternal cavemouth—Bly specifically links him with the protection of the mother—is not yet born; he has not yet emerged entirely from the womb. The irony is that in his unwillingness or inability to enter into the world, his head *has* in effect been cut off, and it is a sacrifice that leads to diminished, not greater, life. The difference between this passive, *de facto* sacrifice and the willing sacrifice affirmed at many points in *Black Coat* is absolute. The former is the small death of stasis and withdrawal, the latter is transformation and openness to the fundamental rhythms of living and dying by which both the world and man truly live.

It is in the context of such sacrifice, of giving one's life to something beyond it, that "Kneeling Down to Look Into a Culvert" should be read—though that theme is beautifully realized within the poem itself. It is a remarkable expression of a remarkable moment of consciousness. Knowing that his child is grown, the poet experiences both great freedom and a fierce and joyful dying. At such moments, living and dying, freedom and sacrifice, a thousand years and the last morning, are of a piece, and are accepted equally. At such moments, a man knows how he belongs to life and to death.

Black Coat contains what is certainly one of the finest "object poems" Bly has written: "Finding an Old Ant Mansion." As an object poem, a prose poem, and a poem containing animals, it is in the line of *The Morning Glory*. But it occurs within the first of Bly's books which focuses strongly on human relationships, and it is the awareness of family ties, sacrifices, labor, and gifts extending across human generations that emerges most strongly from the observation of a natural object here.

The poet awakens, alone, on "the first morning in the North," from a dream which transformed the rubbing of the sleeping bag on his ear into a rattlesnake biting him. Like the sleeper who thought the sound of a door shutting was his head rolling across the ground, he has been "all withdrawn into himself" in his dream. But the self-absorption and anxiety of the dream break up as he awakens. They are replaced by physical pleasure as he goes out and walks in the chill, cloudy morning. His feet feel the earth beneath them—"And how good the unevenness of the pasture feels under tennis shoes! The earth gives little rolls and humps ahead of us . . ."—and once again the body's sensations rouse the mind and imagination:

> The earth never lies flat, but is always thinking, it finds a new feeling and curls over it, rising to bury a toad or a great man, it accounts for a fallen meteor, or stones rising from two hundred feet down, giving a little jump for Satan, and a roll near it for Calvin . . .

That toads and men can be absorbed on equal terms is potentially a depressing thought, but it need not necessarily be so. And perhaps only a person able to entertain that thought with a certain equanimity will also be able to see a human meaning in a piece of natural handiwork, and take satisfaction in the correspondence. The poet comes upon a chunk of wood lying on the ground. He examines it briefly, notices that it has been partly hollowed out, though the wood itself is still solid, not rotted, "only a bit eaten by the acids that lie in pastures." When he carries it back to the house and puts it on his desk, he sees clearly that it was once the home of a colony of ants.

In the passage where Bly describes the interior of the "ant

mansion" we see the logic of association working marvelously. Ideas and feelings enter quickly and smoothly. As the color of the wood is compared to that of workman's benches and eating tables, the ideas of labor and nourishment appear; that the tables are old ones seen in Norwegian farmhouses introduces the idea of ancestry as well. Brief references to caves, barns, cows and mangers, dusk and fall, add to the fabric of associations: the long past, the sturdiness of wood, animal warmth and sacred energies linked with it, and the falling darkness of time, all come quietly into the poem. Then we get a more elaborate comparison: "A little light comes in from the sides, as when a woman at forty suddenly sees what her mother's silences as she washed clothes meant, and which are the windows in the side of her life she has not yet opened . . ." This brings in the motifs of work and generations again, but also thoughts of lives passed in anonymity and the sacrifices and feelings that secretly connect one generation to another. All of these associations will be significant as the poem unfolds, and the beauty of the passage is that it introduces what will be the poem's major themes without our being aware of it. The images and their associations brush against one another here and subtly prepare the mind for what is to follow.

After describing the physical details and the mood of the mansion, Bly pictures the life that went on inside it, when "the ant legions labored" and "the polished threshold [was] passed by thousands of pintaillike feet." The passage is richly alive and lyrical, and Bly allows his imagining a generous range. At one point he speaks of the ants "with their electricity for all the day packed into their solid-state joints and carapaces"; elsewhere he speaks of the ceilings of the "balconies" as being "low and lanterned with the bullheat of their love." The ants are "almsgivers," and "the infant ants awaken to old father-worked halls, uncle-loved boards." Ordinarily no one objects when an insect is thought of as a sort of tiny, organic machine, but comparisons to human beings are likely to arouse not only objections but indignation. Hayden Carruth, in the review of *Tree* cited earlier, was prompted by some of Bly's statements about the consciousness that may exist in the natural world to remind us that "distance and difference are what makes us conscious, not fuzzy homologies."[25] And Philip Dacey, in his review of *Gopherwood*, took Bly to task specifically for his "envy of crickets."[26] The lines on ants just quoted are colorful and impulsive, yet they are not to be explained merely as the product of a fit of warmheartedness, or light-headedness. The interesting thing is that Bly is serious in his admiring fascination for ants, which is actually far from the fanciful anthropomorphism it may sometimes appear to be. Does it mean anything to use the word "love" in connection with ants? The point is worth pausing upon.

In a poem in *The Morning Glory* in which ants also appear, "In the Courtyard of the Isleta Mission," Bly suggested that it is possible, and desirable, "to put ourselves in the hands of the ants." This is a risky statement, no doubt ill-advised since it is almost certain to be interpreted as a dismissal of intellect, moral choice, and individuality, in favor of pure instinct. After all, Bly does celebrate the intelligence of the body and what we could call "the old mind," and he is more than a little suspicious of reason, agreeing with Blake when he says, "May God us keep/ From Single vision & Newton's sleep!"[27] But it is clear, as we look over his work and career, that Bly honors the intellect—the cutting edge of original thought evident everywhere in his criticism—and the independent belief and action, as well as any poet of his generation. How is this compatible with "putting ourselves in the hands of the ants"?

An idea that can help answer these questions occurs in a poem in *Tree* called "An Evening When the Full Moon Rose as the Sun Set." After describing the sun and moon, Bly turns his attention to a pair of pintail ducks. (The use of the word "pintaillike" in "Finding an Old Ant Mansion" makes a slender, no doubt unconscious link between the two poems.) He sees embodied in the ducks, as they swim together, "the life of faithfulness [that] goes by like a river,/ with no one watching it." This river also flowed within the ant mansion, and it flows through human life as well. Among ants it manifests itself as an instinctual rushing about, diligence, and craftsmanship. In the human world it manifests itself as loyalty, affection, willing sacrifice, moral choices, "the indignation of the solitary man . . . that connects this world to the next"--and also in diligence, craftsmanship, and an almost instinctual rushing about.

"The life of faithfulness [that] goes by like a river" is the stream of life the boy-god, or the alienated person, floats above. When Bly says that we should "put ourselves in the hands of the ants," or when he speaks of "the bullheat of their love," running underneath his words is a sense of life lived at one with itself and yet also on behalf of something greater than the life of the individual ant or human being. It is the same sense that is expressed in "Kneeling Down to Look Into a Culvert" and "Mourning Pablo Neruda," and indeed it is what *Black Coat* as a whole affirms.

At the end of the paragraph that describes the ants' love, Bly says of "the sane wood" of the mansion that it was "given shape by Osiris' love." The love of a god which is expressed in the green life of the earth and the death and rebirth of the seasons encompasses the creatures that live and work in the darkness inside wood as well as those who live and work in the light of fire, electricity, and human consciousness.

But the poem does not end with Osiris' love. The motif of human ties and relationships suggested earlier in the poem takes root, and it flowers throughout the next long paragraph. Bly says of the mansion he has described as a physical object and as a vessel of life, "Now it seems to be a completed soul home.

These balconies are good places for souls to sit, in the half-dark."
While he said in "Mourning Pablo Neruda" that the job of the
dead is "to go/ away,/ and not come back,/ even when we ask
them," the longing of the living to keep the bond is powerful.
He thinks of placing the mansion on an altar, as the object of a
small ceremony to honor ancestors; he wants to invite the souls
of the dead to take lodging in this object that both the ants and
his imagination have lived in: "If I put it on our altar, souls of
the dead can come and sit now, I will keep this place for them."
He continues: "The souls of the dead are no bigger than a grain
of wheat when they come, yet they too like to have their back
protected from the wind of nothing, the wind of Descartes, and
of all who grew thin in maternal deprivation."

To Bly, Descartes has a special significance. He symbolizes
the moment of a great schism in the history of human consciousness; he stands for rationalism as it cuts man off not only from
other kinds of consciousness but from the rest of creation as
well. In the anthology *News of the Universe*, Bly makes Descartes
the pivotal figure in the development of what he calls "The Old
Position":

> When Descartes, on November 10, 1619, developed his famous
> sentence, "I think, therefore I am," he intended consciously to
> say something liberating: I think, therefore I am not merely a
> solipsist. But Europe wanted to hear something else. It wanted
> its pride in human reason to be given philosophical underpin-
> ning. Europe had for a long time felt inferior—first to Roman
> culture, then to Holy culture. What I've called the Old Position
> puts human reason, and so human beings, in the superior posi-
> tion. The Old Position may be summed up, or oversimplified,
> this way: Consciousness is human, and involves reason. A serious
> gap exists between us and the rest of nature. Nature is to be
> watched, pitied, and taken care of if it behaves.[28]

Bly's inclusion of the word "too" in the sentence about the
winds in "Finding an Old Ant Mansion" should be noted. What

the dead like is speculation; what the poet wants protection from is clear. The winds of nothing, Descartes, and maternal deprivation are all winds of alienation. As Karl Stern (whose book *The Flight from Woman* Bly draws on in his commentary in *News of The Universe*) has said regarding the Cartesian dualism, or split:

> The sense of mystery which the poet and the contemplative have towards nature; the sense of imbeddedness, of a personal relationship of protectiveness or cruelty, of the familiar or the aweful—all this is not a matter of animism or of a vague sentiment which will eventually be repealed by scientific elucidation. Quite the contrary; if a kind of Cartesian ideal were ever completely fulfilled, i.e., if the whole of nature were only what can be explained in terms of mathematical relationships—then we would look at the world with that fearful sense of alienation, with that utter loss of reality with which a future schizophrenic child looks at his mother. A machine cannot give birth.[29]

As Bly sees it, modern man, in his rationalistic and scientific sophistication, and in his alienation and spiritual poverty, is more than a little like a schizophrenic child.

Bly names some of the dead he hopes will come to the mansion. (The use of the word "mansion" is due to the beauty and elaborateness of the ant-worked wood, but because of the choice of this word the phrase "in my Father's house are many mansions" hovers around the poem.) He says that he will "set out a drop of water and a grain of rye for them." It is when we feed the dead, nourishing their memory and keeping it alive, that they come back to us.

> Vigleik can come here, with his lame knee, pinned in 1922 under a tree he himself felled, rolling cigarettes with affectionate fingers, patient and protective. And my brother can sit here if he can find the time, he will bring his friend if he comes; my grandmother will come here surely, sometimes, with the ship she gave me. This balcony is like her kitchen to the southwest, its cobstove full of heating caves. . . .

Then Bly takes a final step in his meditation, returning to the ants and the motif of anonymous labor. The key correspondence between ants and men is stated directly: "What the ants have worked out is a place for our destiny, for we too labor, and no one sees our labor." And here the poet's father appears once more: "My father's work who sees? It is in a pasture somewhere not yet found by a walker." "And the life of faithfulness goes by like a river/ with no one noticing it." When Bly spoke of the "father-worked halls [and] uncle-loved boards" of the mansion, the ideas of work, love, and generations came together, and indeed they circle close to one another throughout the poem. Work, carried out with some consciousness of the benefit of others, can be a form of love. Likewise, love is a form of work. Together they make up a force that keeps the human colony alive. This force is what the poem envisions and celebrates. In general, such work and love attract little attention, as the poem says, but here they are found in a pasture and well praised.

Why *anonymous* labor? Bly affirms it because he knows that it is through this that most of the important work of the world is accomplished. But there is another reason as well. Insofar as poets are well-known in America, Robert Bly is well-known. When a poet publishes a book or is asked for an interview or wins a prize or applause, he is told that he is special after all. Bly has referred to boy-gods also as "flying boys" or "swans,"[30] taking an image from the fairy tale "The Six Swans."[31] Fame and praise can turn a person into a swan, and a culture which exalts individuality and celebrity encourages this transformation. But in reality we are more like ants working within an old, intricate dwelling than swans. As a poet, as a human being, it is good to remind oneself of this. Ants living out their lives in labor in carved darkness, and a heavy, limping man who resembles rough wood, have at least two things in common: their work attracts little notice, and they are nothing like white, graceful swans that float overhead.

What is it that human beings labor on, comparable to the mansion or hill to which ants devote their labor? In "Finding an Old Ant Mansion," with its concentration on ties extending across generations, it is a family, but by extension also the life of the race itself, the sprawling, elaborately evolving hill parents, ancestors, and the family of man as a whole have created and maintain. In another poem, however, Bly focuses on a particular aspect of the life of that vast hill: language. Fittingly, he dedicates the poem, "Words Rising,"[32] to an elder poet, Richard Eberhart. Here he compares human beings not to ants, but to bees: "We are bees then; language is the honey." Because it nourishes human consciousness and the human spirit, language is crucial to the unique life of our hive.

The nourishment Bly finds in language here is ancient. Language is the means by which stories and histories are preserved, but in "Words Rising" Bly is dealing with an even more fundamental way in which words connect us with the past. They contain what might be called "sensual memory," which, as Bly describes it, goes all the way back to the cave. When we break open a word on our tongues, we find moisture in it from pools that our ancestors drank from in the earliest days. As the poem begins, the poet is writing in his journal and begins to feel an ecstasy—or, in the word Bly increasingly likes and uses here, a "fierceness." Stars and oceans swirl together. Then the past returns:

> All those lives we lived in the sunlit
> shelves of the Dordogne, the thousand
> tunes we sang to the skeletons
> of Papua, the many times
> we died—wounded—under the cloak

> of an animal's sniffing, all of these
> return, and the grassy nights
> we ran in the moonlight for hours.

The poem evokes light, sounds, movement, and smells, but it says that it is not only through the power of imagery that language links us with the past. It does so even more immediately through the sensuousness of words themselves. It is the sound of words that carries the unconscious memory of the old life: "the sound of words/ carries what we do not."

> Watery syllables come welling up.
> Anger that barked and howled in the cave,
> the luminous head of barley
> the priest holds up, growls
> from under fur, none of that is lost!
> The old earth fragrance remains
> in the word "and." We experience
> "the" in its lonely suffering.

Bly pushes his claim as far as he can: no doubt very few of us have noticed the loneliness of "the," or caught the earth fragrance of "and." The poem makes an astounding assertion—one that is beautiful partly because it is so extreme. In it Bly imagines language alive with all the life from which it sprang, and so challenges us to learn to speak and understand it. In *News of the Universe* Bly discusses three dreams which Descartes had the night before his dualistic illumination. The third dream concerned language:

> In his third dream some terrifying tnings happened. A book disappeared from his hand. A book appeared at one end of his table, vanished, and appeared at the other end. And the dictionary, when he checked it, had fewer words in it than it had a few minutes before. I suspect that we are losing some words . . . our vocabulary is getting smaller. The disappearing words are prob-

ably words such as "mole," "ocean," "praise," "whale," "steep-
ing," "bat-ear," "wooden tub," "moist cave," "seawind."[33]

There is a good deal of sensual memory in the words Bly cites,
as there is in "sunlit shelves of the Dordogne," "grassy nights,"
and "the luminous head of barley." Whether through the influence of the Cartesian legacy, or the more blatant influences of
pseudoscientific jargon and advertising, it does seem that our
language is gradually being diminished. Bly dreams of reversing
that trend, and in his poetry he has worked to preserve such
words as "mole," "ocean," and "praise." In "Words Rising" he
imagines a dictionary with no words lost, a language with its
sensual memory intact.

But if language nourishes us, we continually nourish language: "When a man or woman feeds a few words/ with private
grief, the shames we knew/ before we could invent/ the wheel,
then words grow." So with the sentence, "There are eternal vows/
held inside the word 'Jericho,' " the poem moves to a final stanza
in praise of workers devoted to language: "the man who labors/
in his tiny room, writing stanzas on the lamb" (no doubt Blake);
"the dictionary maker, huddled among/ his bearded words"; "the
setter of songs/ who sleeps at night inside his violin case." (One
other person is mentioned: "the woman, who picks the brown/
seeds of solitude in afternoon light/ out of the black seeds of
loneliness." This might only be a description of patient and solitary labor, and not writing in particular. But Bly says that he
was in fact thinking of a worker in language in those lines: Emily Dickinson. The phrase "afternoon light" is the slender reference—to Dickinson's "There's a Certain Slant of Light."[34])
These workers have found a relationship to something beyond
themselves. Though they are alone, they are not alienated in the
sense that I have been using the term; each "*knows* what he should

give." They belong to the generations engaged in long, hidden labor. They are themselves, and at the same time they give themselves up. In this they resemble ants and bees, water that is drunk by trees and men as it flows toward the sea, or the man who feels that he is ready to be torn to pieces fighting.

In one way "Words Rising" is one of the less personal poems in *Black Coat*, but in another way it is personal. In his article on *Sleepers*, Donald Hall commented: "If Bly could write his poems in amino acids or bird calls, he would just as lief; the spirit matters to him, and not the shoulders of consonants."[35] An overstatement, but partly true. While his poetry is not as devoid of sound as it is sometimes made out to be, it has been the spirit that has been foremost for Bly, and language has been, until recently, something of an unpraised servant. But he has not written his poetry in amino acids—though there are points in *Gopherwood* where he seemed about to make the leap. In "Words Rising," while he does not use the pronoun "I" after the first stanza, Bly acknowledges that for him the spirit has lived through language, and that as a poet he has lived through his vocation in language. Bly's emphasis has been on the way psychic energy moves in poetry, and silence and solitude remain important to him, but it is language that connects the poet to the world.

"Finding an Old Ant Mansion" and "Words Rising" are both joyful poems; in them affirmations are made with only a few nods to the grief that is so important an element in *Black Coat* as a whole. I do not mean to withdraw emphasis from that element by ending with them; it is crucial to the overall tone and thought of the book. *Black Coat* is an affirmative book, but its affirmation rises both from the desire for healing and reconciliation (like all of Bly's books) with a father, with the flow of life greater than one's own life—and from an awareness that there are griefs which do not heal: "The Old People's Home/ at dusk, the slow/ murmur of conversation"; the desolation of a man whose wife dies in childbirth; the man who turns and goes back, and does not "climb the hill."

In *Black Coat* we once again see Bly making a book that is not a miscellaneous collection. The unity here is thematic. In this book he extends his meditation on the theme that has been central to him since some of his earliest poems, such as "Where We Must Look for Help," "A Man Writes to a Part of Himself," and "The Fire of Despair Has Been Our Saviour": the dual recognition that we are broken, isolated creatures, and that in our fragmentation lies the purpose of our lives. Before *Black Coat*, Bly had focused on the fragmentation *within* man, and on our need to reestablish our relationship with the nonhuman world. Here he enlarges his vision of fragmentation and healing: it took him a long time to bring human bonds and community into his poetry, but in *Black Coat* he has done so in an impressive and moving way. *Black Coat* significantly enriches both his vision and the body of his work.

In his review of *Sleepers* in 1973, David Cavitch made an interesting statement: "Bly is not really an ecstatic or visionary or even a radical poet. . . . He is a poet who wants intensely to put together a coherent life out of materials that he fears are not enough: personal identity, moral nature, mental attentiveness."[36] At this point I will leave it to the individual reader to judge the accuracy of all the parts of this statement. Its core, however—the part about Bly's desire "to put together a coherent life out of materials that he fears are not enough"—says something important, useful in thinking about Bly's work as a whole. Reading that work, one does sense the urgency of such an effort; certainly in *Black Coat* as much as anywhere we feel him involved in it.

And what is the coherence of the work of a man whose impulses and considered judgments are often paradoxical, whose thought and art are so abundant with opposites—actively related opposites that are as fundamental to Bly's vision as Yeats' were to his—lights and darks, masculine and feminine, exclamations and silence, risings and fallings, ecstasies and griefs? I think it is desire itself. In that too he is like Yeats: the larger pattern of his vision is rich and complex, but it is the desire out of which the vision is created by which the poetry lives. Richard Eberhart has commented that Bly's psyche "has a sun-like radiance."[37] At times it is sunlike, at other times it is moonlike, but in either tone the luminousness of the poems is the sign that desire is moving in them. Bly is not a poet who teaches adjustment to the known, to "what is now proved," nor does he acquiesce to despair, entropy, bitterness, or a studied agnosticism. Sometimes he exhorts, sometimes he draws scenes and images which contain intimations of other worlds, but always he is saying that it is possible to live with greater depth and fullness. His first book, on superficial reading, seems to espouse quietism, but Bly's silences and simple scenes in *Snowy Fields* are compelling largely because they are infused with desire:

> Beneath the waters, since I was a boy,
> I have dreamt of strange and dark treasures,
> Not of gold, or strange stones, but the true
> Gift, beneath the pale lakes of Minnesota.

When he exclaimed about giving up all ambition, it was because more often than not ambition keeps us from the deeper life he desires. Poems of three and four lines record glimpses of that life. Amid the passionate prophecies of *The Light* we find these lines, which amount, as I suggested earlier, to an affirmation of faith:

> We did not come to remain whole.
> We came to lose our leaves like the trees,
> The trees that are broken
> And start again, drawing up from the great roots . . .

This describes a life made up of many deaths and rebirths, and expresses the desire to give oneself to those cycles of being torn and healed. At the center of the long title poem of *Sleepers* lies a fundamental awakening to the conviction that "there is a road." It is desire for the road that lets us see it, and puts it inside us. Even in moments when he realizes that "the older we get the more we fail," the realization draws him on into a more generous sense of life, not a diminished one: "but the more we fail the more we feel a part of the dead straw of the universe, the corners of barns with cowdung twenty years old, the chairs fallen back on their heads in deserted houses, the belts left hanging over the chairback after the bachelor has died in the ambulance on the way to the city" ("August Rain"). He is moved by the deep, sure, ancient life the animals still carry. He celebrates the body not least because it knows desire: "This body longs for itself far out at sea, it floats in the black heavens, it is a brilliant being, locked in the prison of human dullness" ("Going Out to Check the Ewes"). In one sense, the last line of the last poem in *Black Coat* is simply an expression of the desire to live with intensity and openness until the moment of one's death: "I fight—it's time—it's right—and am torn to pieces fighting" ("Kneeling Down to Look Into a Culvert").

Bly's work and career exhibit a unique energy. The poetry of his time would be incalculably poorer without him. No poet of his generation better fits the phrase he used to describe that generation—"lively and fierce servants"—than he himself does. This is true of him in his various interrelated roles as translator, editor, publisher, critic, social critic, anthologist, theorist, lecturer, and speaker of poems. And it is true of the man we discover in his poetry. Here is one of Bly's Kabir versions:

Friend, hope for the Guest while you are alive.
Jump into experience while you are alive!

Think . . . and think . . . while you are alive.
What you call "salvation" belongs to the time before death.

If you don't break your ropes while you're alive,
do you think
ghosts will do it after?

The idea that the soul will join with the ecstatic
just because the body is rotten—
that is all fantasy.
What is found now is found then.
If you find nothing now,
you will simply end up with an apartment in the City of Death.
If you make love with the divine now, in the next life you will
    have the face of satisfied desire.

So plunge into the truth, find out who the Teacher is, Believe in
    the Great Sound!

Kabir says this: When the Guest is being searched for, it is the
    intensity of the longing for the Guest that does all the work.
Look at me, and you will see a slave of that intensity.[38]

Reading Bly's work, one feels the intelligence and desire of a
man who has taken this advice to heart.

Notes

PREFACE

1. William Matthews, "Thinking About Robert Bly," *Tennessee Poetry Journal* (Winter 1969), 2(2):49.

SIX COMMENTS ON POETRY BY ROBERT BLY

1. Bly, "A Wrong-Turning in American Poetry," *Choice* (1963), 3:46. This important essay has been reprinted in Donald Hall, ed., *Claims for Poetry* (Ann Arbor: University of Michigan Press, 1982).

2. "Chinese Poetry and the American Imagination," *Ironwood* (Spring 1981), 17:20.

3. Bly, *Talking All Morning*, p. 98.

4. Bly, "The Dead World and the Live World," *The Sixties* (Spring 1966), 8:6–7.

5. *Talking All Morning*, p. 242.

6. *Ibid.*, p. 233.

1. SILENCE IN THE SNOWY FIELDS

1. Heyen, "Inward to the World," pp. 42–43.

2. Louis Simpson, "Poetry Chronicle," *Hudson Review* (Spring 1963), 16:138.

3. Bly, "Five Decades of Modern American Poetry," *The Fifties* (1958), 1:39.

4. "I Cry, Love! Love!" *The Collected Poems of Theodore Roethke* (Garden City, N.Y.: Doubleday, 1966), p. 92.

5. Bly, "Looking for Dragon Smoke," in Stephen Berg and Robert Mezey, eds., *Naked Poetry: Recent American Poetry in Open Forms* (Indianapolis: Bobbs-

Merrill, 1969), p. 164. This essay differs significantly from its later form, published under the same title in *The Seventies* 1 and *Leaping Poetry*.

6. Bly, *Talking All Morning*, pp. 23, 250.

7. Readers interested in the relationship of American poetry to Chinese are referred to "Chinese Poetry and the American Imagination," *Ironwood* (Spring 1981), 17:11–21, 38–51; and to Jonathan Chaves' "Chinese Influence or Cultural Colonialism," 19:115–23. The former is a compilation, prepared by Gregory Orr, of statements made during a conference sponsored by the Academy of American Poets in 1977, in which Bly participated; the latter is an essay by a writer who is both a translator and a scholar of Chinese literature, and it focuses on three poets: James Wright, Gary Snyder, and Bly. Chaves points out the great simplification involved in speaking of "the influence of Chinese poetry," as if an ancient, enormously rich tradition were monolithic—a simplification my brief comments partake of. As to *Silence in the Snowy Fields*, Chaves calls it "probably the most successful book of American poetry to show the influence of [the] tradition [of Chinese quietistic nature poetry]," and says that it "is filled with wonderful moments and scenes in nature of which a Wang Wei or a Han Shan would have been proud." Chaves also has reservations. He says, "every so often, there is a wrenching movement away from the harmonious unfolding of nature's process, so violent that it threatens to undermine the entire world of the poem," and he feels that the book's surreal effects and the Chinese-influenced nature imagery "sometimes work at cross purposes." I myself do not think these points represent weaknesses in the book, but in any case Chaves' essay is an extremely interesting one.

8. *Talking All Morning*, p. 129.

9. Bly, *Silence in the Snowy Fields*, dust jacket.

10. *Talking All Morning*, p. 56.

11. William Blake, "The Marriage of Heaven and Hell."

12. *Talking All Morning*, p. 53.

13. *Ibid.*, p. 257.

14. Bly made this comment during a reading at Hobart and William Smith Colleges, Geneva, N.Y., in October 1982.

15. *Talking All Morning*, p. 14.

16. *Ibid.*, p. 131.

17. Bly (with James Wright and William Duffy), *The Lion's Tail and Eyes*, p. 6.

18. Bly, "A Wrong-Turning in American Poetry," *Choice* (1963), 3:35.

19. D. D. Paige, ed., *The Letters of Ezra Pound 1907–1941* (New York: Harcourt, Brace & World, 1950), p. 49.

20. T. S. Eliot, ed., *Literary Essays of Ezra Pound* (New York: New Directions, 1954), p. 4.

21. *Talking All Morning*, p. 3.

22. "A Wrong-Turning in American Poetry," p. 47.

23. *Ibid.*, p. 41.

24. *Ibid.*, p. 34.

25. Frank Kermode, ed., *Selected Prose of T. S. Eliot* (New York: Harcourt, Brace, Jovanovich; Farrar, Strauss & Giroux, 1975), p. 48.

26. "A Wrong-Turning in American Poetry," p. 40.

27. *Ibid.*

28. *Talking All Morning*, p. 260.

29. "A Wrong-Turning in American Poetry," p. 40.

30. *Talking All Morning*, p. 260.

31. Bly, "Recognizing the Image As a Form of Intelligence," *Field* (Spring 1981), 24:24–26. This essay was later revised and published under the title "What the Image Can Do" in Donald Hall, ed., *Claims for Poetry* (Ann Arbor: University of Michigan Press, 1982). Throughout this study my quotations from this essay are from the original version.

32. C. G. Jung, *The Spirit in Man, Art, and Literature (Collected Works*, vol. 15), (Princeton, N.J.: Princeton University Press, 1966), p. 81.

33. C. G. Jung, *The Structure and Dynamics of the Psyche (Collected Works*, vol. 8), (Princeton, N.J.: Princeton University Press, 1960), p. 137.

34. James Wright, "Goodbye to the Poetry of Calcium," *The Branch Will Not Break* (Middletown, Conn.: Wesleyan University Press, 1963), p. 12.

35. Bly, *The Lion's Tail and Eyes*, pp. 5–6.

36. Donald Hall, "Notes on Robert Bly and *Sleepers Joining Hands*," in *Goatfoot Milktongue Twinbird*, p. 138. While I am disagreeing with the emphasis of Hall's comments here, I want to acknowledge my indebtedness both to his essay and, especially, to conversations we had in November 1981. Both have been of great help to me in thinking about Bly's work.

37. Erich Neumann, *The Great Mother: An Analysis of the Archetype* (Princeton, N.J.: Princeton University Press, 1963), p. 18.

38. Dacey, "The Reverend Robert E. Bly, Pastor, Church of the Blessed Unity," p. 6.

39. "Contemporary American Poets Read Their Work: Robert Bly" (audio cassette).

40. Michael D. Quam, "Through Norwegian Eyes: Growing Up Among Snowy Fields," *Plainsong* (Fall 1981), 3(2):35–36.

41. Heyen, "Inward to the World," pp. 43–44.

42. Antonio Machado, *I Never Wanted Fame*, p. viii.

43. *Talking All Morning*, p. 133.

2. THE LIGHT AROUND THE BODY

1. Richard Calhoun, "On Robert Bly's Protest Poetry," *Tennessee Poetry Journal* (Winter 1969), 2(2):22.

2. Zweig, "A Sadness for American," p. 419.

3. Smith, "The Strange World of Robert Bly," *The Smith* (1968), 8:185.

4. Louis Simpson, "New Books of Poems," *Harper's*, August 1968, p. 75.

5. Hayden Carruth, "Critic of the Month," *Poetry* (September 1968), 112:423.

6. Heyen, "Inward to the World," p. 49.

7. Leibowitz, "Questions of Reality," pp. 556–57.

8. Rexroth, "The Poet as Responsible," p. 117.

9. William E. Taylor, quoted in "On Bly's Poetry" by Stephen Mooney, *Tennessee Poetry Journal* (Winter 1969), 2(2):17–18.

10. Hall, "Notes on Robert Bly and *Sleepers Joining Hands*," in *Goatfoot Milk-tongue Twinbird*, p. 139.

11. Bly, *Talking All Morning*, p. 99.

12. Bly, "The Collapse of James Dickey," *The Sixties* (Spring 1967), 9:70–79.

13. *Talking All Morning*, pp. 107–8.

14. Molesworth, *The Fierce Embrace*, p. 113.

15. H. R. Hays, *12 Spanish American Poets* (Boston: Beacon Press, 1971), dust jacket.

16. *Talking All Morning*, p. 49.

17. *Ibid.*, p. 118.

18. Bly, tr., *Neruda and Vallejo: Selected Poems*, p. 3. The poem referred to is "Letter to Miguel Otero Silva, in Caracas," which appears on pp. 119–27 in that volume.

19. Bly, "Five Decades of American Poetry," *The Fifties* (1958), 1:38.

20. *Talking All Morning*, p. 38.

21. *Ibid.*, p. 98.

22. *Ibid.*, pp. 79–80.

23. William Matthews, "Thinking About Robert Bly," *Tennessee Poetry Journal* (Winter 1969), 2(2):50.

24. See, for example, "Developing the Underneath," *American Poetry Review* (November/December 1973), 2(6):44–45.

25. Bly, *Leaping Poetry*, pp. 59–67.

26. Bly, "Being a Lutheran Boy-God in Minnesota," in Chester G. Anderson, ed., *Growing Up in Minnesota: Ten Writers Remember Their Childhoods* (Minneapolis: University of Minnesota Press, 1976), p. 213.

27. Bly, "Poems for the Ascension of J. P. Morgan," *New World Writing* (1959), 15:61–77.

28. Leibowitz, "Questions of Reality," p. 557.

29. *Talking All Morning*, pp. 199–200.

30. W. B. Yeats, "Speaking to the Psaltery," *Essays and Introductions* (New York: Collier Books, 1961), p. 14.

31. While traveling in Greece in the spring of 1982 Bly bought a bouzouki, and he began to use this instrument rather than the dulcimer to accompany his

recitations shortly afterward. The effect of the accompaniment remains beautiful.

32. Patricia Goedicke, "The Leaper Leaping," in Jones and Daniels, eds., *Of Solitude and Silence*, p. 105. For another good description, in a different vein, of a reading by Bly, see "Ecstasy and Poetry in Chicago," by Lowell Komie, pp. 129–31. This article, subtitled "A Middle-Aged Lawyer Goes to His First Poetry Reading," is a sharp, self-effacing, funny piece.

33. *Talking All Morning*, p. 208.

34. *Ibid.*, pp. 209–10.

35. Bly, "I Came Out of the Mother Naked," *Sleepers Joining Hands*, p. 48.

36. Bly, "Giving to Johnson What Is Johnson's," in Bly and Ray, eds., *A Poetry Reading Against the Vietnam War*, p. 2.

37. *Talking All Morning*, p. 106.

38. "Contemporary American Poets Read Their Work: Robert Bly" (audio cassette).

39. During the time I was writing this chapter, Garry Wills' article "The Kennedy Imprisonment: The Prisoner of Charisma" appeared in *The Atlantic Monthly*, January 1982, pp. 27–40. I was interested to notice that some of Wills' imagery resembled that of Bly's poem: e.g., "There would be no Sherman Adams in Kennedy's White House. The President would direct his own operation. All bottlenecks to fluidity had to be broken up." "Kennedy's men felt they had broken the logjam caused by Eisenhower's cumbrous way of governing."

40. David Ignatow, letter to the author, July 1981.

41. *Talking All Morning*, p. 124.

42. C. G. Jung, *The Archetypes and the Collective Unconscious* (*Collected Works*, vol. 9) (Princeton, N.J.: Princeton University Press, 1959), p. 279.

3. SLEEPERS JOINING HANDS

1. Donald Hall, "From Death Unto Death," *The National Review*, October 13, 1978, p. 1294.

2. Bly, "A Wrong-Turning in American Poetry," *Choice* (1969), 3:47.

3. Bly, *Talking All Morning*, p. 246.

4. Bly, *News of the Universe*.

5. Bly, "The Network and the Community," *American Poetry Review* (January/February 1974), 3(1):20.

6. Hall, "Notes on Robert Bly and *Sleepers Joining Hands*," in *Goatfoot Milktongue Twinbird*, p. 89.

7. Bly, "Form That Is Neither In nor Out," in Jones and Daniels, eds., *Of Solitude and Silence*, p. 22.

8. *Ibid.*, p. 25.

9. *Ibid.*, p. 27.

10. Bly, "What Whitman Did Not Give Us," in Jim Perlman, Ed Folsom, and Dan Campion, eds., *Walt Whitman: The Measure of His Song* (Minneapolis: Holy Cow! Press, 1981), pp. 321–34.

11. "Form That Is Neither In nor Out," p. 25.

12. Bly, *Leaping Poetry*, pp. 1, 4.

13. *Ibid.*, pp. 46–47.

14. *Ibid.*, p. 4.

15. Bly, *Sleepers Joining Hands*, pp. 32–33. Ellipses are mine; Bly's summary contains additional points of distinction.

16. *Ibid.*, pp. 34–43.

17. *Ibid.*, p. 40.

18. *Talking All Morning*, p. 201.

19. *Sleepers Joining Hands*, p. 48.

20. *Ibid.*

21. *Ibid.*, p. 34.

22. Bly, *The Teeth-Mother Naked at Last*, p. 22.

23. *Sleepers Joining Hands*, p. 43.

24. David Cavitch, "The Poet as Victim and Victimizer," p. 3.

25. James F. Mersmann, *Out of the Vietnam Vortex*, p. 156.

26. *Ibid.*, p. 129.

27. *Ibid.*, p. 130.

28. Cavitch, "The Poet as Victim and Victimizer," p. 3.

29. Joyce Carol Oates, "Where They All Are Sleeping," *Modern Poetry Studies* (1973), 4:341.

30. Hall, "Notes on Robert Bly and *Sleepers Joining Hands*," in *Goatfoot Milktongue Twinbird*, p. 93.

31. Molesworth, *The Fierce Embrace*, p. 126.

32. Bly, letter to the author, December 1981.

33. Michael Atkinson, "*Sleepers Joining Hands:* Shadow and Self," p. 145.

34. David Seal, "Waking to 'Sleepers Joining Hands,' " in Jones and Daniels, eds., *Of Solitude and Silence*, pp. 219–20, 245. Other discussions of the poem are by Charles Molesworth, *The Fierce Embrace*, pp. 126–29, and William V. Davis, " 'At the Edges of the Light': A Reading of Robert Bly's *Sleepers Joining Hands*," in Jones and Daniels, eds., *Of Solitude and Silence*, pp. 260–64.

35. *Talking All Morning*, p. 260.

36. Bly, "Wallace Stevens and Dr. Jekyll," in William Heyen, ed., *American Poets in 1976* (Indianapolis: Bobbs-Merrill, 1976), p. 4.

37. Bly had one brother, James, who died in a car crash in 1971, and doubtless there are links between the dream-brother and the actual one. We get bits of information about Bly's relationship with his brother in the essay "Being a Lutheran Boy-God in Minnesota," and in the poems "Christmas Eve Service at St. Michael's" (*The Morning Glory*) and "Finding an Old Ant Mansion" (*The Man in the Black Coat Turns*). References to family and other specific biographical

details form one layer of "Sleepers," but it is a clouded layer that I do not attempt to speculate on in this reading of the poem.

In an interview made in 1971, while he was at work on "Sleepers," Bly said: "One of the reasons I don't talk about myself much is that I'm a Capricorn. Capricorns love to hide things. And I'm a middle-western Lutheran. Middle-western Lutherans love to hide things. In fact, my whole generation grew up writing 'hiding poetry' . . . that is, poetry that hides the major facts about yourself. I am working on a new long poem, which I've been working on since 1965, in which I try to overcome that somewhat. . . . what I'm trying to put in poems now is my own life" (*Talking All Morning*, pp. 45–46).

"Sleepers" is an inward account. As for specific outward details of Bly's life, they remain in it, whether for reasons of astrological influence or social conditioning, fairly well hidden. Bly's relationship with his father does become a major focus, however, in *The Man in the Black Coat Turns* (see chapter 7).

38. C. G. Jung, *The Archetypes and the Collective Unconscious* (*Collected Works*, vol. 9) (Princeton, N.J.: Princeton University Press, 1959), pp. 214, 216.

39. Edward F. Edinger, *Ego and Archetype* (New York: Penguin Books, 1973), pp. 4, 7. My interpretation's debt to Edinger's book extends well beyond these specific references.

40. *Leaping Poetry*, p. 63. The "three brains" referred to here are the limbic node, the cortex, and the neo-cortex, which Bly calls the reptile brain, the mammal brain, and the new brain. He is drawing here on the theory of the neurologist Paul MacLean that the human brain is not a single thing but three partly independent units. Bly goes on from there to construct a fascinating speculative essay, the fundamental message of which is that "a man should try to feel what it is like to live in each of the three brains, and a poet could try to bring all three brains inside his poems."

4. TINY POEMS

1. *The Sixties* (Fall 1960), 4:9. Charles Reynolds contributed a number of poems and translations to *The Fifties/Sixties*. He was identified in the contributors notes as living "in seclusion in the Black Hills of South Dakota." Like Crunk, the magazine's regular critic, Charles Reynolds is Robert Bly.

2. Bly, *The Sea and the Honeycomb*. Beacon Press reissued a number of titles originally published by the Sixties/Seventies Press. In the cases of these books, the page numbers in my citations refer to the Beacon editions, as these are likely to be more accessible to the reader.

3. *Ibid.*, p. ix.

4. *Ibid.*, pp. ix–x.

5. *Ibid.*, pp. x–xi.

6. Dacey, "This Book Is Made of Turkey Soup and Star Music," p. 43.

7. Bly, *Talking All Morning*, p. 190.

8. Bly, *Sleepers Joining Hands*, p. 50.

9. Yüan Hung-tao, *Pilgrim of the Clouds*, Jonathan Chaves, tr. (New York: John Weatherhill, Inc., 1978), p. 31.

10. Bly, ed., *Lorca and Jimenez: Selected Poems*, p. 77.

11. *Poetry* (August 1981), 138:284.

5. THE MORNING GLORY

1. Russell Edson, "The Prose Poem in America," *Parnassus* (Fall/Winter 1976), 5:322.

2. Bly, "Recognizing the Image As a Form of Intelligence," *Field* (Spring 1981), 24:18.

3. Galway Kinnell, "Poetry, Personality, and Death," *Field* (Spring 1971), 4:65.

4. Michael Benedikt, ed., *The Prose Poem: An International Anthology* (New York: Dell, 1976), p. 43. In addition to Benedikt, Charles Molesworth has also linked Bly's ideas on association and his prose poems to this statement by Baudelaire, in *The Fierce Embrace*, pp. 131–32.

5. Benedikt, *The Prose Poem*, p. 41.

6. Mary Oliver, "Entering the Kingdom," *Twelve Moons* (Boston: Little, Brown, 1979), p. 21.

7. Bly, *Talking All Morning*, pp. 115–16.

8. *Ibid.*, p. 265.

9. Bly, *News of the Universe*, p. 289.

10. *Ibid.*, p. 209.

11. Marianne Moore, "Things Others Never Notice," *Predilections* (New York: Viking Press, 1955), p. 138.

12. *News of the Universe*, pp. 213–14.

13. *Talking All Morning*, pp. 117–18. Bly's memory has slipped here. The caterpillar poem was not his first prose poem; he had written the two prose poems included in *Silence in the Snowy Fields* ("Sunset at a Lake" and "Fall") earlier.

14. For another discussion of the importance of animals in Bly's poetry, see Anthony Libby's "Dreaming of Animals," *Plainsong* (Fall 1981), 3(2):47–54. While I have not drawn on it in my commentary, I would like to quote here from the last paragraph of Libby's essay, which captures something of the complexity of the role of animals in Bly's poetry: "Always creatures of beauty, Robert Bly's animals come to us bearing the deepest messages when they fit his theoretical sense of how they connect with us. They must speak to the extreme poles of our brains, to the ancient instinct of the reptile brain and to the visionary appetite of the luminous new brain. But in doing this they must remain themselves, undistorted by our desires and preoccupations, or by the poet's. Their consciousness must blend with his and ours in the poetry. Impossible, but vital-

ity in this poetry often comes from the animals who somehow live within it. If he dreams them real enough they carry the poet's visions into reality."

15. Bly, "Looking for Dragon Smoke," *Naked Poetry*, p. 162.

16. Rainer Maria Rilke, *The Duino Elegies*, Stephen Garmey and Jay Wilson, tr. (New York: Harper & Row, 1972), p. 61.

17. Bly, *This Body Is Made of Camphor and Gopherwood*, dust jacket.

18. *Talking All Morning*, p. 32.

19. "70 Poets on Robert Bly," *Poetry East* (Spring/Summer 1981), 4/5:112.

6. THIS BODY IS MADE OF CAMPHOR AND GOPHERWOOD

1. Bly, *Talking All Morning*, p. 306.

2. Dacey, "This Book Is Made of Turkey Soup and Star Music," p. 40.

3. Chaves, "Chinese Influence or Cultural Colonialism," pp. 121–22.

4. Bly, "Recognizing the Image As a Form of Intelligence," Field (Spring 1981), 24:18.

5. *One Hundred Poems of Kabir*, Rabindranath Tagore, with Evelyn Underhill, tr. (London: Macmillan, 1915, 1973).

6. Bly, tr., *The Kabir Book: Forty-Four of the Ecstatic Poems of Kabir*, p. 3.

7. John G. Neihardt, *Black Elk Speaks* (Lincoln: University of Nebraska Press, 1961), pp. 198–200. My quotation differs slightly from Bly's; I have included a couple of sentences that he omitted.

8. Bly, *News of the Universe*, p. 33.

9. "Crossing Brooklyn Ferry," section 5.

10. Molesworth, *The Fierce Embrace*, pp. 137–38.

11. *Talking All Morning*, pp. 243–44.

12. Lewis Thomas, *The Lives of a Cell* (New York: Viking Press, 1974).

13. Molesworth, *The Fierce Embrace*, p. 134.

7. THIS TREE WILL BE HERE FOR A THOUSAND YEARS and THE MAN IN THE BLACK COAT TURNS

1. Bly, *Talking All Morning*, pp. 121–22.

2. Bly, *This Tree Will Be Here for a Thousand Years*, p. 11.

3. Eliot Weinberger, "Gloves on a Mouse," *The Nation*, November 17, 1979, pp. 503–04.

4. Hayden Carruth, "Poets on the Fringe," *Harper's*, January 1980, p. 79.

5. Bly occasionally published in *The Sixties* parodies of contemporary poets: Charles Olson, James Dickey, Howard Nemerov, Charles Bukowski, Robert Lowell—and himself. Given this connection and the fact that his poetry has

been especially inviting to parodists, it seems appropriate to include a parody somewhere in a book on Bly's work. The following, based partly on "A Long Walk Before the Snows Began," is by Bruce Bennett. For other examples, see William Zaranka, ed., *The Brand-X Anthology of Poetry* (Cambridge/Watertown: Apple-Wood Books, 1981).

TRACKING THE RABBIT WHOSE TRACKS I DISCOVERED THIS MORNING IN MY BACKYARD

> "I've thrown away many such poems."
> —Robert Bly

I.

I go down into my backyard and discover a rabbit has been there before me.
I can see his tracks in the snow!
He was large, an enormous rabbit, probably white, undoubtedly furry, I can tell from his prints.
Little indentations.
And hungry too. Most of us these days are hungry.
I follow them onto a path where, like a pirate with one good eye, who has misplaced his cutlass, under a half-moon, in a solitary spaceship about to blast off for Mars,
he disappeared into the brush!

II.

Goodbye, old rabbit!
We'll meet again someday, somewhere, just the two of us.
Perhaps on a day like today,
with snow swirling and whirling and twirling around fenceposts,
as I gaze out, now, while I write, at the precise spot,
where—was it only hours ago?—at 5 a.m.
I happened upon your tracks.

III.

Or perhaps it will be spring:
buds will be bursting like shrapnel,
there will be frogs—croakers and peepers! a multitude of the slimy ones!—
mud will be everywhere . . .
I'll pull on my boots and follow,
yes, follow you farther and farther,
farther and farther and farther and farther and farther,
all the way to the edge—
and even beyond, yes, even beyond the edge!—
yes! even over the edge!

6. Bly, "Form That Is Neither In nor Out," in Jones and Daniels, eds., *Of Solitude and Silence*, p. 22.

7. Bly, "What Whitman Did Not Give Us," in Jim Perlman, Ed Folsom, and Dan Campion, eds., *Walt Whitman: The Measure of His Song* (Minneapolis: Holy Cow! Press, 1981), p. 334.

8. Bly, "A Wrong-Turning in American Poetry," *Choice* (1969), 3:38.

9. *The Complete Grimm's Fairy Tales* (New York: Pantheon Books, 1972), p. xiv.

10. Bly, "Being a Lutheran Boy-God in Minnesota," in Chester G. Anderson, ed., *Growing Up in Minnesota: Ten Writers Remember Their Childhoods* (Minneapolis: University of Minnesota Press, 1976).

11. Bly's "boy-god" is closely related to the psychological type, the *puer aeternus*. For a discussion of this type, see, for example, Marie-Louise Von Franz's *The Problem of the Puer Aeternus* (New York: Spring Publications, 1970).

12. "Being a Lutheran Boy-God in Minnesota," p. 206.

13. *Ibid.*, p. 205.

14. *Ibid.*

15. *Ibid.*, p. 217.

16. *The Complete Grimm's Fairy Tales*, pp. 43–51.

17. *The New Republic*, January 31, 1981, p. 28.

18. "Being a Lutheran Boy-God in Minnesota," p. 209–12.

19. E. O. G. Turville-Petre, *Myth and Religion of the North* (Westport, Conn.: Greenwood Press, 1964), p. 42.

20. "Being a Lutheran Boy-God in Minnesota," p. 206.

21. Bly, tr., *Neruda and Vallejo: Selected Poems*, p. 3.

22. *Ibid.*, p. 15.

23. Donald Wesling, "The Wisdom-Writer," *The Nation*, October 31, 1981, p. 447.

24. Anonymous lines from *For Scirnis*, used as an epigraph by Kevin Crossley-Holland for his *The Norse Myths* (New York: Pantheon Books, 1980).

25. Carruth, "Poets on the Fringe," p. 79.

26. Dacey, "This Book Is Made of Turkey Soup and Star Music," p. 39.

27. From a letter to Thomas Butts, *The Portable Blake* (New York: Viking Press, 1946), p. 210.

28. Bly, *News of the Universe*, p. 8.

29. Karl Stern, *The Flight from Woman* (New York: Noonday Press, 1965), pp. 77–78.

30. Bly, "The Witch, the Swan, and the Middle Class," *Plainsong* (Fall 1981), 3(2):25–29.

31. *The Complete Grimm's Fairy Tales*, pp. 232–37.

32. It should be noted that "Words Rising" contains a misprint in *The Man in the Black Coat Turns*. The first two words of the last stanza should read "Blessings then," not "Blessing them." The poem is printed correctly in Jones and Daniels, eds., *Of Solitude and Silence*.

33. *News of the Universe*, p. 125.

34. Bly, letter to the author, March 1983.

35. Hall, "Notes on Robert Bly and *Sleepers Joining Hands*," in *Goatfoot Milk-tongue Twinbird*, p. 137.

36. Cavitch, "The Poet as Victim and Victimizer," p. 3.

37. *Of Solitude and Silence*, dust jacket.

38. Bly, *The Kabir Book*, pp. 24–25.

Selected Bibliography

I would like to acknowledge my debt to the bibliography compiled by James Doss and Kate Daniels, which appears in *Of Solitude and Silence: Writings on Robert Bly*. It has been invaluable to me throughout my work on this book.

WORKS BY ROBERT BLY

Poetry
The Lion's Tail and Eyes: Poems Written Out of Laziness and Silence. (With James Wright and William Duffy.) Madison, Minn.: The Sixties Press, 1962.
Silence in the Snowy Fields. Middletown, Conn.: Wesleyan University Press, 1962; London: Cape, 1967.
Chrysanthemums. Menomenic, Wis.: Ox Head Press, 1967.
Ducks. Menomenie, Wis.: Ox Head Press, 1967.
The Morning Glory: Another Thing That Will Never Be My Friend. San Francisco: Kayak Books, 1969; revised 1970.
The Teeth-Mother Naked at Last. San Francisco: City Lights Books, 1970.
Christmas Eve Service at Midnight at St. Michael's. Rushden, Northhamptonshire, U.K.: Sceptre Press, 1972.
Water Under the Earth. Rushden, Northamptonshire, U.K.: Sceptre Press, 1972.

The Dead Seal Near McClure's Beach. Denver: Straight Creek Journal, 1972; Rushden, Northamptonshire, U.K.: Sceptre Press, 1973.

Jumping Out of Bed. Barre, Mass.: Barre Publishers, 1973.

Sleepers Joining Hands. New York: Harper & Row, 1973.

The Hockey Poem. Duluth: Knife River Press, 1974.

Old Man Rubbing His Eyes. Greensboro, N.C.: Unicorn Press, 1974.

Point Reyes Poems. Half Moon Bay, Calif.: Mudra, 1974.

The Morning Glory. New York: Harper & Row, 1975.

Climbing Up Mount Vision With My Little Boy. Pittsburgh: Slow Loris Press, 1976.

Four Poems. Birmingham, Ala.: Thunder City Press, 1976.

The Loon. Marshall, Minn.: Ox Head Press, 1977.

This Body Is Made of Camphor and Gopherwood. New York: Harper & Row, 1977.

Visiting Emily Dickinson's Grave. Madison, Wis.: Red Ozier Press, 1979.

This Tree Will Be Here For a Thousand Years. New York: Harper & Row, 1979.

What the Fox Agreed to Do. Athens, Ohio: Croissant, 1979.

The Man in the Black Coat Turns. New York: Dial Press, 1981.

Translations

For the translations, I have not listed small press books, such as those from the Sixties Press, if the material they contain was later reissued within larger collections.

Hans Hvass. *Reptiles and Amphibians of the World*. New York: Grosset & Dunlap, 1960.

Georg Trakl. Twenty Poems. (Translations by Bly and James Wright.) Madison, Minn.: The Sixties Press, 1961.

Selma Lagerlöf. The Story of Gösta Berling. New York: New American Library, 1962.

Knut Hamsun. *Hunger*. New York: Farrar Straus and Giroux, 1967; London: Duckworth, 1974.

Issa. *Ten Poems*. Privately printed, 1969.

Pablo Neruda and Cesar Vallejo. *Selected Poems*. (Translations by Bly, James Wright, and John Knoepfle.) Boston: Beacon Press, 1971.

Miguel Hernandez and Blas de Otero. *Selected Poems*. (Translations by Timothy Baland, Bly, Hardie St. Martin, and James Wright.) Boston: Beacon Press, 1972.

Basho. *Basho.* San Francisco: Mudra, 1972.

Federico Garcia Lorca and Juan Ramon Jimenez. *Selected Poems.* Boston: Beacon Press, 1973.

Harry Martinson, Gunnar Ekelöf, and Tomas Transtromer. *Friends, You Drank Some Darkness.* Boston: Beacon Press, 1975.

Vincente Aleixandre. *Twenty Poems.* (Translations by Bly and Lewis Hyde.) Madison, Minn.: The Seventies Press, 1977.

Rolf Jacobsen. *Twenty Poems.* Madison, Minn.: The Seventies Press, 1977.

Kabir. *The Kabir Book: Forty-Four of the Ecstatic Poems of Kabir.* Boston: Beacon Press, 1977.

Antonio Machado. *I Never Wanted Fame: Ten Poems and Proverbs.* St. Paul: Ally Press, 1979.

Antonio Machado. *Canciones.* West Branch, Iowa: Toothpaste Press, 1980.

Mirabai. *Mirabai Versions by Robert Bly.* New York: Red Ozier Press, 1980.

Tomas Transtromer. *Truth Barriers.* San Francisco: Sierra Club Books, 1980.

Rainer Maria Rilke. *Selected Poems.* New York: Harper & Row, 1981.

Rumi. *Night and Sleep.* (Versions by Bly and Coleman Barks.) Cambridge, Mass.: Yellow Moon Press, 1981.

Göran Sonnevi. *The Economy Spinning Faster and Faster.* New York: Sun, 1982.

Other Books

Bly has published a great many essays and reviews; in the interest of a more concise bibliography, I haven't listed them individually here. The prose contained in the following books represents the greater part of Bly's critical writing, and together with the additional essays cited in the text it will give the reader a good sense of Bly as critic and theorist.

The Fifties/Sixties 1–10. All numbers have been reissued by the Hobart & William Smith College Press, Geneva, N.Y.

A Poetry Reading Against the Vietnam War. (Edited with David Ray.) Madison, Minn.: American Writers Against the Vietnam War/The Sixties Press, 1966.

The Sea and the Honeycomb: A Book of Tiny Poems. Madison, Minn.: The Sixties Press, 1966; Boston: Beacon Press, 1971.

Forty Poems Touching on Recent American History. Madison, Minn.: The Sixties Press, 1966; Boston: Beacon Press, 1970.

Leaping Poetry: An Idea with Poems and Translations. Boston: Beacon Press, 1975.

Selected Poems of David Ignatow. (Edited and with commentary by Bly.) Middletown, Conn.: Wesleyan University Press, 1975.

News of the Universe. San Francisco: Sierra Club Books, 1980.

Talking All Morning. Ann Arbor: University of Michigan Press, 1980.

SECONDARY SOURCES

A brief listing of selected books, special issues, essays, and reviews that will be useful to the reader studying Bly's work.

Altieri, Charles. *Enlarging the Temple.* Lewisburg, Pa.: Bucknell University Press, 1979.

Atkinson, Michael. *"Sleepers Joining Hands:* Shadow and Self." *Iowa Review* (Fall 1976), 7(4):135–53.

Cavitch, David. "The Poet as Victim and Victimizer." *New York Times Book Review,* February 18, 1973, pp. 2–3.

Chaves, Jonathan. "Chinese Influence or Cultural Colonialism: Some Recent Poets." *Ironwood* (Spring 1982), 19:115–23.

Dacey, Philip. "The Reverend Robert E. Bly, Pastor, Church of the Blessed Unity: A Look at 'A Man Writes to a Part of Himself.' " *Pebble* (1979), 18/19/20:1–7.

——"This Book Is Made of Turkey Soup and Star Music." *Parnassus* (Fall/Winter 1978), 7:34–45.

Davis, William V. "Hair in a Baboon's Ear: The Politics of Robert Bly's Early Poetry." *The Carleton Miscellany* (Winter 1979–80) 18:74–84.

Ellmann, Richard and Robert O'Clair, eds. *The Norton Anthology of Modern Poetry.* New York: Norton, 1973.

Faas, Ekbert. *Towards a New American Poetics: Essays & Interviews.* Santa Barbara: Black Sparrow Press, 1979.

Friebert, Stuart and David Young, eds. *The Longman Anthology of Contemporary American Poetry 1950–80.* New York: Longman, 1983.

Friedman, Norman. "The Wesleyan Poets. III: The Experimental Poets." *Chicago Review* (1967), 19:52–73.

Gunn, Thom. "Poems and Books of Poems." *Yale Review* (October 1963), 53:142–44.

Hall, Donald. *Goatfoot Milktongue Twinbird*. Ann Arbor: University of Michigan Press, 1978.

Hammer, Louis Z. "Moths in the Light." *Kayak* (April 1968), 14:63–67.

Heyen, William. "Inward to the World: The Poetry of Robert Bly." *The Far Point* (Fall/Winter 1969), 3:42–50.

Howard, Richard. *Alone With America*. New York: Atheneum, 1969.

——"Poetry Chronicle." *Poetry* (June 1963), 102:182–92.

Janssens, G. A. M. "The Present State of American Poetry: Robert Bly and James Wright." *English Studies* (April 1970), 51:112–37.

Jones, Richard and Kate Daniels, eds. *Of Solitude and Silence: Writings on Robert Bly*. Boston: Beacon Press, 1981.

Komie, Lowell. "Ecstasy and Poetry in Chicago: A Middle-Aged Lawyer Goes to His First Poetry Reading." *Harper's*, March 1978, pp. 129–31.

Leibowitz, Herbert. "Questions of Reality." *Hudson Review* (August 1968), 21:553–57.

Lensing, George S. and Ronald Moran. *Four Poets and the Emotive Imagination*. Baton Rouge: Louisiana State University Press, 1976.

Libby, Anthony. "Robert Bly Alive in the Darkness." *Iowa Review* (Summer 1972), 3:78–91.

Malkoff, Karl. *Crowell's Handbook of Contemporary American Poetry*. New York: Thomas Y. Crowell, 1973.

Mersmann, James F. *Out of the Vietnam Vortex*. Lawrence: University Press of Kansas, 1974.

Mills, Ralph J. *Contemporary American Poetry*. New York: Random House, 1965.

Molesworth, Charles. *The Fierce Embrace*. Columbia: University of Missouri Press, 1979.

Poetry East. Special Double Issue on Robert Bly. Spring/Summer 1981, vol. 4, no. 5.

Rexroth, Kenneth. "The Poet as Responsible." *Northwest Review* (Fall/Winter 1967–68), 9:116–18.

Tennessee Poetry Journal. A Robert Bly Issue. Winter 1969, vol. 2, no. 2.

Zweig, Paul. "A Sadness for America," *The Nation*, March 25, 1968, pp. 418–20.

AUDIO-VISUAL MATERIALS

A Man Writes to a Part of Himself. Videotape. University Community Video, 425 Ontario Street Southeast, Minneapolis, Minn. 55414.

Contemporary American Poets Read Their Work: Robert Bly. Audio cassette. Everett/Edwards, Deland, Fla. 32720.

Robert Bly: Interviews and Readings. Videotape. Brockport Writers Forum, Department of English, State University College, Brockport, N.Y. 14420.

Index

Howard Nelson is a Professor of English at Cayuga Community College in Auburn, New York. He is the author of poems and essays that have appeared in numerous magazines and journals, and a book of poems entitled *Creatures*.